5/00

D1084556

Edmund Spenser in the Early Eighteenth Century

Medieval & Renaissance Literary Studies

Edmund Spenser in the Early Eighteenth Century

Education, Imitation, and the Making of a Literary Model

RICHARD C. FRUSHELL

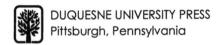DUQUESNE UNIVERSITY PRESS
Pittsburgh, Pennsylvania

Published by

DUQUESNE UNIVERSITY PRESS
600 Forbes Avenue
Pittsburgh, PA 15282

Library of Congress Cataloging-in-Publication Data
Frushell, Richard C., 1935–
    Edmund Spenser in the early eighteenth century: education,
imitation, and the making of a literary model / Richard C.
Frushell.
        p.   cm.—(Medieval & renaissance literary studies)
    Includes bibliographical references (p.) and index.

    ISBN 0-8207-0305-2 (acid-free paper)

    1. Spenser, Edmund, 1552?–1599—Criticism and
interpretation—History—18th century.   2. Spenser, Edmund,
1552?–1599—Study and teaching—England—History—18th
century.   3. English poetry—Study and teaching—England—
History—18th century.   4. English literature—18th
century—History and criticism.   5. Spenser, Edmund,
1552?–1599—Parodies, imitations, etc.   6. Spenser, Edmund,
1552?–1599—Adaptations.   7. Criticism—England—History—
18th century.   8. Spenser, Edmund, 1552?–1599—Influence.
9. Canon (Literature).   I. Title.   II. Series.
    PR2364 .F73 1999
    821'.3—ddc21   98-40136
                                                                CIP

For Kristen, Marcantonio, Sarah, Olivia,
Kraig, Peter, Emma Rose
and Those To Come

Contents

Introduction

On the 18-foot walls of the Maryland Department Room, a large second-floor reading room in Baltimore's Central Enoch Pratt Free Library, 18 murals, much in need of restoration, cover 1,800 square feet. The scenes, from Edmund Spenser's *The Faerie Queene*, demand the attention of the library's patrons. Begun in the 1930s, the first panel was executed in 1941, and the murals were completed in 1945 by the hand of Baltimore native Lee Woodward Zeigler. The library's catalogue, *Murals Based upon Edmund Spenser's Faerie Queene* (1945), describes the making of this prodigious display and notes that the project had its inception when Zeigler's father gave him a copy of Spenser's epic. In just this way, nearly two centuries earlier, Thomas Warton Jr. received the book from his grandfather.

I mention this indebtedness because it was a common way for the neophyte to experience the "poet's poet" for the first time. Since Spenser's death at the very end of the sixteenth century, the record is quite full, even if hard to get at, of how Spenser was first encountered, particularly by the young, in school, during school years, or afterward, through the ministrations of relatives, friends, or especially teachers, whose encouragement toward the poet resulted in some 318 Spenser imitations and adaptations in the eighteenth century alone, efforts fully described in the bibliography at the end of this volume. That age was also the first one for consistent, considerable Spenser scholarship, criticism, regard, and influence, a statement applicable to the first half of the century as well, a time not usually understood as particularly rich in matters Spenserian.[1]

Spenser has universally and properly been understood as a mighty influence on the British romantic writers, particularly Wordsworth, Coleridge, and Keats, with his heyday in the second half of the eighteenth century and several decades beyond, when demonstrably he made an indelible imprint on the romantic imagination and its artistic working out. Yet the stately, moral, sage, Rubenesque, capacious Spenser—all descriptors used by commentators in the eighteenth century[2]—was taken seriously and increasingly and variously imitated in the first six decades of the century. I suggest that during this time the making of the poet into a literary model of first consideration took place, and this elevation was effected in part through teachers such as the three Wartons, who were themselves devoted, "practicing" Spenserians; through the schools's regimen of imitation, the standard pedagogical method and often the very stuff of learning; through the changing sensibility of what poetry should do and be and increasing vocalization against requiring exclusively classical models for *imitatio* and *aemulatio*, the latter a different sort of changing sensibility; and through the collateral interest in Spenser by critics and editors, almost all of them directly influenced at a young age by Spenserians. All these forces combine to form a Spenser renewal or revival, after his first flowering in the first quarter of the seventeenth century—which, one hurries to add, had almost no direct influence on the Spenserianism of the chronological eighteenth century.

Of the four greatest native British writers, after Milton it was Spenser who was imitated in the eighteenth century more frequently, uninterruptedly, and experimentally than either Shakespeare or Chaucer. Unremarked heretofore, Spenser's influence in the schools and universities, at least in part the result of his being a model for imitation, contributes crucially to what we now call the profession of English. In a sense, truly the English major was born and the course set for curricular and canonical change in the schools largely because of the growing popularity, ubiquity, and importance of such native models for imitation as Spenser.

Further examples of and reasons for Spenser's influence in the early eighteenth century—from 1706 and Matthew Prior's important Spenser imitation "Ode to the Queen" (in 35 "Prior Stanzas")[3] to 1762 and Richard Hurd's manifesto-like *Letters on Chivalry and Romance* (these denote this study's onset and terminus dates)—would include Spenser's increasingly frequent appearance in literary criticism and anthologies. The latter were impressively represented by Robert Dodsley's popular collections around midcentury; such volumes often featured imitations of Spenser.

The pivotal years of the Spenserian fashion in the century are 1747–1762, when a clustering of significant Spenserian "events" occurred and when he was established unequivocally as a literary exemplar and inspiration; these matters have not been examined in the environment I give them. The direction that Spenserianism and the poet's celebrity took in the second half of the century was shaped substantially by the 1750 reprinting of John Hughes's edition of the *Works* (1715), William Kent's "romantic" illustrations for *The Faerie Queene* (1751, illustrations comparable to those in Hughes and the *Calendarium Pastorale*), the landmark John Upton edition of *The Faerie Queene* (1758), by the exponential increase in imitations, the progressive popularity of Spenser in the anthologies, the Wartons' and Hurd's substantial appreciations of Spenser's "gothic" *inventio* and *executio*, the availability of Spenser editions and commentaries in school libraries, and an alteration generally in attitudes about the nature and role of the poet and poetry.

Of course, throughout the century Spenser (and here I mean his work and his image as a poet) was adapted to the gradually changing poetic fashions, modes, and emphases. In the early part of the century, for example, the Rev. Samuel Croxall convincingly imitates the poet in two politico-allegorical poems, then a well-known subgenre: *An Original Canto of Spencer* (1713) and *Another Original Canto* (1714). Early-century Spenser imitations, at one with other poetic efforts of the times, include bucolic poems such as Moses Browne's minor *Piscatory Eclogues* (1729) and William Melmoth's "The Transformation of Lycon and Euphormius" (ca. 1743).

But a more substantial and attractive poem of this type in the manner of Spenser is one of the century's finest poems, William Thompson's *An Hymn to May* (ca. 1740), a work with palpable Popean influence as well—not an uncommon admixture in the eighteenth century. These imitations do not differ in their subjects from other poems produced in the same years; only the literary model is new. One, then, should expect to find that almost all the century's elegiac and panegyric Spenser imitations—such as Prior's "Ode to the Queen" (1706), William Thompson's "An Epithalamium on the Royal Nuptials of Frederick and Augusta" (1736), and William Mason's *Musaeus: A Monody to the Memory of Mr. Pope* (1744)—appeared before midcentury, when the taste for such poems was keenest. And the same assertions and matchings could be made for the satirical Spenser imitations by Pope, Shenstone, Pitt, Cambridge, Akenside, and Lloyd. As one may assume, the quality of many imitations make them a burlesque to their readers, even though unintended as such by their authors.

As expected from the age under consideration, generalized allegories imitative of Spenser were written and published throughout the century, perhaps best exemplified by James Thomson's *Castle of Indolence* (1748) and typified by Robert Bedingfield's "The Education of Achilles" (1747) and Robert Lowth's "The Choice of Hercules" (1747), a subject the

eighteenth century imitators favored. This last effort, significantly, was written as a school exercise. Also conformable to
the times which gave them rise were the physico-philosophical
imitations in the second half of the century, the most famous
and influential of which was James Beattie's *The Minstrel*
(1771, 1774). One is bemused by the miscellaneous, occasional
topics selected by the Spenser imitators as well as the variety
of Spenserian verse forms: such subjects as hope, pain, music,
suicide, sun, sexes, traveling, health, and silk; such verse forms
as that of Spenser's *Faerie Queene, Shepheardes Calender,
Mother Hubberds Tale, Amoretti,* "Epithalamion," and *Complaints*—or adaptations of them into blank verse, decasyllabic
couplets, or Prior stanzas (all published from the century's
earliest days). But in all this multeity the Spenserian model
remained constant, even if at times fissured by imitators with
few lights or little gust for the task.

Such remarks speak to the scope of my study, give an indication of how the three terms of the subtitle will play, and
offer an example or two of the content itself. I have cast my
lot with eighteenth century education, imitation, and modelmaking, three inextricable topics that I believe better show
the poet than would an exclusively anecdotal account of
Spenserian sightings and citings in the age, even though some
of those are indeed part of the discussion. Since this is a first
study of these subjects in the milieu I set forth, this Introduction need say little more, except for intention. The aim of the
pages below is primarily to explain Spenser's progressive importance in the eighteenth century as seen in the pertinent
and largely unexamined primary documents of the age.

The movement in the opening chapters is from Spenser as
the poet's poet for the young, who was encountered both in
and outside the schools; to an account of some general linea-
ments of Spenser imitations and adaptations and of his being
anthologized. That is, these chapters offer a taxonomy of sorts,
of those works created by young writers who were led to, or

found on their own, Spenser as a worthy model, as well as a study of the anthologies that served as popular forums for reading the poetic products of those imitators. The introduction of Spenser to young men and women directly led to many of them becoming Spenser imitators. The range of imitators and imitations, some of their relational ties, and the anthologies that presented them are the subjects of chapter two and its companion bibliography C of eighteenth century imitations and adaptations. This bibliography is augmented from my *Spenser Encyclopedia* account of imitations and adaptations, which selectively lists some 250 items. The 318 items below in bibliography C attempt a full listing.

The aim of such an arrangement in the opening chapters is to create a foundation, an overview, a spine for the diverse Spenserian manifestations, treated in the final chapters, that also contributed to the making of him as a literary model. I would suggest that Spenser "criticized" and edited cannot be so well understood without the circumstantial account I provide, of how he was realized by young writers who read and imitated him. In brief, *ex nihilo nihil fit*.

For the poet's advent in anthologies, I examine some key imitations, at the midcentury particularly, when the fashion for Spenser was quickly gathering momentum, for their Spenserian likenesses, their reflection of the time of their composition, and their anticipation of a changing poetic sensibility. The increasing frequency of appearances and the "packaging" of Spenser in the early eighteenth century *directly* led to the poet's grand climacteric in the middle and final decades of the century. The anthologies have not been studied for Spenser *per se* and his contributions to taste, sensibility, and a "romanticism" that was not inimical to poets such as Pope. Indeed we shall see examples of Spenser imitations where Pope, Milton, and Spenser are all models, at times in a single poem.

The imitations, however, ineluctably look forward in tone, in manner, and in subjects treated, rather than back. The anthologies have not been part of the Spenser historians' primary material, but they are revealing of poetic taste and practice at each of their publication dates. One sees more clearly than is possible in other forms of publication the poetic environment in which Spenser was read as well as his prominence. Chapter 2 thus looks at the sweep of the imitations in the period under consideration as well as the particulars of several representative imitations: as poems, as barometers of the times, and as pieces crafted with a model in mind.

A truncated picture of Spenser in the early eighteenth century, and a loss of symmetry, would result from the omission of criticism and editions of the poet's work. Yet their inclusion and the placement I give them may perhaps raise the question of cause and effect. Would critical commentary on Spenser's art, and would editions of his works, have been produced without the experience of Spenser that I describe in my first two sections? I believe not. I am sure that most eighteenth century critics and editors were part of the educational formation I delineate; as such, their Spenserian work is rightly and logically understood in the context I give.

For the discussions of Spenser in works of criticism and of editions of his poetry, I purposefully and fully highlight relevant passages of primary works, since many are rare and since having the setting of the Spenserian material reveals more about the several topics at hand and remains with the reader better than would thematic snippets, the more common presentation of such material. I also believe that chronological ordering, for the same reasons, proves to be a more satisfactory approach than other schemes. I keep to a chronological arrangement in the final chapter as well, where the subject is Spenser in the fulcrum sixth decade of the century: a time of evolving critical theory, strikingly but not exclusively about imitation, within which the decade's important and various Spenserian activities, including imitations, are better seen. Also, time order, for my purposes, best allows for comparisons of Spenserians and their practices along with intimations of new literary directions and Spenser's place within them.

The general presentational shape can be seen perhaps as hourglass, with the large-picture sections on either end and the midbook devoted to Spenserian activities that logically flow from the crucial first chapter. This figure is not to suggest that *Edmund Spenser in the Early Eighteenth Century* is exclusively or primarily a work of literary criticism or a pure history in the usual sense of those terms. It surely partakes of both, but mostly this study is a tool and primer for future critical scholarship as well as a guide to primary material. I should nonetheless like to have it considered as an investigation of a major writer's advent, reception, employment, growth, and influence in an age other than his own. In the service of such aims, I provide three bibliographies, the nature of which are clear from the table of contents. To avoid a packed presentation, throughout the text I give only short references to the works about Spenser, including imitations, and give full publication information in the several bibliographies gathered at the end of the volume.

If at all successful, the work that follows should mean most to Spenserians and Miltonists and those generally interested in Renaissance and eighteenth century studies; but it should also mean something to students of romanticism, the history of education and the profession of English, biography, and librarianship.

Because I have been favored by uncountable intellectual and affectional kindnesses over the many years I have been at the research for this project, I owe mightily. Only a sign of my gratitude and indebtedness can be communicated by the mere mentions that follow. To the many teachers, scholars, and critics who have contributed to my education on matters treated in this study, I am deeply grateful, especially to G. Foster Provost: *magister et amicus*. I am pleased to acknowledge the help extended to me in many libraries. Particularly generous of time and expertise were the librarians at the Folger Shakespeare Library, the Milton Eisenhower Library of The Johns Hopkins University, The Library of Congress, The Boston Public Library, several Harvard University libraries, Biblioteca Nationale Centrale, Firenze, Biblioteca Nationale Vittorio Emanuele, Roma, Biblioteca Universitaria Alessandrina, Roma, as well as the libraries of the University of Chicago, University of Illinois, and Indiana University's Lilly Library where, for a pleasant summer in the early 1980s, I was a Fellow working on Spenser imitations in the early eighteenth century.

I am pleased to thank the following for their patient and full answers to my queries about texts, curriculum, and teaching at English schools in the eighteenth century: Roger Custance, Peter Gwyn, and J. M. G. Blakiston of Winchester College, as well as Fellows' Librarian of that school, Paul Yeats-Edwards; Patrick Strong, Keeper of Eton's College Library and Collections; Alan Woolley of Merchant Taylors' School and A. Hugh Mead of St. Paul's; Hazel Anderson, Harrow School Archivist; and Charterhouse Librarian, Mrs. B. Freake. I acknowledge the early support of Bernard J. Vondersmith, William A. Oram, William B. Hunter Jr., the late Vernon Sternberg, and, more recently, Nancy L. Herron, who as my academic officer has been a vigorous and generous supporter of this project. And I am pleased to remember with affection my graduate students in Bibliography and Literary Research 600 at Indiana State University some years ago, wherein our research interest was Spenser in the eighteenth century: Janice Borders, Jerald Clayton, Maria Knepp, Gene Melendy, Brenda Rogina, and Bobby Stockwell. Last, I much appreciate the correspondence of Peter Beal, Ernst Häublein, R. L. Arrowsmith of Amerley, Sussex, and Tsokan Huang's considerable assistance with holdings on education subjects in American libraries. I am pleased to thank Joseph Weixlmann, R. C. Alston, Donald Cheney, and, more recently, David H. Radcliffe, who aided my work on imitations.

I also appreciate the guidance and editorial work on essays I published on Spenser and the eighteenth century given by Thomas P. Roche Jr., and Patrick Cullen of *Spenser Studies,* and A. C. Hamilton, Donald Cheney, David A. Richardson, and the magnificent research and copy editors of *The Spenser Encyclopedia.* I acknowledge permission to reprint two essays (centerpieces for, but not the entirety of, my first two chapters), which were originally published by AMS Press, Inc., and the University of Toronto Press: "Spenser and the Eighteenth-Century Schools," *Spenser Studies* VII (1987): 175–98; and "Imitations and Adaptations, 1660–1800," *The Spenser Encyclopedia,* ed. A. C. Hamilton *et al.* Toronto: University of Toronto Press, 1990: 396–403 (second edn. forthcoming). For their assistance in the involved mounting of an early version of bibliography C, I am happy to thank David A. Richardson and Lenora Brzoska of Cleveland State University.

Two versions of parts of chapter 2 on Spenser anthologized were given in 1996 as papers, presented at the Yale Center for British Art in the conference on *"The Faerie Queene* in the World, 1596–1996" ("Spenser's Advent as Literary Model: 1706–1762"), and at the University of Texas in the annual conference of the American Society for Eighteenth Century Studies ("Edmund Spenser's Role in the Expanding Canon after Pope"). I appreciate the helpful oral and written responses to my papers, particularly since they come from representatives of the two scholarly communities most interested in the larger study below. I was gratified to find that my *Spenser Encyclopedia* essay served as the basis for much of the display mounted at The Yale University Beinecke Rare Book and Manuscript Library for the 1996 Yale conference on *"The Faerie Queene* in the World." I can only hope that the pages below similarly encourage others' work on Spenser in the eighteenth century.

I acknowledge the financial support given by the Indiana State University and the Pennsylvania State University Research Committees for part of the research. For schooling me, a very reluctant pilgrim in the *selva oscura* of academic computing, my thanks go to Donald Cassidy. And for the four-month sabbatical benefice to prepare the knottier parts of this manuscript for publication, I thank the Pennsylvania State University.

Finally, for his crucial support of this work over the years, I express my indebtedness to Albert C. Labriola, General Editor of the *Medieval & Renaissance Literary Studies* series that now includes my work. Also, I am grateful for the perfect advice and professional kindnesses of Susan Wadsworth-Booth, Editor in Chief of Duquesne University Press.

ONE

"As a Ramping Young Horse"

୫

The Young Poet's Poet in School and Out

Imitation theory and practice was much engaged-in during the eighteenth century, and Edmund Spenser's increasing prominence in both is of first importance for his progress as a formidable literary model. The very fact of his being imitated is, of course, a solid sign of Spenser's stature and influence and thus a measure of the respect and affection which redounded to him. The education of imitators seems to be a rich and reasonable investigation, for much of how Spenser was first realized at that time comes directly from school or school-age experiences of him. *Imitation* herein does not mean merely echoing, alluding to, quoting, or otherwise employing Spenser. Rather, imitation denotes "written in the manner of" or "in continuation of," these the usual practices of eighteenth century imitators instead of, say, *aemulatio*, which often involves an attempt by the imitator to overgo the model. No imitator I know presumed to that.[1]

An important discussion of imitation theory in terms of Spenser and Milton merits examination at this point for it reveals pertinent assumptions that underlie much of what follows. Ronald S. Crane's 1908 study of the "Imitation of Spenser and Milton" presents a persuasive case for the importance of Henry Felton's (1679–1740) enormously popular *Dissertation on Reading the Classics and Forming a Just Style*, written in 1709 and published in 1713. Indeed, the year-span of my own study embraces subsequent editions of Felton's work: the second in 1715, the third in 1718 and 1723, the fourth in 1730, and the fifth in 1753. Crane's thesis is that Felton "brought the . . . Spenser and Milton revivals into close and explicit harmony with a thoroughly traditional conception of poetical imitation" (195). Felton's fourth and fifth sections, on principles of imitation and past and present noteworthy English writers, are of most interest here. He distinguishes between true and false imitation, the latter merely translating, paraphrasing, or transcribing models. The former sets out actually to rival the models *in their own manner and theme*; thus, my assertion holds true: no imitator presumed to overgo the model, especially such gifted models as Milton and Spenser.

Imitators realized this perfectly and often qualified their imitations with titles that included "in the manner of" or "a further canto of" or some such locutions. Crane points out that most of the period's critics wrote against slavish, uninspired imitation (see Dr. Johnson and Young below) and remained faithful to the classical education, which included imitation of the Ancients. Addison, Trapp, Welsted, Young, Blackwell, Melmoth, Lloyd, and Johnson would embrace that position. I am concerned to show not only that exclusive imitation of the Ancients breaks down as the century wears on but the particulars of this changing attitude and practice.

Important to the question of which models to imitate is

Felton's support of Spenser and Milton, who are just as deserving as the Ancients. Felton's contemporary Matthew Prior quite comfortably recommends both Spenser and Horace, showing that the early years of the eighteenth century were a crucial time for seeing the Ancients and Moderns as coequal models. The heads that Felton uses for his remarks on Spenser are to become some of the most common and important ways to speak about the poet in the century's criticism. For example, Felton considers Spenser's antique lines as ravishing music with "the softest, sweetest Numbers" (Crane, 206); Spenser's pastorals equal Theocritus, and his *Shepheardes Calender* is superior to Virgil, the favorite Ancient. Felton's placement of Milton is even higher than Spenser's, with the *Paradise Lost* ranking higher than Homer and Virgil because of its scriptural roots (206). Since Felton's book was so popular, his recommendation of Milton and Spenser could not but be a spur to the discussion and practice of those of his readers who would have their own "just" writing style (to quote Felton's title), based upon new models. In effect, Felton's title "Reading the Classics" suggests Milton and Spenser as the new "classics" for imitation.

The Young Poets: Making Free with their Model

When attempting to see the imitations within the general poetical setting, the student of this subject notes, as I do in my Introduction, that they generally parallel the slowly changing critical fashions of the age while reflecting similar stylistic features of other poetry then published. The range of kinds of imitations is similar also: political, bucolic, elegiac, patriotic, allegorical, panegyric, seasonal, religious, and otherwise topical poems. One also finds a similar consonance in the range of tonalities: serious, playful, reverential, whimsical, wry, jejeune, mock-heroic. The variety found in the general run of poetry, then, is found in the Spenser imitations.

An important common element in this diversity is the youthfulness of the imitators, both men and women (at least nine of the latter, including the popular Mary Tighe and the talented Anna Barbauld, Mary Leapor, Anna Seward, and Jane Bowdler),[2] who first turned to Spenser in their early years. An example of Spenser and the youths at Oxford at the midcentury is Spenserian Thomas Warton Jr.'s *The Oxford Sausage* (London, 1764; a "new edition" 1814), which communicates the joyance of the enterprise as well as how embedded imitation was in the academic—and as we shall see, popular—imagination and practice. The anthology presents Hawkins Browne's "A Pipe of Tobacco" wherein six writers are imitated in one poem. Also imitated in the volume is Spenser (including Warton's own imitation "Morning an Ode" and Christopher Pitt's scurrilous imitation about a chamber pot, "The Jordan"). Included is a spoof of the current poetical fads such as graveyard poetry, in "Ode to Horror, in the . . . Style of Our Modern Ode-Writers and Monody Mongers" (n.d., 611–64), a carefree effort that satirically and easily yokes and invokes Spenser (3.12), Pope, Tasso, and Milton.

The youthful efforts continue with drinking songs, broadsides, parodies, and such saucy epigrams as the anonymous "Epigram Written by an Exciseman, and addressed to a young lady, who was courted at the same time by an Apothecary":

> What though the doctor boasts to fit
> Your *mortar* to his *pestle;*
> Are not my *inches* ev'ry whit
> As good to *gage* your *vessel?*

The Oxford Sausage is a commentary on education as a man discerned it in the exuberance of young writers expressing themselves through imitation of their betters. Perhaps of some interest, as an indication of the times at Oxford midcentury and beyond, is a political section of the collection called "Verses of the Oxford Newsmen, from the Year 1754 to the Year 1772."

The remainder of the volume also reveals something of the educational scene, through James Shergold Boone's "The Oxford Spy," a dialogue of hundreds of generalized—and numbing—couplets.

Much earlier than *The Oxford Sausage*, many young poets attempted imitations of Spenser. The evidence makes one confident in asserting that Spenser is the poet for young poets, whether British or American. Not only the writers treated below admired him in their youth, but so did all the major romantics—Byron perhaps reluctantly so—turn to him seriously and embrace him when young, as Tennyson did in the following generation. Later still, a very young Yeats was strongly influenced by Spenser. Perhaps all this gives a newness to the old epithet for Spenser, the poet's poet. And it is helpful to recall that Spenser himself was a rather regular, deep, creative imitator both of the Ancients and the Moderns, his own contemporaries in England and on the Continent. Since Spenser himself was an imitator in his own youth—thus allowing a nice ambiguity in this chapter's title—the role in that practice of Spenser's teacher at Merchant Taylors' School, Richard Mulcaster, is interesting to ponder.

The playfulness and energy of many imitations in the eighteenth century can thus be accounted for through the youthfulness of their authors; Alexander Pope's "The Alley" (ca. 1706) and Mark Akenside's "The Virtuoso" (1737) are striking examples. And later in the century, on a different continent, John Trumbull's saucy liberties with Spenser's "Epithalamion" argue against the notion that the writings of such "high" models are sacred texts. The stanzaic experimentation and adventuresomeness of many imitations are also thus accounted for. These satiric efforts were anticipated, if not caused, by the likes of the anonymous 1619 parody titled "Pasquins Palinodia, and His Progresse to the Taverne" where the opening of *The Faerie Queene* becomes "Loe, I the man whose Muse whilom did play, / A *horne-pipe* both to Country and the Citty." Young poets behave this way in verse more than do seasoned poets. A perusal of the imitators' biographies along with the prefaces and notes attending their imitations show them as early readers of the poet, some during school days, and some, formally, *in* school. Such writers as Southey, Wordsworth, Coleridge, and Lamb at the century's end would be included in a listing of youthful Spenser imitators. The eighteenth century imitations themselves reveal that the opening books of *The Faerie Queene*, "Epithalamion," and *The Shepheardes Calender* were the most persistent models for imitation, just the pieces one would estimate that would attract young writers.[3] Early books of *The Faerie Queene* were imitated rather than later books, probably because students only read into the poet that far—not a wild-eyed surmise from the perspective of today's experience.

Spenser in and about the Curriculum

Most imitators attended one of only a handful of public schools. While Spenser, or any other Modern, was not part of the curriculum at such schools as Westminster, Winchester, and Eton—these the three with the highest number of alumni imitators—he was made available for study through editions and criticism of his works placed in the schools, a matter attended to below. Most important I should guess, study and imitation of Spenser was encouraged informally. While one can not offer abundant proof from extant school exercises (but do see Robert Lowth, William Mason, James Scott, and William Whitehead in bibliography C) or evidence from memoirs of Writing Masters (these were in the early years most often only penmanship tutors) who were Spenserians,[4] enough circumstantial evidence exists, particularly about teachers, to make a case for imitating Spenser in the eighteenth century schools. Demonstrably, imitation of models, classical models by the formal dictates of the schools's founders, was a basic, an unwavering mode of learning, writing, and teaching in the eighteenth century as it was earlier, and as it would continue to be for generations thereafter. Evidence survives, although it can be a considerable struggle to get at, that Moderns were offered for imitation at school even though not as part of the formal course timetables. This should not be surprising, since English literature as a subject for study would not become part of curricula until late in the nineteenth century, and then at the universities.

Several Spenser imitations are on the subject of school and schooling: for example, William Shenstone's celebrated "The School-Mistress" (1737, rev. 1742, rev. 1748), the Rev. Robert Bedingfield's "The Education of Achilles" (1747), Gilbert West's *Education: A Poem* (1751, in 96 Spenserian stanzas), and Thomas Ager's "The Schoolmaster" (1794, an imitation of an imitation, which is not unusual for this century). While Shenstone's poem is the most famous of this group, the others are equally significant for the topic under consideration here, particularly West's allegorical attack on blind adherence to the Ancients as models. In this, a kinship is discernible between West and John Locke, who attacked the curriculum at Westminster School, Locke's school, for its failure to relate to practical life outside the academy.

Many imitators were themselves teachers or the sons or daughters of teachers—a few, of librarians. A listing of noteworthy imitators, some who wrote noteworthy imitations, who themselves were teachers or schoolmasters would include James Beattie, Robert Lloyd, James Ralph, Elijah Fenton, John Bidlake, Robert Potter, Mary Robinson, Jerome Stone, James Thomson, Samuel Wesley, Samuel Whyte, and, of course, Thomas Warton Sr. and his sons Joseph and Thomas. At least some of these names will register in my readers' minds even though probably for other reasons.

Some Spenser imitators discovered Spenser largely themselves, clearly without benefit of "regular" schooling. This gathering would include Alexander Pope, Thomas Chatterton,[5]

Henry Kirke White, and William Blake, all of whom read Spenser assiduously when quite young, imitated him when young, and wrote works influenced by him when young.[6] The privately educated imitator of Spenser's sonnets, Thomas Edwards, the father of the eighteenth century sonnet, hoped never to be "ashamed of imitating such great originals as Shakespeare, Spenser, and Milton, whom to imitate with any degree of success is no small praise."[7] Other imitators encouraged to attend to the poet by a parent, relative, friend, or teacher would include Anna Letitia Barbauld, who could read before the age of three and, very soon after that, knew the most famous of the English authors.

As the *Dictionary of National Biography* and general anthology sketches indicate, the blind Scots poet Dr. Thomas Blacklock, friend to Robert Burns and landlord for the Rev. Hugh Downman, both Spenser imitators, had Spenser read to him by friends and parents. Robert Fergusson, dead in his twenties, was first taught the British poets "carefully" by his mother, as was Elizabeth Smith, the prodigious linguist. The Swan of Lichfield, Anna Seward, was quite early urged to write poetry by Erasmus Darwin and probably also by her teacher and grandfather, who taught Anna's enemy Dr. Johnson. Christopher Smart wrote verse when a youth through the financial patronage of the Duchess of Cleveland. Robert Southey's aunt's library in Bath was the location of his early encounter with Spenser, before age eight. Southey once boasted to have read *The Faerie Queene* 30 times. All these writers were Spenser imitators, as are those who follow.

The three Wartons, Spenserians of distinction, were intimately affiliated with schooling. All three were explicitly or subtly involved with the training of other Spenserians. Especially prominent for purposes of this chapter is Joseph Warton and Winchester College, where he was involved for nearly 40 years as either student (beginning 1735), Usher (that is, assistant teacher, beginning 1755), or Master (beginning 1766).

Needless to say, Thomas Warton, Joseph's father and Master of the grammar school at Basingstoke, encouraged his sons to study Spenser.[8] It should be noted that while many Spenser imitators were to enter Holy Orders or become medical doctors, many others would not enter any profession and had no university training.

So far as I can determine the matter from the evidence, the "tradesman" imitators of Spenser first met him when schoolboys or at least of school age. That youngsters with no particular acumen, desire, or opportunity for academic or professional pursuits would be taken with Spenser is striking testimony to the power of the poet as well as to the talents of those who presented him. And the standard general bibliographies of the holdings of the Library of Congress and British Library make clear that many children's editions of Spenser were published at the end of the nineteenth century and in the early twentieth century; they, too, are testimony to the power and attractiveness of the fabulist dimension of Spenser's work for the unsophisticated reader, including children.

One wonders how many teachers followed the example of William Taylor, William Wordsworth's young headmaster at Hawkshead School, by lending students their books. Surely Wordsworth's two early teachers, his father and Taylor, had much to do with the genesis of "The Female Vagrant" (1791–1794, in 26 Spenserian stanzas).[9] Nor should one forget the influence of his Spenser-loving sister Dorothy.[10] Last, surely one of the century's most charming and affecting Spenser imitations is a remembrance of a teacher, William Shenstone's first, Sarah Lloyd, in "The School-Mistress" (1737, in 35 Spenserian stanzas).

A significant group of poets imitated Spenser—to give one reason at least—because of the influence of other imitators. Lines of influence are traceable from James Thomson's *The Castle of Indolence* (1748) to the last-revised edition of 1748 of William Shenstone's "The School-Mistress" (the first version of which in 1737 was also influenced by Pope's playful 1706 imitation "The Alley," possibly the century's first Spenser imitation). Shenstone's poem in turn influenced Robert Fergusson's "The Farmer's Ingle" (1773), a model for Robert Burns's more famous imitation "The Cotter's Saturday Night" (1786), a poem also influenced by James Beattie's important Spenser imitation The Minstrel (1.1771; 2.1774). "The School-Mistress" contributed to the composition of William Vernon's "The Parish Clerk" (1758), which also imitates William Whitehead's stanza (ababcC), all Spenser imitations.[11] Many other lines of influence could be drawn for others of the English, Irish, and Scots Spenser imitators, but suffice it to say that many imitators of Spenser attempted to render the poet because of earlier imitators. Especially is this true of the Scots. Some imitators, Robert Burns for example, probably knew Spenser not at all first hand;[12] and, as indicated below in the Keats example, eighteenth century Spenser imitators like Thomson, Shenstone, and Beattie influenced the imitations of the major romantic poets, all of whom also knew Spenser's works *per se*.

It may be clear, in miniature at least, that many imitators were influenced by school teachers. This hardly startles when one remembers that the century is anticipated by such Spenserians as John Milton, whose teacher Alexander Gill, High Master of St. Paul's School (1608–1635), *directly* taught him Spenser, an encounter I shall examine later. For historical accuracy, it is worthwhile to recall that Spenser himself was always regarded as a great teacher, beginning at least as early as Milton—himself a teacher for several years—who in his *Areopagitica* calls Spenser "a better teacher than Scotus or Aquinas," and continuing through the next century. One also recalls that soon after the eighteenth century ends, John Keats, an avid Spenserian, was introduced to the poet by his teacher Charles Cowden Clarke at the Rev. John Clarke's private school at Enfield, where Keats was first ravished by the "Epithalamion" and *The Faerie Queene*. Like his eighteenth century forebears, Keats was a close reader of previous Spenser imitators: James Thomson's *Castle of Indolence* (1748), one of the best imitations ever;[13] the Irish Spenserian poet Mary Tighe, whose mid-1790s *Psyche* ran to over 300 Spenserian stanzas; and also James Beattie, whose *Minstrel* was a favorite since its first book was published in 1771 (in 60 Spenserian stanzas). While the short-lived Keats was always a Spenserian, who went through the Elizabethan poet as a "ramping" young horse by his own admission, he was less consistently a devotee of the poet's eighteenth century imitators.

In a letter to his brother and sister, 31 December 1818, Keats says, "Mrs. Tighe and Beattie once delighted me—now I see through them and can find nothing in them but weakness, and yet how many they still delight!"[14] A few months later, 19 March, though, he says to the same correspondents: "This morning I am in a sort of temper, indolent and supremely careless: I long after a stanza or two of Thomson's Castle of Indolence." I have remained with Keats (whose youthful reaction to the poet serves as part of my chapter's title) because I find the nature of his exposure to and involvement with Spenser typical of the eighteenth century, and Keats's own nineteenth century as a whole. It hardly seems imprudent, then, to believe that many schoolchildren between Milton and Keats would have been directed to Spenser by a teacher who was himself or herself a Spenserian. But what of the schools themselves?

As part of their school's curriculum, students learned to imitate classical models. A revealing poem in·this regard, albeit not a Spenser imitation, is "Westminster-School," which appeared in *The Gentleman's Magazine* in the thirties.[15] The anonymous author first pays tribute to such alumni worthies as Abraham Cowley, John Dryden, and Matthew Prior. He or she also might have added alumnus Giles Fletcher the Younger who in *Christs Victory and Triumph* (1610) imitated Spenser and adapted the Spenser stanzaic form into the eight-line *ababbccC*, itself further adapted in the eighteenth century, with the alexandrine retained or dropped. The Westminster School poet describes the school itself and expatiates on the portrait of its most indelible teacher, Dr. Richard Busby, in mock-heroic style.[16] The primary aim of the piece is to "Describe the diff'rent rules they all obey, / And paint the various labours of the day," as the seven forms or "classes" are described.

In the first class, Aesop's tales are studied, for they are instructive for the innocent and "unlearn'd." Here, "Busby's ever-honour'd precepts teach / By easy rules the rudiments of speech." In the second class, the boys have more Aesop wherein "they perceive to what his fables lean." Martial, Justin, and Ovid are *imitated in the schoolboy's own verse* in the third class: "Here first how Poets write, you're taught to know, / And learn to make your lines in numbers flow." But imitation and not emulation is the aim even in a comic passage regarding Grubstreet hacks and poor Colley Cibber:

> See this bright class to genial lines give birth,
> Tho' not superior, yet of equal worth
> To your admir'd profundity of verse;
> For if they don't write better—they can't write worse.

So much for the under school, the first three forms.

Virgil is the subject of the fourth class, where a student "pursues / Books more sublimely penn'd, more noble views." The fourth class is "taught to speak / In diff'rent accent of the hoarser greek." Identified in the fourth form are future "sparks," "lawyers clerks," and apothecaries who try to impress with only the simplest understanding of Greek. The fifth form studies Horace as well as unnamed Greek sages for their "precept" and "virtues." The penultimate class is "in every learned classick [unspecified] skill'd," but the poem's author is more concerned to list distinguished students who won through this class, among them, once again, Dryden, Prior, and Cowley, the latter who read Spenser "all over before . . . twelve years old" since his mother had a volume of his works in her parlor. Noteworthy graduates also included Nicolas Rowe and the Duke of Newcastle. In the seventh form, the Ancients are combined for study, "Eastern tongues [read: Hebrew] are counted rough no more," and "lofty Homer sings." Yet the final pictures in the poem are the "birch-room" ("Ye awful twigs!") and the late Master, the Rev. Dr. Robert Freind,[17] who is compared to no less than Phoebus in brilliance and power and whose "grateful infl'ence and his fire displays / Smiles on his sons, and warms their rising lays." Even though John Locke could criticize the school, Matthew Prior ranked Westminster above the French *lycées* and actively recruited students for its classes.

This airy glimpse of Westminster School in the early eighteenth century has intrinsic merit for its remarks about the awe-inspiring teachers, its alumni, and, more to the point, its by-class list of readings, what the boys were to gather in from the readings in terms of pleasure and instruction, and intimations of what the boys were to write. The "rising lays" of the last lines were certainly imitations, albeit imitations of the Ancients, and begun as early as the third form, the highest class of the under school where "make Latin or English themes" was included.[18] If imitation was so habitual in the schoolboy's early experience, the possibility of students rendering more modern authors like Spenser is not remote, particularly if Phoebus, the teacher, is a Spenserian, as many teachers clearly were.

There is ample evidence that Restoration writers translated the Ancients and "paraphrased" the Psalms, Job (scripture was seldom "imitated"), and Chaucer, but there is also substantial evidence that they imitated such contemporaries as Milton, Butler, Dryden, and even Defoe.[19] Spenser was not as popular a model *for imitation* in the second half of the seventeenth century—a great age for imitation but not of the

Elizabethans—as he was in the first third of that century for Giles and Phineas Fletcher, Joseph Beaumont, and Michael Drayton. This is not to say of course that Spenser was not a considerable *influence* on late seventeenth century writers. Before the eighteenth century proper, then, there was precedent for imitating models other than the Ancients. It is interesting to notice that the seed ground for revolt against exclusively imitating or regarding classical models was the seventeenth century and not later, which is perhaps a more common surmise. Beginning with the 1715 John Hughes edition of Spenser's works, his poems were readily available for study.[20]

At this point it may be instructive to compare two famous, influential schoolmasters who were devoted to Spenser, but for different reasons and with quite different sensibilities. Many years ago, Donald Lemen Clark made clear in his *John Milton at St. Paul's School* the influence exerted on the young Milton at St. Paul's by its High Master, Dr. Alexander Gill Sr.[21] Milton was most explicitly imitative of Spenser in his earlier works such as *Comus* and the stanzaic "minor" (shorter) poems, those closest in time to his St. Paul's days when, according to Clark, Milton "was encouraged to write verses in English as well as in the learned tongues." Clark accounts for Milton's schoolboy experience with Spenser in this way: "As English poets began to produce a classical English literature, the study of English literature was gradually introduced into the school. Dr. Gil, a leader in this movement, wrote an English grammar, the *Logonomia Anglica* (1619), which explained English grammar and rhetoric, in Latin to be sure, but illustrated and embroidered [*copia* being the technique] many of the beauties of the language with quotations from Spenser, Sidney, and Wither." Spenser was Gill's favorite, and Milton's.

Highmaster Gill's pedagogical emphasis in Spenser was tropes. "Our Homer," as he calls Spenser, was a lode for prosody and figures, especially his *Faerie Queene,* and after that poem, *The Ruines of Time* and *The Shepheardes Calender.*[22] Gill's

imitation exercises mostly involved memorization, translation, and paraphrase ("false imitation" R. S. Crane, after Felton,
would judge). His aim was typically the *style* of the model,
and he mustered many examples to this end, emphasizing
Spenser's meters and rhetorical figures. This emphasis was
indeed part of Erasmus's Humanist program of *copia*, or expanding an image or notion used by a literary model. Milton
was good at this technique; Spenser was great at it.

In the first form of the upper school, Gill's students for the
first time were to "turn and prove verses," from Ovid. When
he wanted the example of a Modern, Gill offered Spenser as a
model for his boys. Clark puts the matter this way, "Whether
Dr. Gil let the boys [in the fourth form, of eight] at St. Paul's
School 'taste the sweetness of poetizing in English' before they
were allowed to versify in Latin we have no means of knowing," but Gill certainly did know his English meters and did
admire Spenser's gifts therein. And Milton himself says that
he wrote English verse as a schoolboy. Since Milton was also
being tutored at home by his father and hired teachers while
attending St. Paul's during the day, Gill may not have been
the only influence on Milton's Spenserianism. But he was indisputably the greatest influence. One might generalize with
some assurance that Gill's "taste" in Spenser predominated
throughout the remainder of the seventeenth century, for
Dryden at Westminster School was equally instructed and
pleased by Spenser's figures and versification. How different
from Gill's, however, was the emphasis with Joseph Warton,
Headmaster at Winchester College ("School" to Americans)
for 26 years, beginning in 1766.

The imaginative, romantic (that is, in the manner of the
romances) Spenser was Joseph Warton's Spenser, and this predilection must have been at the center of Warton's teachings
on the poet to the Winchester students during his long tenure
there (dating from 1755 when he began to teach as Usher).
Warton was in his own poetry and criticism passionately in

favor of "Invention and Imagination" as the "chief faculties of a Poet"; he was unfriendly to "the fashion of moralizing in verse." Warton's pronouncements appear in the famous Advertisement for his volume of 14 *Odes on Various Subjects* (1746), poems that he hopes will "bring back Poetry into its right channel."[23] For Warton, Spenser's work exemplifies this "channel." Warton reports on a distinguished (unnamed) person who "after reading a book of the *Dunciad,* always *sooths* himself, as he calls it, by turning to a canto in the Fairy Queen" (2.383n). As a chief exemplar of poetry's right channel of inventiveness and imagination, Spenser influenced Warton's classmate William Collins, who was at Winchester College in his own schoolboy days, commencing in 1735 when he was first elected Scholar there.

Warton's "Gathering Book," written at Winchester College (1739), survives among the Warton manuscripts collected at Trinity College, Oxford. In it are "Subjects for a Picture" and "Similes" such as "The Dark gloomy Scenes in Mines . . . Griping of a Serpent or a Crocodile. A Lamp in a lone Tow'r. Noises heard at Hell-Gates, that were shut . . . Evening Dances in Arcadia . . . Loathsom as the twining of a Serpent round one's Body . . . Oedipus and His Daughters in the Storm a fine Subject for a Picture. Woman with child meeting a devouring Serpent in a Desart."[24] While not identifiably and exclusively Spenserian, they indicate Warton's disposition toward romantic "pictures" in Spenser, images also seen in Warton's own poems. In his *Essay on Pope*—Pope he admired; Spenser he loved—Warton rhapsodizes about Spenser, declaring that "the pencil of Spenser is as powerful as that of Rubens, his brother allegorist"; but Warton allows Spenser more "grace" than Rubens and calls the poet just as "warm a colourist" (2.34). Warton gives as evidence two Jealousy passages from books 2 and 3 of *The Faerie Queene.* One seriously doubts that Dr. Gill would have had such "subjects for a picture" in his own gathering or commonplace book, and one can be rather certain he would not have had his students keep such a journal.

Warton's more romantic attitude is concerned with wildness, dream, fancy, and isolation in instructive repose in nature. These Spenserian elements are caught well in his own "Ode I. To Fancy" where he requests

> Then lay me by the haunted stream
> Wrapt in some wild, poetic dream,
> In converse while methinks I rove
> With Spenser thro' a fairy grove.

Such scenes and vocabulary are iterated throughout Warton's poems. He sees the poet as a welcome companion, since "sweet Spenser caught her [the Italian poetic spirit's] fire" ("Ode V," 25). But Warton can also "wish for tender Spenser's moving verse, / Warbled in broken sobs o'er Sydney's herse" ("Ode XII," 42). Spenser's tenderness is yet another descriptor in evidence in Warton's diction and sensibility. It is pleasant to imagine the reaction of Dr. Gill's boys, and Dr. Gill himself, to Warton's treatment of Spenser were he able to be a guest lecturer at St. Paul's.[25] Gill had few remembered Spenserian progeny (although the one he did have will do!); Warton had many.[26]

Warton's remarks about fellow Spenser imitators are indicative of his own taste as well as of the direction, in sensibility at least, that imitations would take in the next two generations: "It has been fashionable of late to imitate Spenser, but the likeness of most of these copies, hath consisted rather in using a few of his ancient expressions, than in catching his real manner." Warton believed that three imitations go beyond the standard effort: Shenstone's "The School-Mistress," Bedingfield's "The Education of Achilles," and Beattie's *The Minstrel*, all three significantly having to do with education. These three poets have the "simplicity," "tenderness of sentiment," and "touches of nature" of Spenser himself, Warton judges. He calls a fourth imitation exquisite: Thomson's *Castle of Indolence* is "wild" and "romantic" in its imagery. These adjectives, along with *fairy, fancy* and those others already noted, are often used by that other Warton, Thomas, when he writes of Spenser, often at the same time he talks about his favorite subject, Oxford education. All this is quite a distance from the primary concerns of the seventeenth century Spenserians. There has been a traceable movement toward a different sensibility and poetic emphasis coming from the work of the most influential Spenserians.

Other Spenser imitators to study at Westminster School were Sir James Bland Burges, William Cowper, Robert Lloyd (there as student, Usher, and Master), Matthew Prior (who wished to be buried at the feet of Spenser and was),[27] Edmund Smith (early, under Dr. Busby), Robert Southey, and Samuel Wesley ("near Twenty Years Usher" at Westminster, according to the titlepage of his 1736 *Poems*).[28] As we shall see, Wesley's relative John included *The Faerie Queene* on his list of recommended readings for Methodists in the second class of their formation at Kingswood School. Such schools as Wesley's and the dissenting academies (similar, one should think, to the one attended by Daniel Defoe, the Rev. Morton's academy at Newington Green) seem to have been alone in *formally* offering a nonclassical curriculum.

Spenser imitators connected with Winchester College included the cleric William Lisle Bowles (pupil of Joseph Warton), Joseph Warton, Dr. Robert Lowth, Gloster Ridley, Christopher Pitt, William Whitehead, and William Collins.[29] The latter entered Winchester at age 12 and in 1733, according to the testimony of his friend Joseph Warton, Collins, *while a student at Winchester*, composed his *Persian Eclogues* (published 1742), which are in part Spenser imitations. One is certain that Collins' practice in this was not unique. Of course, Collins' "Ode on the Poetical Character" is one of the milestone usages of Spenser's *The Faerie Queene* at the midcentury, 1747. While there were more Spenserians in the making at

Westminster School and Winchester College than at any other schools, Eton could boast of better Spenser imitators. Alumnus Thomas Gray, who by his own admission never wrote poems before rereading Spenser (and his poems reflect this practice), of course wrote the century's most beautiful reflection on Eton, "Ode on a Distant Prospect of Eton College" (1742).

Eton was also the alma mater of the elder of two of Spenser's first imitators: Phineas Fletcher (*The Purple Island*), brother to Giles, a Westminsterite. As did his brother, Phineas further adapted the Spenserian stanza (*ababababccC*). The second early Etonian imitator was Henry More, whose *Praexistency of the Soul* (1647) appeared in 104 Spenserian stanzas, which, while good in Spenser's diction and form, are innocent of Spenserian content. Another Etonian, William Pitt, according to his sister Anne's report, "knew nothing accurately except Spenser's *Faerie Queene*."[30] Eton's Assistant Master at one time was James Upton, whose second son John went on to become the century's greatest *Faerie Queene* editor.

Eton spawned as well the Rev. Samuel Croxall, the eighteenth century's first accomplished imitator of Spenser's diction and nine-line stanza in the 1713 *An Original Canto of Spencer* (46 Spenserian stanzas). In the next year, he wrote two imitations: *Another Original Canto of Spencer* (54 Spenserian stanzas) and *An Ode Humbly Inscrib'd to the King* (42 Spenserian stanzas). As good as any of the century's satirical imitations in its approximation of Spenser's antique language was Etonian Richard Cambridge's mock-heroic *Archimage* (1742, in 29 Spenserian stanzas). George Sewell's couplet "The Force of Musick: A Fragment after the Manner of Spenser" (ca. 1710) is at once an early example of Spenser rendered into a verse form quite un-Spenserian and an early anticipation of the many general subjects Spenser imitators would treat. The final noteworthy Etonian Spenser imitator was Gilbert West (whose 1751 *Education: A Poem* has already been referred to), who in 1739 wrote about *The Abuse of Travelling*, published that same year as *A Canto of the Fairy Queen* (58 Spenserian stanzas). This is to say nothing of those several Spenserians trained at Harrow, St. Paul's, Merchant Taylors', the dissenting academies, or those 20 or so imitators prepared in schools in Edinburgh and Ireland.[31] School records and alumni anecdotes shed some light on a few of these schools.

Spenser Reposited

Texts and teaching were similar it seems at all the major English public schools in the century. The situation at Winchester College is elucidated by the introduction printed for the June 1971 exhibit titled *Winchester College 1679–1832*, held at the school and mounted by the predecessor of Archivist Roger Custance, Peter Gwyn, and Fellows' Librarian J. M. G. Blakiston. An excerpt from the exhibit's printed introduction may serve as a useful generalization for the three major schools:

> Not everybody in the 18th century thought that a classical curriculum was the only one possible [witness Gilbert West]. So influential a person as John Locke could plead quite vigorously for a wider programme. In practice, however, Latin and Greek completely dominated the education provided in all schools which, like Winchester, might contemplate sending boys to the Universities. It is true that probably for most of the 18th century a Writing Master was employed, who might give private tuition in elementary mathematics as well as helping a new boy to write well; but until the appearance of Thomas Bowyer in 1800 he is a very shadowy figure. . . . Modern languages made only a faint appearance before 1821. . . . The fact that a most successful English Grammar was produced by the Wykehamist Robert Lowth and that a man with such a love and knowledge of English literature as Joseph Warton was Headmaster for twenty-six years might suggest that English would have found a place in the timetable, but the evidence of any formal instruction in this subject is very slight.

It is important to note, as the authors go on to suggest, that English writers would have naturally been included with the Ancients in such classrooms as Warton's. Matching the evidence in the Westminster poem quoted earlier, Gwyn and Blakiston concede that a "boy's time was heavily occupied in speaking and translating Classical authors and in writing his own compositions, especially verse compositions, in the ancient languages"; but "There is some evidence that once a boy had risen from the lower forms he could encounter less emphasis on Grammar at Winchester than elsewhere." One on the trail of Spenser *in* the eighteenth century schools would be led to believe that valuable information was available from the mysterious Writing Master.[32] One would also mightily wish to discover just *how* such teacher-Spenserians as Warton departed from and enlivened the unremitting curriculum by using such Moderns as Spenser. That he used Spenser in his classrooms cannot hereafter be seriously contested.

As an indication of what school library holdings were in Spenseriana in the eighteenth century, Winchester had three editions of Spenser's works and a paraphrase of *Faerie Queene,* book 1, all given to the College library by Old Wykehamists: the 1611 *Faerie Queene* and *The Shepheardes Calender,* the 1687 *Spencer Redivivus Containing the First Book of the Fairy Queen,* and the 1679 *Works.* In addition, the library had Thomas Warton Jr.'s *Observations on the Faerie Queene of Spenser* (1754), William Huggins's *The Observer Observ'd. Or, Remarks on a Certain Curious Tract intitled Observations on the Faiere Queene of Spencer by Thomas Warton* (1756), and Sir Kenelm Digby's early *Observations on the 22 Stanza in the 9th Canto of the 2d Book of Spencers Faery Queen* (1644). Of this trio, Warton and Digby were Wykehamists. Spenser and selected (by Warton?) studies of him were thus available in print to the boys in school.[33]

The case with teaching and texts seems to be little different at Eton in the eighteenth century, when Greek and Latin filled the curriculum. As well, precious little mathematics figures in the schoolboy's education until after the first quarter of the next century. The practice of sending "up for good" meritorious exercises to the Headmaster after each half—the pieces still housed in the College library as they have been since the eighteenth century—may have trained the boys to try to excel in composition, a discipline that would have made them more competitive later for Cambridge and Oxford poetry prizes, some of which were given for Spenser imitations. Certainly, however, as late as 1832, prize exercises in schools were still almost exclusively involved with translating into Latin and Greek, as the *Charterhouse Prize Exercises, From 1814–1832* makes clear. For most of the century, the curriculum at Harrow School was probably the same one offered by the school's founder John Lyon (1571): classical languages and literatures, scripture, and English grammar. But later in the eighteenth century, English verse and prose writing became more prominent and important. At Harrow, the extant composition exercises, dating from ca. 1770, are in Latin and Greek, and unfortunately not many detailed records or timetables regarding curriculum survive. Yet, Harrow schoolboys did read English literature, and the practice of English prose and verse composition were significant in the final quarter of the century. The dramatist Thomas Sheridan's teacher, Dr. Samuel Parr, remembers him, at Harrow 1762–1768, as not distinguished in either Latin or English composition, in either prose or verse. A schoolmate of Sheridan is remembered, however, for having "excelled in English verse."[34] Apparently no evidence survives of the verse the boys were directed to study as models for their writing.

Among the English literature read in the schools were works by Edmund Spenser. As the record of imitations of the poet for each decade of the eighteenth century makes clear, Spenser was a popular model for writers. My purpose up to this point has been to suggest that Spenser was often first encountered in a serious way in the schools or during the school years, but outside of school, student and poet were most likely introduced by a parent, tutor, or friend. One has the impression that young readers then, as now, needed to be instructed in Spenser, what he was about as moralist, fabulist, and belle-lettrist.[35] The more one studies the factual record, the more confidence one has in suggesting that the eighteenth century schools, notwithstanding their rock-ribbed conservative curricula, fostered, through those teachers who loved Spenser, a spirit of liberating experimentation as they, perhaps formally, perhaps not, presented the Moderns as models. As a model for imitators in the areas of a variety of subjects and verse forms, Spenser was second to no other; that is, Spenser, among the native writers, was rendered more variously than was Milton, and certainly more than Shakespeare and Chaucer.

SPENSER AS THE SPRING OF ENGLISH LITERATURE

While one hopes that what has been said is worth knowing for its own sake, one also is emboldened to suggest that an important result of imitating native models is the beginnings of the profession of English literature.[36] While rumblings were heard intermittently a century earlier, it is in the eighteenth century that for the first time an educational revolution was begun, one giving birth to the "English profession" by a group of teachers and curricular reformers not of a cabal and not confederated. These revisionists, while adhering to the ancient and prescribed teaching and learning method of imitating models, elevated three native writers "of the last age," particularly Spenser, to the stature of such great classical pedagogical exemplars as Aesop, Martial, Justin, Ovid, Horace, and Virgil, who for generations were among those writers deemed most worthy of study and imitation. The importance of this fact for the development of English studies and teaching is incalculable and surprisingly unnoticed heretofore.

The few recent historical accounts of the English profession are similar to that of James R. Squire's "History of the Profession," wherein the eighteenth century is ignored, the late nineteenth century recognized as the "beginnings," and the twentieth century the study's heart.[37] Scholars in this area must adjust the inception date and their understanding of the formulative forces identified above as efficient cause for the English profession as it is today, even though the proper models for study remain a continuing discussion and presumably always will. "Profession" has two senses: first and most pointed, an open affirmation of English writers over Latin and Greek writers as most appropriate models for imitation; second, and closer to what most readers probably would understand by the term: canonical and curricular matters, the rise of departments of English, and the training and credentialing of teachers. These last three are in part the result of the first sense of the word.

Thanks to the efforts of eighteenth century reformers, "beauties" from Shakespeare, Spenser, and Milton increasingly appeared in grammars, books of instruction, anthologies, literary criticism, imitations, adaptations, editions, and, as seen above, in classrooms. At that time, Shakespeare's influence on the English profession was comparatively diffuse, somewhat superficial, and often only aesthetic. Needless to say, Shakespeare's influence otherwise in the century was profound. For the history of the profession, of the three great Renaissance writers, Shakespeare was third in importance. Milton is ubiquitous in the century and without question the most commonly cited of the native models; his presence on the pages that follow is not surprising. Spenser's importance is perhaps more surprising, since he is today regarded mostly as an influence on the taste and sensibility of the age's second half, when the floodgates of Spenserianism were opened and that poet became the major native model for the English romantics. The Wartons, as we have seen, contributed significantly to the movement to loosen the curriculum, but their voices and practices were not the only ones in the land.

There is direct evidence of the call to action away from strictly classical models. One J. F.'s couplets, "Verses spoken at Westminster School" (Dodsley *Collection* 4:111–17), are light social satire about this important nursery for Spenserians, where "we speak like Romans, and like Romans write" (116). Increasingly, even conservative classicists saw the efficacy of English along with classical models. Henry Felton's popular and important 1713 *Dissertation*, remarked upon by R. S. Crane and myself, extols Spenser and Milton as proper models for study and imitation, equal to Theocritus and Virgil. The significance of such pairing of Ancients and Moderns is difficult to overstate, but one young woman's reaction to Felton's work is recorded by "Mr. Harte." In the notes to his 1727 translation of "The Sixth Thebaid of Statius" (*Poems on Several Occasions*, 105–225), Harte quotes Spenser several times and reports on a young lady's response to Felton's *Miscellany*: "Like *Vinci's* strokes, thy verse we behold; / Correctly graceful, and with labour bold . . . Here *Spenser's* thought in solemn numbers roll, / Here lofty *Milton* seems to lift the Soul." The reader does not fail to see that the writers impressing her were native and modern or to note that it is Spenser's thoughts that are indelible.

Some reformers sided with John Clarke, whose 1720 *Essay upon the Education of Youth* posits alternatives. Master of Hull Grammar School, Clarke praises John Locke's essay on education but implies he does not go far enough in his reforms. Clarke wants to give students a "variety of proper *English* examples to their Rules" (16), and, concurring with Locke, allow theme-making in English at the expense of verse-making in Latin. He sounds like a further liberated Dr. Gill, but Clarke wants theme writing for the purpose of training the reason and judgment and not for the flowers of wit, fancy, or rhetoric (120). For such efforts as these and his other giftedness, historian T. A. Laughlin considers Clarke one of Hull's "Four Great Headmasters" (22–31). The anonymous author of the 11-page *Proposals for the Reformation of Schools and Universities* (1704) adds that learning has decayed, few can write well, and reforms are needed; therefore, the suggestion is, teach the English language, read English authors in whole books, and include "Modern [unspecified] Books of all sorts" (8). *Tatler* 234 (1710) is among several defenses of its day in favor of reading more English over Latin grammar. Of course some commentators like "Anti-Paedagogus" of *The High Road to Parnassus* (1720) hated both the Ancients and Moderns in the schools and hit at curriculum, pedantry, poets, and religious instruction with equal venom.

As suggested earlier, the two-score dissenting academies seemed to agree: their influence was broad, and their curriculum was to become the standard after several more generations passed. University trained and thereby indoctrinated into the fixed classical curriculum of Oxford and Cambridge, tutors at dissenting academies ignored traditional strictures by teaching modern writers. Milton was a favorite along with Spenser, Milton's own favorite model. Oxonian John Wesley taught Spenser at Kingswood, a Methodist academy where history was emphasized. After the first year, a track was offered each year in English literature. In year two, Spenser was the only belletristic author studied. In year three, Milton; in four, Shakespeare.[38] The importance of this curricular ventilation is great in the long view and hindsight. Not wishing to appear novel, defenders of such an opened curriculum wanted traditionalists to know that their academies offered a substantial "higher" education. Wesley himself claimed that four years of his curriculum were worth seven at Cambridge or Oxford. Samuel Palmer's 1703 pamphlet *Defence of the Dissenters*

Education recommends Milton while taking pains, in its 21 pages, to show that a dissenter's education is distinguished, serious, nonfactional.

An undated manuscript commonplace book of the period 1700–1725 (Folger MS W.A. 126) shows that Spenser was read not only for the purpose of stylistic improvement but also for his moral fabling: "Spenser was a great genius. The heathenish religion being woven into the contexture of all the ancient poets, the moderns affected to give that of phanity a place in theirs; but as these attempts seemed rather to debase religion than to heighten poetry, Spenser endeavourd to supply this defect with morality & to make instruction instead of story the object of an epic poem. His execution was excellent, and his flights of fancy very noble and high, but his design was poor and his morality lay so bare that it lost its effect" (25).

The instructive, moral and even "bare" Spenser seems to have been the Spenser the 1835 diarist chose to see. In the Wordsworth Collection of Indiana University's Lilly Library resides a manuscript "Prose redaction" of the first nine cantos of book 1 of Spenser's *Faerie Queene*, dated 16–30 September, which shows that the writer, whom I believe to be William Wordsworth, was impressed with the morality of Spenser's allegory more than his pictures. Since the manuscript was— carefully—written over a two-week span in the early autumn of 1845, the emphasis on the instructive over the imagistic may seem faintly anachronistic for such a late-romantic document, particularly if Wordsworth indeed is the diarist. If so, the manuscript shows that he, at age 75, was a lifelong reader of Spenser and concerned with different excellencies in his work from those that captivated him during the years of "The Female Vagrant" (26 Spenserian stanzas), in the early 1790s, and its revisions in the later 90s into *Salisbury Plain* and *Guilt and Sorrow* (respectively, 54 and 74 Spenserian stanzas).

Picture-making Spenser seems ever to have been of first interest to young readers of the poet. Gill realized this in presenting Spenserian posies to his students. But posies or the versification interests of Dryden or the fancy and gothicities of Warton and Hurd are not emphasized in the Wordsworth Collection's prose redaction of book 1 of *The Faerie Queene*, which goes some distance to show that the romantics were not exclusively aesthetes in their appreciations of Spenser. The redaction also goes some distance to say that the eighteenth century Spenserians did not have the edge in seeing instruction in that Elizabethan poet.

Only a few examples from the manuscript need serve. Along with a neat, full paraphrase, the commentary, apostrophes, and moral-ethical opining show that Spenser's first book teaches. While the subject of holiness naturally lends itself to didacticism, one would expect Wordsworth to linger in scenes, emotions, and pictures in his notations, but one finds little of that. It is as though the privately meant poem is the occasion of meditation for the poet, who writes with only five years of life remaining to him. His rendering of the Error episode is straightforward with no interpretational intrusions, but his selection of what to quote, Una's and the Dwarf's warning, and Una's caveat before and after Redcross's victory, betray the drift of the highlighting that follows.

For the opening Archimago episode, interest is shown in the wizard's invitation to rest; spiritual sloth is of course allegorically the opening for temptation. Redcross's temptation is moralized in spots, almost comically. The knight sees the false Una, described thusly: "There stood his Lady before him, hiding her bated hook under her black stole." In canto 2, the sexual intercourse between the false squire and false Una is given in patent eighteenth century language, "the shameful chains of Venus." Archimago's duplicity earns "O who can understand the hidden power of words and might of magic!" Clearly the apostrophizer either reads Spenser as a moral teacher or shows himself to be one, or both.

Next comes a fleshed-out description of the Redcross-Sansfoy battle. Wordsworth's few crossouts and careful, accurate paraphrases suggest that he wanted to get Spenser right, even explaining the similes. He interpolates often; for instance, Redcross, after hearing of Duessa's false lineage, is described as "moved with passion, more busying his eyes to view her face, than his ears to hear what she told." This remark says something worthwhile about the psychological state of Redcross in the moral allegory and not merely at the fictive level. The paraphrase also injects little pieties, such as in the episode of the tree people, Fradubio-Fraelissa: grief is hard to speak about, "but the grief is double which is concealed like flowers, which burn inwardly." Canto 2's paraphrase ends with this demi-Spenserian description of Redcross's revival of (falsely) swooning Duessa: "Too simple, and too faithful, he took her up with a trembling voice of trembling solice, and often kissed her." The emphasis and manner of the paraphrases of the following seven cantos are like those above.

Canto 3, titled "Una," sensuously shows Una with "limbs beautiful" and body "tender." Adversity is examined fully, as is "true love." Canto 4's center is the procession of the Seven Deadly Sins and their matching animals, including filthy Lechery, unfit for ladies; but Lechery did fine with the ladies, "For who can tell what is the bent of a woman's fancy?" Canto 5's paraphrase, the second longest at 11 pages (canto 7 is longest), is the first to contain no commentary. Wordsworth seems to like this canto with its imagery of dark and light, especially dark. As revealed by the dating log of the manuscript, he spends two days on its paraphrase; some cantos receive only one day's notations. Canto 6's treatment of the attempted rape of Una causes an apostrophe on heaven beholding this noisome act. The writer is seemly in his treatment of the poem's sex: he never becomes explicit, never lingers.

The manuscript's omissions are of some interest, too; Wordsworth does not interpret the symbolic meaning of clothing, demeanor, physiognomy, and so forth. Thus in canto 7 one does not read that Duessa's triple crown and dress are to be associated with the Whore of Babylon and the Roman

Catholic Church. In the penultimate canto, Orgoglio's smelly dungeon and the pitiful sight of Redcross did not dissuade his rescue by Prince Arthur because, we are told, "entire affection regards not niceties." Through manuscript underlining, Arthur's instruction to the weakened Redcross is emphasized: *"that bliss may not abide in the state of mortality"*; then, as if talking to Redcross, the writer instructs the knight to go forth and "master these misfortunes with patience." Canto 9, the final section of book 1 treated, is well done in carefully wrought English; but the seven pages, the briefest of the lot, stop abruptly just before one of the poem's great moments, the Despair encounter.

Likewise, perhaps such a moral, instructive, serious Spenser was the main attraction for the protestant and Protestant dissenting academies, which were in many ways the clearest forerunners of our own curricula. Their instructive Spenser (and Shakespeare and Milton) rather than the virtuoso "poet's poet" of Gill and Busby was a commonly held view of this poet in the eighteenth and nineteenth centuries. And this view influenced choices for textbook and curricular canons in our own century, at least until recently. In the nineteenth century, two contemporaries of Wordsworth, Leigh Hunt and Cardinal Wiseman, engage in a battle over the morality of Spenser and in Spenser, reported from Hunt's point of view in a 94-page autograph manuscript (circa 1859; Folger N.a.74 case 84) titled "English Poetry versus Cardinal Wiseman."

Hunt quotes the Cardinal's charge that Chaucer and Spenser never give a "'description of natural beauty' without 'wantonness, voluptuousness, and debauchery'" (unnumbered ms.). In a "series of countercharges," which accuse Wiseman of proselytizing for Catholicism, Hunt labels Spenser a moralist through his allegorical portraits of "excess" (27). Like Chaucer, Spenser wrote as he did because of his Catholic sources and the times. In a provocative observation still of interest today, Hunt allows that Spenser did not degrade women as did the

Catholic Dante. Of interest also, especially when one remembers the manuscript paraphrase above, is Hunt's appeal to the authority of Wordsworth, who saw Spenser and Milton as "'two grand store-houses' of poetical imagination" (39). And Hunt quotes Wordsworth's appreciation of Spenser's being "free" by virtue of his "allegorical spirit."

In a remark that is applicable to almost all the major nineteenth century writers, and many earlier ones, Hunt boasts that "I, for one, have been a reader of Spenser during almost the whole of my life" and Spenser has given "content" and "retreat from care, full of comfort and beauty inexpressible, with his woods, his visions, his virtues, his music, his mythologies, his masterly and most pictorial paintings, his noble and most refined sentiments." He continues his affecting defense with "I am not aware that [he] . . . ever did me an atom of harm" (39). Later, Hunt charges Wiseman with misunderstanding Spenser's merely "classical mind" (53), a key to which are John Upton's *Faerie Queene* notes (1758 edition). Last, Hunt gives a moving portrait of the dead Keats, who was hurt by Wiseman's attacks. Scrutiny of this appreciation and defense by Hunt reveals that there is no important difference in what is said about Spenser from earlier remarks, even as early as a century or more before.

But back to the century under consideration. By the mid-century, writers such as Gilbert West felt fully comfortable in allegorically attacking unthinking adherence to the Ancients in *Education* (1751). And the important anthologist and some-time Spenser imitator Robert Dodsley was not renegade in giving generous examples from Shakespeare, Spenser, and Milton in his popular school text. Dodsley's 1748 two-volume *Preceptor: Containing a General Course of Education* (7 eds. by 1783) gives, for analysis by students, excerpts from Milton and Shakespeare. For imagery and personification, Dodsley offers passages from *Faerie Queene* book 2 along with a Spenser imitation, "The Choice of Hercules," fittingly in the section on Human Life and Manners (2:534–44).

Many students, perhaps between schooldays and those at the university, during the university experience (rather like our semester abroad), or shortly thereafter, commonly took the Grand Tour. It was one of the most pleasant of eighteenth century rites of passage, particularly but not exclusively for "gentlemen" in the making. Apparently Jonathan Swift was not a supporter of the whole-person educational ideals of the Italian Renaissance as reflected in, say, Baldesar Castiglione's *Il cortegiano* and the French practices. Swift writes against the trend, in the education of the privileged, away from book learning of the classics and toward such enterprises as dancing, fencing, and French tutors: in short, against what some today would call holistic education. "Education is always the *worse* in Proportion to the *Wealth* and *Grandeur* of the Parents," Swift complains in his 1735 *Works* (1. 286). His reader has the impression that he would not be enthusiastic for all aspects of the Grand Tour.

With similar sentiment and in the same year as Swift's *Works*, Hildebrand Jacob's "To *** Concerning Travel and Education" advises his friend's collegiate son to study and forget the fashionable Grand Tour travel. Indeed, the boy himself wants to return to school:

> He went, and grudges all his pains,
> Till Cam [Cambridge] or Isis he regains,
> . . . Had it not better been to stay,
> And *Educate* the good, old Way,
> With *solid Learning* store his Mind
> From *Books*, he left unread behind
> . . . The dark'ning *Age* declines apace:
> With Tears I think upon the *Race*
> Our future *Progeny* must breed,
> And fear, our *Grandsons* will not *read*.
>
> (*Works*, 119–21)

Gilbert West satirizes the Grand Tour as "vain Travel" (stanza 2) in *A Canto of the Fairy Queen* (1739). Orgoglio tempts Redcross by taking him to a country resembling the

Bower of Bliss—Italy, I assume—where the "Arts of slavery / were taught" (stanza 18). West calls the place a "Seminary of Fashions Vain" that causes travelers there to think "meanly of their Native Land." In Swift, Jacob, and West, nationalism probably was as much in play as pure educational concern.

To a large degree, English and what has been called the vernacular movement was tied to nationalism, and most ferment on this issue took place in the schools. Richard S. Tompson's appraisal of education in the eighteenth century is accurate and in keeping with my own findings. His "English and English Education in the Eighteenth Century" makes several pertinent points. First, "Instead of a quiescent period [in education], we must consider the 18th century to be a period of activity, spurred by the traditional philanthropic motive of social stability, the prevailing notions of utility [I presume this means the practical subjects of the dissenting academies] and concern for building the strength of the national state" (1). These are not unlike the reasons one finds proffered today for legislating that English solely be the language of the United States.

Second, the vernacular movement was led by teachers and educational writers such as Thomas Sheridan, Daniel Defoe, and Jonathan Swift, who wrote reform theory rather than reform praxis in curricular matters (Tompson, 4–5). Third, new schools proliferated most in the first half century, textbooks most in the second half. Last, of the kinds of fast-growing eighteenth century elementary schools (endowed schools, charity and Sunday schools, and tuition schools), the swiftest growth was in schools endowed "specifically for nonclassical instruction," especially between 1700–1740 when about "35% of all the schools in existence in 1818 were founded." Also, elementary schools endowed as classical schools "included provisions for English instruction in their foundation" (5). Thus, the primary materials, generalizations, and assumptions I offer are consonant with Tompson's data.

Spenser at University

The educational rigors at Cambridge and Oxford were much less malleable and open to the sense of new days dawning. The old opinions about the eighteenth century's poor university teaching and eye-glazing curricula seem to be true. On the authority of A. D. Godley's 1908 study of *Oxford in the Eighteenth Century*, one concludes that Cambridge was more liberal in formal educational matters than Oxford, but teaching at both was generally inferior, with the first half of the century better than the second. Apparently the nadir was reached in the 1790s. For those interested in literary study, "college teaching generally did little more than to lay a meagre foundation" (65). The required reading lists were narrow and classical. And the reading of Moderns and native writers such as Shakespeare, Milton, Pope, and Spenser, even though encouraged by enthusiasts such as the Wartons, was accomplished on one's own time.

At the universities Spenser was read informally as well as taught by Spenserians. *Some Account of the Studies of English Universities in the Eighteenth Century*, the subtitle of Christopher Wordsworth's 1877 *Scholae Academicae*, shows that as early as 1707 students at Cambridge, Spenser's own university, were encouraged to read daily some "Piece of the best and most genuine English" written by historians, but still and nonetheless in comparison with model ancients (338–39). By the midcentury, the Rev. Thomas Zouch's "Scheme of Study at Trinity College Cambridge" is to "Occasionally read Some of our best English Poets, whenever you find youself fatigued with more severe studies" (347). In the ten letters (1707–1710) written by the Earl of Shaftesbury to a "Young Man at the University," the youth is directed: "If the Ancients, in their Purity, are as yet out of your Reach, search the Moderns, that are nearest to them. If you cannot converse with the most Antient, use the *most Modern* [my emphasis]. . . .

Gain the Purity of the *English*, your own Tongue; and read whatever is esteem'd polite or well writ, that comes abroad."[39] Probably more students than Thomas Warton Jr. had the now-familiar experience with Spenser while at university. Warton often read "romantic Spenser's moral page" (the adjectives of interest in tandem) while lying on Cherwell's shore at Oxford, when Upton came

> To chase the mists that hung o'er fairy ground:
> His wisard hand unlocks each magic value,
> And opes each flowery forest's guarded bound.
>
> ("Ode V. Sent to Mr. Upton,
> on his [1758] Edition of the *Faerie Queene*," 41)

The Connoisseur No. 42 (14 Nov. 1754) mentions a newly formed "English Club" aimed at cultivating English language usage by having English classics read to its members: "They have instituted annual festivals in honour of Spenser, Shakespeare, Milton, &c. on each of which an oration, interspersed with encomiums on the English language, is spoken in praise of the author" (1:247). Even if it is satirically intended, this worthy effort to encourage the native tradition still did not salve the dissatisfaction felt by a new Cambridge B. A., expressed in a piece written for *Connoisseur* 107 (12 Feb. 1756). His evaluation of studies there serves as a typical judgment on fossilized university education, for his four years at Cambridge were cluttered with a "miscellaneous heap of nonsense"; so now, after his undergraduate years, he must "begin the world of literature anew" (2:643–44).

Once again, Spenser figures importantly in many poems about education, this time at the university level. A good example is Samuel Whyte's 1772 collection of lyrics, *The Shamrock; or, Hibernian Cresses*. Therein in "A Familiar Epistle, from a Law Student, in the Country, To his Friend, at the Temple" (1761), Spenser is an inspiration during university days:

When, thus, 'midst solemn Dons, at last
Six lingering loitering Hours are past,
O! who the Pleasure would refuse
Of listening to the chearful Muse?

(293)

After lunch, while walking in the meadow near the river, the student is far from boring studies: "Here oft in pensive Mood I stray, / Recalling many a tuneful Lay," of Spenser (295). English literature was thus engaged in by students at universities.

In a concluding section of "Thought on the Prevailing System of School Education," Whyte, himself a schoolmaster, is regardful of the sentiments expressed in Gilbert West's *Education*. He also agrees with curricular reformers such as Locke and Thomas Sheridan who wanted more English language and literature. In Sheridan's 1769 *Plan of Education*, the upper school would accommodate career choices, but curricular constants would be religion, history, oratory, and English literature. Whyte recommends Shakespeare and Spenser but particularly Milton's *Paradise Lost*. An advocate of women's education, Whyte, in the tradition of Daniel Defoe and several others a generation earlier, calls for the "female Right to literature"; but—in keeping with his time—he wants women to be educated separately (507). His recommendations for the "Teaching of English in a Classical Manner" (510) were not to be heeded for another century in Great Britain. Although English literature was incorporated into the "Pass Examination" at Oxford in 1873, the English School at Oxford was not founded until 1894 (Cambridge's occurred a bit earlier); nevertheless, as seen above, efforts were made in the direction of such study for nearly 200 years before. In his 1909 account of *The School of English Language and Literature* at Oxford, C. H. Firth concludes that although the "development of the study of English literature in the universities was less rapid than that of Anglo-Saxon, there were always men who read it with delight," for there is a "critical spirit" about English literature which "encourages its study" (11).

The struggle to unmoor the unrelenting classical curriculum begins in earnest and from varied perspectives and degrees of intensity in the eighteenth century, and this effort, although only partially successful, has to do significantly with the course of "English" thereafter. It is possible to add that the introduction of native models in the schools and out, both formally and informally, helped to elevate national pride; to establish three shining lights, including Spenser, as the epicenter of a native literary tradition; to whet taste for events, themes, and personages real or imagined from the British tradition (Arthurian materials and Medieval ballad, drama, and romances, for example); and to create what will become standard native allusions and styles: Miltonic blank verse and Spenserian verse forms and meters are only two examples. The advent of native writers in the schools of the seventeenth and eighteenth centuries also started a palpable, traceable curricular dialectic in literature that we today still engage: namely, deciding which writers best match with what may be termed the *oughtness* of a particular educational enterprise, or such concerns as the mission of the school(s), or the "product" one wishes to fashion, or the intrinsic merit of the literature itself as art. In the remarks of the curricular reformers, modern teachers are certain to see something of themselves and their own professional musings, questions, and struggles. And Spenser's role as played in the early eighteenth century has had surprising resonances in such matters. He thus contributed to the maturation of several movements and fashions in the eighteenth century particularly, when his celebrity and importance as a literary model grew directly out of educational encounters with him.

Two

"Methinks I Rove with Spenser thro' a Fairy Grove"

ﻰ

Some Lineaments of Imitation and Spenser Anthologized

Faced by a rising enthusiasm for Spenser, Samuel Johnson expressed dissatisfaction over typical imitations of the poet's style, particularly of his diction and stanza, a practice which, at midcentury, "by the influence of some men of learning and genius, seems likely to gain upon the age" (*Rambler* 121, May 1751). And some 30 years later, when he came to write *The Lives of the Poets* (1779–1781), Johnson did not change his mind.

In his *Life of Gilbert West*, Johnson praises West—a skillful imitator of Spenser—for "the metre, the language, and the fiction" of his imitations, three matters that contemporary commentators on Spenser usually addressed. However, Johnson adds that such works

> are not to be reckoned among the great achievements of the intellect, because their effect is local and temporary; they appeal not to reason or passion, but to memory, and presuppose an accidental or artificial state of mind. An imitation of Spenser is nothing to a reader, however acute, by whom Spenser has never been perused. Works of this kind may deserve praise, as proofs of great industry and great nicety of observation, but the highest praise, the praise of genius, they cannot claim.

As we shall see, poet and critic Edward Young's evaluation is cannily similar to Johnson's. Despite such animadversions, imitating Spenser occupied the talents of a wide range of poets, all of whom were perhaps content to fall short of "the praise of genius," but whose work is nonetheless an extraordinary testimony to the "great industry and great nicety of observation" of the age. Spenser was the second most imitated; the first, Milton, also had imitators who were attacked, and much earlier in the century. Sir Richard Blackmore complains about imitators such as John Philips in his 1718 *Collection of Poems*:

> No more let Milton's Imitator dare
> Torture our Language to torment the Ear,
> With Numbers harsher than the din of War
> ... So many Masters of this tuneful Skill,
> With their melodious Songs the Kingdom fill.

(14)

In this period, no major writer's imitator, regardless of his or her competence, totally escaped close critical scrutiny if the imitations were often put before the public.

The vogue for imitating Spenser in the eighteenth century began in 1706, the year of Matthew Prior's "An Ode, Humbly Inscrib'd to the Queen." But a perusal of the imitations listed in bibliography C will show other candidates for "first" than Prior. On or about the year 1706 were written or published

Alexander Pope's pert "The Alley," William Atwood's remarks on Prior's *Ode*, "A Modern Inscription," Elijah Fenton's "Ode to the Sun," and Thomas Warton Sr.'s "Philander." Before Prior and his fellow imitators at the beginning of the eighteenth century, there were only a handful of Spenser imitations; after 1706, they multiplied rapidly.

The most intense period of imitation was 1746 to 1758, though imitations are found in abundance throughout the century. Of 318 verifiable imitations and adaptations (not including works only influenced by, or alluding to, or echoing Spenser), some 62 come from this period, so it is little wonder that Johnson wrote as he did in his *Rambler* essay of 1751. These 13 years produced James Thomson's *The Castle of Indolence* (1748), one of the best imitations, and the writing of Moses Mendez, one of the most authentic imitators of the age. Also from the midcentury came the imitations of the influential anthologist Robert Dodsley, himself a minor Spenser imitator, whose collections of *Poems* (1758–63) contain many Spenser imitations which are at once reprises of the efforts of earlier imitators and harbingers of the kinds of imitations to appear in the second half of the century. Particularly are they the latter.

During these few years, there were at least 20 imitations of *The Faerie Queene*, totaling many hundreds of Spenserian stanzas. There were as well eight more that adopted the quasi-Spenserian stanza which Prior introduced in his "Ode" of 1706. There were imitations of Spenser's sonnet form by writers such as Thomas Percy, an unidentified "Dr. P.," and Thomas Edwards, who in 1748 wrote his sonnet 8, "On the Cantos of Spenser's Fairy Queen, Lost in the Passage from Ireland." Other Spenserians imitated *The Shepheardes Calender*, *Epithalamion*, *Amoretti*, *Fowre Hymnes*, *The Ruines of Time*, and *Mother Hubberds Tale*. There was also a 1758 blank-verse adaptation of *The Shepheardes Calender* by one "Philisides." This concentrated output shares many characteristics with other imitations and adaptations of 1660–1800, the years of the (now standard term) "long" eighteenth century.

Ways and Means of Imitation

The midcentury produced imitations in several major categories: (1) allegorical imitations, (2) "new" or substitution cantos, (3) continuation cantos, (4) bucolic and "season" poems, (5) elegies and panegyrics, (6) political and satiric pieces, (7) school or education poems, and (8) major-author imitations. These divisions do not include such miscellaneous adaptations of Spenser as Blake's "Head of Spenser" (ca. 1800; see, too, his tempera entitled "The Characters in Spenser's *Faerie Queene*," ca. 1825); the anonymous *New Occasional Oratorio* (with the text of recitative and chorus adapted from Milton and Spenser), "rehearsed at Handel's lodging" and performed 14 February 1746 at Covent Garden; a prose rendering of *The Faerie Queene* called *Prince Arthur: An Allegorical Romance* (1779, perhaps by Alexander Bicknell); *Colin Clout's Madrigal* (1728); and the anonymous *Cetus: A Mask* (ca. 1783), a three-act imitation both of Spenser's *Faerie Queene*, books 2 and 4, and Milton's *Comus*.

Like their fellows throughout the century, midcentury imitators were fond of generalized or partial allegories (some of which I return to more fully in the second half of this chapter). For example, in 1747, the Rev. Robert Bedingfield published "The Education of Achilles," a passable imitation of *The Faerie Queene*'s form and diction; the content, however, is strictly of the eighteenth century. In this poem, Thetis takes her son Achilles to the famous centaur Chiron, in a wood where Aesculapius, Jason, and her husband Peleus were educated. Modesty lives nearby, close to Temperance, Fidelity, Benevolence, Experience, Contemplation, and Exercise. "The fond parent left her darling care" with this group to learn discipline. In the final stanza (14), after "The stern-brow'd boy in mute attention stood" to learn his lessons from the sages, he ends up shaking his shield "And braves th'indignant flood, and thunders o'er the field." Seemingly all that instruction did little to teach Achilles control. There is nothing Spenserian here, not even the slightest situational humor. A synecdoche of sorts for nearly all imitations of this type, Bedingfield's piece is characterized by feeble, transparent allegory, absence of literary ornamentation, or *copia*, emphasis on instructive elements, and roots which cannot be tied to any specific episode, character, or meaning in Spenser.

Although many are interesting as period pieces, few of the many eighteenth century allegorical imitations like Bedingfield's are as literarily excellent as James Thomson's *Castle of Indolence* (1748), with its Spenserian sensuousness and its clash of seemingly opposite personifications of Indolence and Industry, the former portrait superior to the latter. Even its wry humor is reminiscent of Spenser. Second to Thomson's *Castle* in literary distinction, but equal in influence on later Spenser imitators, is James Beattie's more philosophically murky *The Minstrel, or The Progress of Genius* (1771, 1774), in two books totaling 123 Spenserian stanzas; Wordsworth was impressed by its hero, Edwin, the nature lover.

"New" or substitution cantos are exemplified by John Upton's *New Canto of Spencer's Fairy Queen* (1747), curiously—in terms of its title—in 42 Prior, not Spenserian, stanzas. Seen occasionally throughout the century, this sort of imitation is usually an ambitious effort to copy authentic Spenserian detail and to adhere to Spenser's stories. In a decidedly non-Spenserian touch, however, Upton includes scholarly notes to explain his allegory. His motto promises a tale indebted to *Faerie Queene* book 1, but he uses book 3 as well:

> From ill to ill, through various Scenes,
> Led is the Fairy Knight:
> Him Arthur Heav'n directed saves,
> From Archimago's Spite.

Upton's fairy knight is Sir Paridel rather than Redcross, perhaps because Paridell had also been saved by Arthur (*Faerie Queene* 4.9). He also has some of the sensualism of Spenser's Paridell (3.9–10).

Closely related to substitution cantos are what I can only call continuation cantos. Both types are represented in works by the Rev. Samuel Croxall, Moses Mendez, and William Julius Mickle. The first masterly imitator of Spenser's stanza, diction, and pictorialism, Croxall wrote two important imitations early in the century: *An Original Canto of Spenser, Design'd as Part of His Fairy Queen, but Never Printed* (1713), and *Another Original Canto of Spencer* (1714). Both are topical pro-Whig allegories in verse startlingly similar to Spenser's own.

An important transitional imitator writing at midcentury, Mendez helped turn the fashion away from more purely political-allegorical content and manner with his emphasis on description and narration. Especially noteworthy are *The Squire of Dames* (1751) and *The Blatant Beast* (ca. 1755), his loose imitations of *The Faerie Queene*. The former poem is in two cantos, the second of which is much better, especially in its Castle of Bon-vivant and L'Allegro episodes. Also in two cantos, *The Blatant Beast* shows Sir Pelleas's adventures and misadventures with the Blatant Beast, Peter the Eremite, Talus, and Florella. It is a good imitation of Spenser's diction, form, and humor.

Another noteworthy practitioner of the continuation canto is William Julius Mickle, who revised his popular *Concubine* (1767, 4 eds. by 1772) into *Sir Martyn, or The Progress of Dissipation* (1777), two cantos totaling 136 Spenserian stanzas. This piece is worth one's attention for its tongue-in-cheek humor and its imitation of Spenserian similes, antique diction, and painterly descriptions. This domestic tale features Sir Martyn and his domineering Lady Kathrin, who is perhaps the model for Tabitha Bramble in Tobias Smollett's *Humphrey Clinker* (1771). Canto 1 is a good imitation of Spenser, and canto 2 has attractive country scenes and a competent imitation of a Spenser cave scene in its Cave of Discontent; but Mickle's fable of Martyn's dissipation in canto 2 is digressive.

Bucolic imitations including rural-life and pastoral poems, and "seasons" imitations including "days" and time poems, are fully represented at the midcentury in Robert Potter's "Farewell Hymne to the Country" (1749, which I closely examine below), Moses Mendez's "Seasons" (1751), Thomas Warton Jr.'s "Pastoral in the Manner of Spenser" (1753), and William Vernon's "Parish Clerk" (1758). Among the century's finest poems in imitation of Spenser is William Thompson's *Hymn to May* (ca. 1740, 75 stanzas *ababccC*). The poem is a paean to May with Popean echoes, and with some surprising images, diction, and descriptions of moods, flowers, and creatures such as the bee (stanza 25) and fairy elves (stanza 34). Thompson's May is no time for owl, raven, ghost, witch, "Ponk," rumor, misery, or martial trumpet. Rather, it celebrates patriotism, innocence, simplicity, shepherds, and Venus' birthday. Ianthe is invoked in an excellent stanza beginning "Come then, Ianthe! milder than the Spring" (stanza 61), and later, "Ianthe! now, now love thy Spring away; / Ere cold October-blasts despoil the bloom of May" (stanza 68).

Other such imitations are anticipated if not influenced by Ambrose Philips's *Pastorals* (1708–09). Pope's *Pastorals* of the same date were strongly influenced by Spenser but are not, to my mind, strictly imitations. John Gay humorously combines the bucolic and seasonal in *The Shepherd's Week* (1714). The conduct and quality of rural life figure in imitations such as Moses Browne's *Piscatory Eclogues* (1729), William Melmoth's "Transformation of Lycon and Euphormius" (ca. 1743), as well as Robert Burns's "Cotter's Saturday Night" (1786). Other anonymous imitations include "The Country Parson" (1737, published with its parody "The Country Curate"), *Thames: A Canto . . . in Imitation of Spenser* (1741), "A Pastoral Digon Davy and Colin Clout" (1743?), and *The Progress of Time* (1743). A more *Sturm und Drang* nature setting is part of Andrew MacDonald's two 1782 imitations, *Verlina* and "Minvela."

Rural-life imitations were written through the end of the century, among them Samuel Hoole's "Edward, or The Curate" (1787), three imitations in 1788 by Gavin Turnbull ("Pastoral 1," "The Bard," and "The Cottage"), Richard Polwhele's *Influence of Local Attachment* (1796), John Bidlake's well-received *Country Parson* (1797), John Merivale's continuation of James Beattie's poem *The Minstrel* (ca. 1798), and two end-of-century anonymous imitations: the first a copying of Burns's poem called "The Peasant's Sabbath," and the second, *The Village Sunday* (both ca. 1799).

Since most eighteenth century readers and imitators of Spenser considered him a lofty and wise poet, it is not surprising to find him adopted and adapted in several elegiac and panegyric pieces mostly written before midcentury. Two of these poems, both written in 1706, are noteworthy. Thomas Warton Sr.'s elegy, "Philander: An Imitation of Spenser, Occasioned by the Death of Mr. William Levinz," is significant only because of its author and its early date of composition (first published 42 years later).

Matthew Prior's much more significant "Ode, Humbly Inscrib'd to the Queen" has already been noted for its ten-line adaptation of Spenser's stanza. Largely concerned with the battle of Ramillies (1706) and the Duke of Marlborough's puissance, it is as well a commendation of Queen Anne. Its adaptation of Spenser for panegyric, patriotic purposes was the century's first such effort. Reading the "Ode" as a satiric attack, William Atwood in 1706 severely reviewed it in *A Modern Inscription to the Duke of Marlborough's Fame*. But Prior's piece was not hindered. It was often reprinted (for instance, *The Grub-Street Journal* 153, 30 November 1732, uses lines from it for its motto), and its stanza form was clearly influential.

No elegies imitative of Spenser were written after 1754 except for Robert Burns's "Stanzas on the Same Occasion," that is, the prospect of death (1784) in three Spenserian stanzas of little distinction. Panegyrics faded even earlier—perhaps the final one was published in 1748—partly because the fashion for such praise had declined. Imitative panegyrics include Prior's "Colin's Mistakes" (ca. 1717), William Thompson's "Epithalamium on the Royal Nuptials" of Frederick and Augusta (1736), Samuel Boyse's "Olive: An Heroic Ode" (1736), his equally poor "Ode, Sacred to the Birth of the Marquis of Tavistock" (1740), and William Hamilton's "On Seeing a Lady [Mary Montgomery] Sit to Her Picture" (1748).

The Spenserian elegies are more substantial and interesting, beginning with William Mason's variously imitative *Musaeus: A Monody to the Memory of Mr. Pope* (1744). Pope's death in 1744 was also the occasion of Robert Dodsley's "On the Death of Mr. Pope," part of which imitated *The Shepheardes Calender.* Four more elegies come from the early fifties: in 1751, the anonymous "Thales: A Monody, Sacred to the Memory of Dr. Pococke" and Thomas Warton Jr.'s "Elegy on the Death of the Late Frederick Prince of Wales"; in 1752, Thomas Blacklock's "Philantheus"; and in another monody, Thomas Denton's "Immortality, or The Consolation of Human Life."

Most satirical and political imitations were also written before midcentury. Although often the two types cannot be separated, a few works are more one than the other. Alexander Pope's "Alley" (ca. 1706), most likely the earliest eighteenth century satirical imitation, is in its six Spenserian stanzas a puerile send-up of Spenser and a treatment of noisome experiences in alleys along or near the "silver" Thames. The poem is, however, a poor and misleading indication of Pope's respect for and indebtedness to Spenser; its few imitators include—in muted fashion albeit—Shenstone and the more scurrilous six Spenserian stanzas of Christopher Pitt's "The Jordan" (1747), a

poem about a chamberpot, a jordan. A better satire is Richard
Cambridge's "Archimage" (1742), a buoyant mock-heroic piece
of 29 Spenserian stanzas replete with old diction about a boat
trip with a belle. Mark Akenside's "Virtuoso" (1737), in ten
Spenserian stanzas of fossilized and overwrought diction, is a
youthful spoof of that type of projector called the virtuoso.
Nonetheless, it is the best of this group, all of which made
some light fun of Spenser, as Henry Mackenzie was to do in
the mid-sixties with his companion poems in Prior stanzas,
"The Old Batchelor" and "The Old Maid."

Political imitations, which also commonly touch upon
religion and patriotism, lack the satires' mocking tone. Of
the 13 political poems, excluding Prior's "Ode," eight were
published before 1752. These are better imitations than the
largely patriotic examples following Thomas Denton's 1762
attack on the Catholic church, "The House of Superstition,"
which is reminiscent of Spenser's Error episode. Other late
political imitations are the anonymous *Land of Liberty* (1775)
in two cantos totaling 120 Spenserian stanzas, the anonymous
"Liberty" (1783) in Prior stanzas, Richard Polwhele's "Ancient
and Modern Patriot Contrasted" (1795) in 6 Spenserian stanzas, and Sir James Burges's incredibly prolix *Richard the First*
(1800) in 1,849 Spenserian stanzas. No one has wished the
poem longer.

The political poems before midcentury are characteristi-
cally "occasional" and specific, for example Robert Lloyd's
"Progress of Envy" (1751) in 30 Spenserian stanzas on the
occasion of William Lauder's attack on Milton in 1747. After
Prior's 1706 "Ode," an anonymous imitator wrote a political
satire in couplets on the Earl of Oxford's administration: *A
Protestant Memorial, or The Shepheard's Tale of the Pouder-
Plott* (1713). In that same year and the next appeared Samuel
Croxall's two *Canto* poems. *An Original Canto* (1713), in 46
fine Spenserian stanzas, was immediately popular. It purports,
not very seriously, to be a lost canto by Spenser himself, a

claim made by almost no other Spenser imitator. The motto
of Croxall's poem indicates its content:

> Archimage with his Hell-hounds foul
> Doth Britomart enchain:
> Talus doth seek out Arthegall,
> And tells him of her Pain.

Another Original Canto of Spencer (1714) is in 54 Spenserian
stanzas of somewhat lesser quality than *An Original Canto*;
its motto hints that the later poem may be a covert political
satire:

> Archimage goes to Faction's House,
> Deep delved under Ground:
> The Hag adviseth how he may
> Fair Britomart confound.

Both are good Spenser-like narratives, which the Whigs glee-
fully read as attacks on the Tories; "party" was specially important in 1713–1714. Three additional political imitations
are an anonymous, supposedly Jacobite, parody of Spenser's
Mother Hubberd, "Mother Hubbards Tale of the Ape and Fox"
(1715); an anonymous elegiac-panegyric-patriotic effort called
"The British Hero . . . Sacred to the Immortal Memory of . . .
Marlborough"; and Samuel Boyse's dismal "Albion's Triumph"
(1743).

School or education imitations, as has been stated, include
poems written by university students, some of them writing
prize poems, as well as a small group of poems dealing directly
with education. At least nine student pieces date from midcentury, beginning with Thomas Warton Jr.'s "Morning" and
the anonymous "Imitation of Spenser," both published in 1750
in *The Student, or The Oxford and Cambridge Miscellany*.
Warton's stanza rhymes *ababcC*; the anonymous poem is in
six Spenserian stanzas. Two others are Lewis Bagot's "Imitation of the Epithalamion" (1755), published in *Gratulatio Academia Cantabrigiensis*, and the anonymous "Morning:

An Ode, Written by a Student Confined to College" (1772, *ababcC*), published in *The Gentleman's Magazine*. Five other school poems were Cambridge Prize winners published in the 1808 *Musae Seatonionae*. Beilby Porteus's "Death" (1759) is in blank verse; the rest are in Prior stanzas: James Scott's "Heaven: A Vision" (1760, in 31 stanzas indebted to the Bower of Bliss episode), James Scott's "Hymn to Repentance" (1762), Samuel Hayes's "Hope" (1783), and Charles Philpots' "Faith: A Vision" (1790). Clearly, Spenser's own university (unlike his school, Merchant Taylors') continued to be mindful of its famous son.

The four major imitations about education are longer, more challenging poems. Two of them are perhaps less significant: the Rev. Robert Bedingfield's "Education of Achilles" (1747) and Thomas Ager's "Schoolmaster" (1794), an imitation of an imitation by William Shenstone. The other two are quite good as imitations and as poems in their own right: Shenstone's justly celebrated "School-Mistress" (1737, 1742, 1748) and Gilbert West's entertaining and instructive *Education: A Poem, in Two Cantos, Written in Imitation of the Style and Manner of Spenser's Faery Queen* (1751), which is treated below. A call for educational reform, West's *Education*, in 96 Spenserian stanzas, is one of the better imitations of the century. Shenstone's school piece is one of the century's five or six best imitations of Spenser's stanza, even if not diction, and one the age's better minor poems. "The School-Mistress" began as an imitation of Pope's "The Alley," then expanded in subsequent editions from 12 to 28 to 35 Spenserian stanzas while adopting a tone somewhere between Pope's "Alley" and Thomson's *Castle of Indolence*. Largely because of its gentle burlesque of Spenser and humorous treatment of the school-mistress, Shenstone's appealing poem became exceedingly popular and led to other Spenser imitations. Although no enthusiast for the type, Dr. Johnson approved of West's and Shenstone's imitations.

A final category can only be termed miscellaneous imitations on a broad range of subjects. Near the midcentury, Glocester Ridley publishes *Psyche* (1747), a 51-stanza pastiche of Spenserianisms. *Psyche* is also the title and subject of 372 Spenserian stanzas by Mary Tighe (1795), who was very likely the most influential of the nine eighteenth century women who imitated Spenser.[1] Several poets who today often appear in collections of eighteenth century poetry also imitated Spenser under various topics: Christopher Smart in his 1756 "Hymn to the Supreme Being," William Cowper in his 1781 "Anti-Thelyphthora," and Thomas Chatterton in several of his 1760s Rowley poems. Adding to the variety of subjects are the imitations by William Collins and Thomas Gray. For Collins, a quick look at the Lonsdale 1969 edition of his poetry displays how imitative of Spenser the 1739 *Persian Eclogues* are; for Gray, the same edition demonstrates his indebtedness to Spenser for the 1746 *Odes on Several Descriptive and Allegoric Subjects.*

Other subjects of imitations are hope (William Bowles 1796, an imitation of Spenser's Masque of Cupid), pain and patience (Samuel Boyse, ca. 1740 and Robert Dodsley, 1742), the sun (Elijah Fenton, 1707), music (George Sewell, ca. 1710), taste (Alexander Thompson, 1796), sickness (William Thompson 1745, in blank verse), the sexes (Samuel Wesley, 1723), traveling (Gilbert West, 1739, whose Redcross is an English xenophobe), and suicide (Alexander Wilson, 1790). Less generalized miscellaneous imitations include Thomas Morell's "Verses on a Silk Work" (1742), William Rider's "Westminster Abbey" (1735), and William Thompson's "Nativity" (1736). Three good allegorical imitations complete this selective listing: William Wilkie's "Dream in the Manner of Spenser" (1759, in 18 Spenserian stanzas), Hugh Downman's *Land of the Muses* (1768, in 85 Spenserian stanzas recast in couplets in 1791), and the anonymous "House of Care, in Imitation of Spenser's Faery Queen" (1786, in 8 Spenserian stanzas). One imitator attempted

more topics than any other. Thomas Dermody's 14 imitations—
some generalized, some quite specific, in several Spenserian
measures written from 1792 to the turn of the century—speak
of the pleasures of poetry, enthusiasm, ignorance, joy, pedantry,
hope, fancy, the Reverend Mr. Sterling, the Countess Moira,
winter's night, and even coffeehouses.

The great number of Spenser imitations and adaptations
leads to several informed generalizations. First, the imitations
follow the changing styles and emphases of eighteenth century poetry generally. Second, received opinion about which
are the best imitations still holds true; but the names of
Croxall, Edwards, Mendez, Mickle, Thompson, and West, and
perhaps even Downman and Wilkie should be put in the com-
pany of better recognized imitators such as Akenside, Beattie,
Burns, Shenstone, and Thomson, whether for belletristic or
historical reasons, or both.

Third, most imitators were college men, many educated at
Spenser's own Cambridge University. A surprising number
were schoolboys at Westminster or Winchester; many of the
better imitators were educated at Eton. As my first chapter
shows, there is no doubt that encouragement came from teachers or fathers or other Spenser imitators, resulting in literary
genealogies such as Downman-Blacklock-Fergusson-Burns or
Warton-West-Thomson. (There were at least 16 Scots among
the 100 imitators, and many Irish men and women.) The playfulness of some works is largely explained by the fact that
nearly all imitators were young men and women who were
attracted to Spenser, some through school imitation exercises,
in a spirit of stanzaic experimentation and poetical adventu-
rousness, away from the strictures and conventions of couplet verse. The evidence shows, however, that favorites such
as Pope were not abandoned.

Finally, many imitations of Spenser's stanza still have the
couplet feel, and imitations of Pope or the Ancients are occasionally combined within Spenser imitations throughout the

century. Except for Croxall, Thomson, Mendez, and Mickle, imitators did not succeed in approximating Spenser's diction. Many did not want to imitate his diction, as I indicate later. When they attempted "old" words at all, they randomly sprinkled their archaisms around a text. Eighteenth century imitations of Spenserian measures were more successful. A few writers caught something of his incidents and "types." Judging from their comments as well as their imitations, most seemed to like Spenser's seriousness, pictorialism, and poetic virtuosity. Many, but certainly not all, eighteenth century critics did not seem to care as much for Spenser as fabulist or allegorist, and many of the poet's enthusiasts found *The Faerie Queene* stanza tedious. But Spenser was never ridiculed, seldom burlesqued. He was, however, at times, played with.

The imitations tell an important part of the story of Spenser's reputation during the period under consideration.[2] Their frequency and distribution throughout the century, with no appreciable lacunae, show that many writers, and not only the preromantics, cared about him and for him as moral teacher and inspirational literary model. Their imitations contributed to Spenser's proceeding a peer of the classical writers long before the century's end.

SPENSER AND THE BEST FOUR: SOME GENERALIZATIONS

Surprisingly little sustained work has been done on the Spenserianism of the major authors of the early-to-mid eighteenth century, namely Dryden, Pope, Swift, and Dr. Johnson. Except for Pope's brief, youthful "Alley," neither he nor Dryden wrote direct whole-work imitations of Spenser (in accordance with the definition I offer at the outset of my study) although both, and particularly Pope, were profoundly influenced by Spenser and often employed him in their own works. Dryden admired Spenser and learned much from him; but, as has been suggested, his age preferred to imitate or "paraphrase" the Psalms, classical authors and a very few Moderns. The task of discerning the influence of Spenser on the more major of the early eighteenth century writers is at least threefold. Very few of today's scholars and critics of the period have seemed to be interested in writing about the connectedness; those who have done so have understandably had difficulty seeing precisely wherein the influence lies; and distinguishing between influence by Spenser and the general influences of other writers and forces is a daunting endeavor. Thus, deciding on how and to what extent Spenser figures in the art of the period's major writers remains to be accomplished by future students of this topic. In *Edmund Spenser in the Early Eighteenth Century*, I provide the Spenserian milieu for such an investigation. Yet some connections have been made, largely by Renaissance scholars.

Dryden

For earlier Dryden critics, the Spenser-Dryden relationship was seen mainly in figures, diction, and versification. In his dedication to *The Spanish Friar*, Dryden—as Pope will later—mentions reading Spenser when a boy. Also, since Spenser was related to his forebears, Dryden would naturally be disposed toward him. It is most likely that Spenser's works were for Dryden a model for heroic poetry moreso than for pastorals, even though Dryden considered the *Shepheardes Calender* superlative in its subgenre. Dryden owned Spenser's 1611 folio *Works*, but it was his copy of the 1679 *Works* that he marked up carefully, including *The Faerie Queene* where the marginalia for book 7, canto 7.12.12 includes "Ground work for a song on St. Cecilias Day."

Dryden's plans for writing an epic included Virgil of course but also Spenser as model, and Reginald Berry's *Spenser Encyclopedia* article on Dryden demonstrates how pervasive Spenser's influence was: borrowings from *The Faerie Queene* such as those in *Heroique Stanzas*, the Lucretius translation in *Silvae, Albion and Albanius,* and *Palamon and Arcite*—borrowings, says Berry, that show Dryden's view of Spenser as a "pictorialist after his own poetic temperament" (228). Dryden also recognized in him the justification of his own technical innovations, as when he defends his fondness for the alexandrine (preface to *Aeneis*) and his revival of obsolete words (*Discourse concerning Satire,* 1693).

All this attention by Dryden should not lead us to ignore the fact that he ranks Shakespeare above both Chaucer and Spenser or the few negative comments in his otherwise positive treatment of the poet in *Discourse concerning Satire.* Dryden sees Spenser as cavalier in the unity of action and structure and boring in his overly homogenized heroes, his use of antique words, and his metronomic stanza. As we shall see, these are charges commonly brought against the poet in the eighteenth century.

Since the work of Richard Ringler and John Steadman in the 1960s, a bit more attention has been given to the heroic dramas of Dryden and Spenser's contribution to them. Berry's remarks on the relationship are fresh, however, in noting that as early as 1672 and *Of Heroic Plays* Dryden thought of *The Faerie Queene* in "terms of his own heroic drama": spirits, visionary objects, myth, for instance. And Dryden ranks *The Faerie Queene's* Bower of Bliss episode (2.12) with Virgil's ghost of Polydorus and the Enchanted Wood of Tasso (1.160–61). Long before Joseph Warton and Richard Hurd, then, Dryden naturally saw Spenser's romantic possibilities—that is, once again, in the manner of the romances—along with possibilities from the French heroic romanticists.

Berry observes that *The Conquest of Granada* (part 1, 1670, part 2, 1671), *All for Love* (1677), and *Don Sebastian* (1690) "have aspects of a romantic structure strongly resembling Spenser's": the joining of love and pathos; anarchic women (compare Duessa, Acrasia, or Malecasta with Zempoalla, Lyndaraxa, or Nourmahal). And, "most important, Spenser provided

Dryden with one method of reconciling the classical and Christian conceptions of the hero," such as in *The Conquest's* Almanzor (228). In his planned King Arthur epic, Dryden envisioned that legendary ruler as his "greatest 'Spenserian' hero." Even the opera he wrote in place of the epic has strong Spenserian influences, and differences as well: "Unlike Spenser, Dryden's Arthur is conceived as an overtly nationalist, political character; but politics is leavened by Dryden's 'Fairy kind of writing, which depends only upon the Force of Imagination'" (dedication to *King Arthur*, 3). This statement could have come from many of the eighteenth century's preromantic writers and any of the major romantics, particularly Coleridge and Keats.

Berry concludes by giving some consonances between the allegories of Spenser and Dryden and a reasonable assertion that Dryden *continued* rather than imitated Spenser's allegorical manner in *Absalom and Achitophel* (1681), *The Hind and the Panther* (1687), and especially *Fables Ancient and Modern* (1700). Certainly the first problem with discerning the influence of Spenser on Dryden is not so much seeing an influence but rather reassessing Dryden because of it. One may go so far as to hold that this important neoclassicist (a name and "attitude" that Howard Weinbrot and the late Donald Greene have written about deeply and long) is, in part at least, romantic to the degree of Spenser's influence upon him.

In Thomas Warton Jr.'s 1754 *Observations on the Fairy Queen* we are told that Dryden "learned his art of versification" from Spenser (2. 440); and in the index to the 1762 second edition of that work Dryden is explicitly called an *imitator* of Spenser. In the special sense of being regardful of Spenser, of extolling him, and of borrowing from him, Dryden is his imitator. And Dryden's most immediate literary heir did all three as well as directly imitate.

Pope

In *The Garden and the City,* Maynard Mack's magisterial study of a generation ago that still demands attention, we are reminded that Alexander Pope's Twickenham library displayed busts of Homer, Shakespeare, Milton, Dryden, and Spenser. Mack is also helpful in pointing out that, like Spenser's Proem to book 1 of *The Faerie Queene,* Pope's later poetry puts aside the "oaten reeds" of pastoral and takes up the "trumpets sterne" of epic in order better to "moralize [his] song." Arthur Hoffman (1970) and John Preston (1966) studied, respectively, correspondences between Spenser "Prothalamion" and "Epithalamion" and Pope's *Rape of the Lock* as well as *The Faerie Queene*'s relationship to that mock epic. Critics such as Audra, Durling, Melchiori, and Provost have seen significant ties between the two poets' pastorals. And Spenser's influence on Pope's diction and poetic practice have received the attention of Butt, Chernaik, Groom, Sutherland, and particularly Wyld.

But Howard Erskine-Hill more recently has extended the discussion of indebtedness in his *Spenser Encyclopedia* essay by comparing *Dunciad* book 2 and Spenser's *Mother Hubberds Tale.* Interesting also is the suggestion that Pope, always attentive to the history of English poetry and his part in it, planned in the mid-thirties his own history featuring Spenser. Erskine-Hill ends with an important assessment of similarities between Spenser and Pope that may serve as a pattern for future criticism on this topic, in that the poets' relationship "involves the evolution of a poetic mode highly mobile between the comic and the sublime, capable of remarkable visual and aural beauty, especially in the setting forth of temptation and danger, reaching often towards the emblematic and allegorical, using marvels and metamorphoses for strongly moral and religious ends" (555).

Swift

As many of my readers will suspect, Addison, Steele, and Swift do not have entries in *The Spenser Encyclopedia*. In *Spence's Anecdotes* (sect. 1, 1728–1730), Pope charges that Addison's "character" of Spenser in his letter to Sacheverell is just as false as his portrait of Chaucer. Pope waggishly adds, "I have heard him say, that he never read Spenser till fifteen years after he wrote it." I have found no full studies and few mentions of Spenser and Addison, Spenser and Steele, or Spenser and Swift beyond those I present later. That the Renaissance writer is not onmipresent in Addison and Steele is perhaps understandable, for Spenser wrote in genres very different from theirs and was, although their countryman, an alien in poetic sensibility, especially to Addison. Steele probably warrants scrutiny in this regard. But why not Spenser and Swift?

Spenser's absence in Swift scholarship is curious, albeit he too mostly wrote in genres different from Spenser's. Pope's enthusiasm for the older poet well might have whetted the interest of his close friend, correspondent, and sometime collaborator Swift (on *Martinus Scriblerus*, for example) as was the case with Spenser and Dorothy and William Wordsworth and Spenser and Coleridge. Was *Mother Hubberds Tale* not congenial in tone and manner with Swift's own sensibility and taste, and specially congenial to *A Tale of a Tub* and *Gulliver's Travels*? In the least, the "body" materials (physiognomy, fluids, appearance-reality treatments) and general scatalogical strain in Swift is tonally and texturally precisely that of Spenser. Even if Spenser were not to Swift's taste, Swift had available to him some politicized filterings of Spenser such as the 1715—just the right time for the genesis of *Gulliver's Travels*—eight-page Jacobite satire of Spenser's *Mother Hubberds Tale* called *Mother Hubberds Tale of the Ape and Fox, Abbreviated from Spenser*. In the least, Spenser and Swift's experiences in Ireland and their writings and ambivalent attitudes about that country are tellingly alike and underreported by critics. Most likely, then, this absence of scholarly notice should not be interpreted as Spenser's lack of influence on Swift, or as Spenserian echoes not being evident in the satirist's work.

Johnson

The final major writer within the central purview of this study, Samuel Johnson offers an equally complex and yet more satisfying case for one who searches for Spenser's imprint on writers beyond his own day. Since I return to Johnson and Spenser in the discussion of the sixth decade, here I only suggest some broad lines of inquiry. As we have seen, Dr. Johnson (*Rambler* 121), while seeing his friend Gilbert West's imitations of Spenser as a cut above midcentury efforts of a host of lesser poets, withholds his highest praise, since imitation is a parasitic enterprise. While this judgment is unambiguous about the impossibility of imitation as reaching the level of high art, it reveals nothing tangible about Johnson's attitude about Spenser. His *Idler* 60 essay, however, sides with Spenser against his defamers, who are as vacuous as his (poorer) imitators. What is Johnson's attitude about Spenser, then? Was he influenced by him; did he imitate him?

As Claudia L. Johnson properly observes in her *Spenser Encyclopedia* remarks on Johnson and the poet, Dr. Johnson "never wrote at length on Spenser; his scattered, sometimes contradictory remarks are almost always made either with reference to other writers or on their authority" (411). He owned editions of Spenser's *Works*; read him thoroughly; incorporated his poetry and prose, some 3,000 citations, into his *Dictionary*; acknowledged Spenser as one of the English Renaissance group—along with More, Ascham, and Hooker—who formed his style (see Hawkins' biography of Johnson); credited Spenser and Shakespeare with smoothness and harmony

(*Preface to Shakespeare*); recommended Spenser and Sidney as crucial for the "dialect of poetry and fiction." Also, according to contemporary Hannah More, Dr. Johnson attempted to include Spenser in his *Lives of the English Poets*, but his bookseller would not allow it (*Memoirs* 1.174). And both More and James Boswell speak of Johnson's refusal of King George III's request for a biography of Spenser, turned down only because of the paucity of fresh biographical information. The last fact of use to the pursuer of Spenser in Johnson is that Johnson championed his friend Thomas Warton's *Observations on The Faerie Queene*. Some of these matters appear in chapter 4.

Such positive attitudes must counter Johnson's calling Spenser's style "vicious, obtuse" (see *Rambler* 121). This judgment seems to contradict his approbation of that same style elsewhere. Too, Johnson finds noisome the Italianate Spenserian stanza (same *Rambler*) and indeed, as his famous *Lycidas* indictment shows, he is no friend to pastorals (see *Life of Milton*). Echoing Pope's *Guardian* 40 attack, Johnson hits at the "studied barbarity" of the *Shepheardes Calender*'s "September" (1–4), where shepherds dilate on fallen Rome. About that, Dr. Johnson sniffs "Surely, at the same time a shepherd learns theology, he may gain some acquaintance with his native language" (*Rambler* 37). Even though he himself engaged in allegory—in his hands mostly an act of giving abstractions "form"—in *Theodore the Hermit* and some *Rambler* pieces, he objects to polysemous allegories; one suspects that Johnson had in mind straying and intersecting plot lines and characters such as those of Ariosto and Spenser.

Claudia Johnson astutely observes, however, that when Dr. Johnson "censures Spenser, he generally does so indirectly, through another poet: Milton on rhyme, Jonson on diction, and Dryden on unity. Such obliqueness is uncharacteristic and suggests that he may not have identified fully with the judgments he cites" (412). The balancing of the evidence for and against Dr. Johnson's affection for Spenser's art would probably yield this trenchant appraisal, again by Claudia Johnson: "his occasional remarks do not represent his last words on Spenser. He would probably have praised Spenser's invention and morality" while giving him credit for "creating a literary language and initiating a formidable national literary tradition in the process: 'We consider the whole succession from Spenser to Pope as superiour to any names which the continent can boast,'" avers Englishman Johnson in *Idler* 91.

The complexities and ambiguities of discerning Spenser and Spenserianism in Dr. Johnson reflect the problem in finding with precision and hard evidence the poet's influence in the period in general, whether for the major writers, the minor writers, the would-be writers, or the "common reader." A plan for remedy would include, first, knowing well what Spenser actually wrote; looking for him and not only his name in the works of, for example, Swift and Johnson; examining his influence on professed Spenserians such as Dryden and Pope; analyzing and explaining the meaning of the connections found, or, if not found, speculating on why not.

SPENSER ANTHOLOGIZED: *"WOND'ROUS TRUTHS IN PLEASING DREAMS"*

For the introduction and dissemination of Spenser's work and imitations of it to the popular reader, it is difficult to overestimate the importance of his being anthologized in the early and mid-eighteenth century. All the anthologists were Spenserians who came to the poet in one of the ways I examine in my first chapter. A noteworthy example is Elizabeth Cooper whose 1738 *Historical and Poetical Medley* remarks on Spenser in ways that by that time were commonplace: biographical sketch, then selection of works. A sometime playwright and the widow of an auctioneer, Cooper is an oddly overlooked figure who favored Elizabethan writers, perhaps because of the help of the antiquarian, book collector, editor, and Raleigh biographer William Oldys. On Spenser's works, Cooper is barometric and vatic rather than deep. She is helpful to the student of Spenserianism for she has the pulse of her day in that regard.

She begins, "And tho' Chaucer, and Spencer are ever nam'd with much Respect, not many are intimately acquainted with their Beauties," a situation she wishes to correct by her anthology: "No writer ever found so near a Way to the Heart as he," (Spenser, that is), and "When I read Him, I fancy myself conversing with the *Graces*, and am led away as irresistibly, as if inchanted by his own *Merlin*"—all these effusions of "Female Fondness" for which she apologizes (255). She would agree with Spenserian Matthew Prior's description of Spenser's allegory as "Wond'rous Truths in Pleasing Dreams" (1706 "Ode to the Queen"). She is too self-effacing. Rather than a reaction caused by or typical of her gender, the remarks soon thereafter become the mainstream reaction to Spenser. In fact, Cooper's "fanciful," enthusiastic response is exactly that of Joseph Warton, who together with his brother Thomas prove to be the age's seers in matters Spenserian.

It goes without saying that the faculty Cooper most admires in Spenser is his imagination, which makes him the most evocative and fecund of writers. She correctly judges that with all his flaws, "no Writings have such Power as his, to awake the Spirit of Poetry in others: And 'tis probable many Geniuses, beside *Cowley's*, have ow'd their Inspiration, to the reflected Fire [exactly Warton's word], they caught originally from Him" (255). Cooper's affective reaction to Spenser and her accurate estimation of him are of considerable interest, in particular her claim that he spawned many poets.

In some ways more important is a same-year three-volume collection by Thomas Hayward, one which includes many Spenser passages, *The British Muse*, which Warton considered the best anthology he knew. An attorney from Hungerford,

Berkshire, Hayward had a collaborator in common with Elizabeth Cooper, William Oldys, who wrote the preface to the 1740 version of *The British Muse,* called *The Quintessence of English Poetry.* In his collection of posies, Hayward conveniently reviews earlier "Collections of this Kind" including those by Edward Bysshe (*The British Parnassus,* 1714, a two-volume distillation of his 1702 *Art of English Poetry*), Charles Gildon (*The Compleat Art of Poetry,* 1718), and the author of *England's Parnassus* (a 500-page octavo miscellany of 1600), the latter annotated by who else but William Oldys.[3]

Even though, as we have seen, Henry Felton's enormously popular early eighteenth century *Dissertation on Reading the Classics* (Felton was a student of Dr. Busby at Westminster College) did much to launch the Milton and Spenser revivals, Hayward gathers unto himself this credit: the selections he presents, admittedly indebted to the 1715 edition by Hughes, "as from *Spenser,* &c. appear almost entirely new, having never been quoted in this manner and perhaps little observed before" (22). Oldys' preface reviews earlier poetry and play anthologies, some of which are severely treated: one such anthologist is Edward Bysshe for omitting "unexcelled" Spenser because his, and Shakespeare's, language is obsolete; another is Charles Gildon for being too sketchy.

Gildon, though, is praised for resurrecting Spenser and Shakespeare by introducing "with some extent" their imagery (17). Oldys points out that Hayward eschewed the Moderns such as Milton, Cowley, Waller, and Dryden in order to "devote himself to [Spenser's] neglected and expiring merit" (20). Oldys claims that Spenser is therein anthologized for the first time. With some justification, he sees Hayward and himself as innovators, rescuers, and arbiters of taste. As anthologists, both were significant in the Spenser revival as the crucial middle decades of the century approached.

After the Spenser imitations of Matthew Prior and Samuel Croxall, as well as the Hughes edition early in the century, the midcentury collections of poems edited by the Spenserian Robert Dodsley gave the strongest *single* impetus to Spenser's growing popularity, reputation, and influence. Dodsley did so primarily by gathering and publishing some of the best Spenser imitations; one misses, however, the lovely 1740 "An Hymn to May" by William Thompson. The student of this subject will want something of the Spenserian environment of the Dodsley volumes, given here for the first time, which point the direction of eighteenth century poetry and dramatize the changing poetic sensibility.

Thoroughgoing literary entrepreneur, educator, poet, bookseller, dramatist, and projector with both Pope and Dr. Johnson, Robert Dodsley the younger (1703–1764) was most influential with his surpassingly popular *Collection of Poems by Several Hands*, begun in 1748. A host of editors prepared their poetic collections in the manner of Dodsley's, George Pearch, Moses Mendez, and John Bell among them. Indeed, Bell's 1789–90 multivolume *Classical Arrangement of Fugitive Poetry* has as its tenth and eleventh volumes respectively, *Poems in the Stanza of Spencer* and *Poems in the Stanza of Spenser; and, In the Manner of Milton.*

In the 1748 first edition of three volumes appear these Spenser imitations: William Shenstone's "School-Mistress" (vol. 1); Gilbert West's "On the Abuse of Travelling. A Canto in Imitation of Spenser" (vol. 2); and, in volume 3, Robert Lowth's "Choice of Hercules," Glocester Ridley's "Psyche," the Rev. Robert Bedingfield's "Education of Achilles, and William Mason's "Musaeus." One imagines these imitators behaving as the dreamer in "An Ode to Fancy" by "Mr. Warton" in that same third volume: "Then lay me by the haunted stream, / Wrapt in some wild, poetic dream" (80). Given the great regard accorded the Dodsley miscellanies during this period, these Spenser imitations, adaptations, and remarks could not but have had an influence on the common reader and on future Spenserians by being placed so prominently before them. Some indication of the reach of the Spenser imitations is, as indicated earlier, their spawning other imitations, several of them Spenserian, examplified below. Other indications of influence would include adaptations such as Handel's 1751 music to Lowth's "The Choice of Hercules."

The second edition of *A Collection of Poems,* also of 1748, includes the Spenser imitations of the first edition unchanged, except for the expansion of "The School-Mistress" to 35 stanzas and an addition to volume 2, of sonneteer Thomas Edwards's (irregular) "Sonnet VIII. On the Cantos of Spenser's *Fairy Queen,* lost in the Passage from Ireland." Even more important for Spenser's progress in the second half of the century is Dodsley's six-volume *Collection* (1751–1758), for some of the earlier imitations are once again reprinted but five new ones are added, for a total of 11: mostly long poems, more by half than of any other writer included therein.

Volume 4 (1755) presents two imitations I examine below, including Gilbert West's "Education a Poem: in two Cantos" and Moses Mendez's "Squire of Dames" (82 Spenserian stanzas followed by a glossary). Volumes 5 and 6 (1758) offer other imitations I remark on later: the anonymous "Epithalamium," Thomas Denton's "Immortality: or, The Consolation of Human Life. A Monody" (31 Prior stanzas), and the anonymous "Country parson" (12 stanzas *ababbcC*).

Dodsley's six-volume *Collection* is, then, among the fulcrum Spenserian events in the century's middle, not only because of the imitations but also because of the forward-pointing hybrid pieces, presented "to preserve to the public those poetical performances, which seemed to merit a longer remembrance than what would probably be secured to them by the Manner wherein they were originally published" (vol. 1, Advertisement).[4] There is a strong strain in the early eighteenth century to resurrect, introduce, and preserve Spenser. In the second half of the century, more precisely the final 40 years, with those good offices already performed, Spenser settled in for his many admirers as a native "classic" model of what a poet and poetry should be.

Some ephemera and societal poems are included in Dodsley along with more memorable pieces: Johnson's "London," Dyer's "Gronger Hill" and his equally physico-ruminative blank verse "Ruins of Rome," and three Collins odes including "Ode to Evening." The numerous imitations of both ancient and modern writers attest to how common that manner of poetic expression continued to be. That Spenser is the chief native poet imitated and presented is important to his fame and durability, and, as I attempt to show in chapter 1, to the beginnings of English literature as a profession.

The title page advertisement, actually part of the *Collection*, for the 35 Spenserian stanzas of William Shenstone's "School-Mistress" gives good reasons for Spenser's inclusion in the anthology and his popularity: "What particulars in Spenser were imagin'd most proper for the author's imitation on this occasion are, his language, his simplicity, his manner of description, and a peculiar tenderness of sentiment remarkable throughout his works." Each of these except for description, as we shall see, is the opposite of early-century judgments of this poet. This change is due to maturation and a dramatic turn of taste. I suggest that the Dodsley volumes are a tidy *locus* for seeing the change. Tenderness of sentiment is a characteristic that was not usually noticed in the poet, who in stanza 19 of Shenstone's poem is spoken of as "sighing" as he sung, who did in "tears indite" (255).

Three odes by Gray and two attractive poems on friendship by William Whitehead are highlights of volume 2, which ends with 14 sonnets, one an imitation of Spenser's sonnets. (Did Dodsley, one wonders, have a role in the revitalization of the sonnet that had lain fallow since Milton?) The eighth sonnet, "On the Cantos of Spenser's Fairy Queen, lost in the Passage from Ireland" (331), argues that Ireland partially achieved revenge for English exploitation when the Irish Sea claimed Spenser's cantos, purportedly lost in the passage from its shores.[5]

The student of romanticism will find God's plenty in Dodsley's crucial third volume, for therein are Joseph Warton's blank verse "Enthusiast: or the Lover of Nature" and the "Ode to Fancy" as well as James Thomson's "Hymn on Solitude" and "An Ode on Aoleus' Harp." Also found there are Spenser imitations, firstly Robert Lowth's 1747 "Choice of Hercules" (27 Prior stanzas). It is not a work of the first rank, but it offers a useful example of an eighteeth century generalized psychomachia, wherein Jove's son Hercules, now an adult, like Rasselas and Candide ponders his "path of life," whether to pursue virtue or "pleasure's flow'ring way" (stanza 2).

As he muses, he is presented with two large, beautiful women, one Virtue and the other Happiness (Sloth, really). Each is described in believable Spenserian detail. Happiness tempts Hercules with persuasive come-with-me-and-be-my-love enjoinments. The diction is not fake antique as are many of the imitations that deal with abstractions, and there are competent approximations of Spenserian sensuousness. To Hercules comes Virtue, an amazon who speaks to him in a "manly tone" (stanza 11), asking him to eschew soft ease since his roots are divine. But her instruction to him is interrupted by Sloth, false happiness, who tries to win him over to her. Earlier, in stanza 5, she was introduced in detail not unlike Spenser's:

> All soft and delicate, with airy swim,
> highly she danc'd along, her robe betray'd
> Thro' the clear texture every tender limb,
> Height'ning the charms it only seem'd to shade:
> And as it flow'd adown, so loose and thin,
> Her stature shew'd more tall; more snowy-white, her skin.

(3)

We discover that Sloth, or manifest indolence and sensuality, was thrown from heaven by Jove and condemned to "man's degenerate race" (stanza 10). Virtue, on the other hand, dwells "with the gods, and godlike men" (stanza 21). Thus Hercules' choice comes down on the side of Virtue, and upon this decision, Sloth is revealed as repulsive, not unlike the stripped Duessa later in *Faerie Queene* book 1. Of course, Virtue's beauty thereupon becomes more lustrous and soft; and armed with what she represents, Hercules "free'd the earth" and through her "gain'd the skies" (stanza 27). Most midcentury "simple" allegories work this way; namely, this allegory is an unnuanced one-to-one relationship in meaning between the vehicle, or fiction, and the tenor, which is always singular and not plural.

A better imitation of Spenser and another poem of abstractions is Gloster Ridley's 1747 "Psyche: or, The Great Metamorphosis" (Dodsley vol. 3, 17–37) in 51 Spenserian stanzas. The poem begins in the garden of Adonis (cf. *Faerie Queene* 3.6) with a youth and the seasons playing around the god-man: "Sich gardens now no mortal wight can see, / Ne mote they in my simple verse descriven be." The garden is full of such Spenserian touches as bursting vegetation, songful birds, and stable climate. Adonis in "unfading youth" bickers with Venus; Eros and Anteros observe. Venus has no part of them but her son Cupid does, along with his beloved Psyche who, gaily appointed in black, green, and gold of changing hues, "In that enclosure happy sojourn made" (stanza 6). Like Milton's Eve, wanting to travel through the garden, Psyche is warned by Cupid to beware of the rose's prick. The fine leavetaking scene (stanza 15) also is reminiscent of Milton's Eve and Adam's parting before her temptation by Satan. Such conflating of Milton and Spenser is not unusual in the century.

Cupid enlists the protective aid of his mother, Venus, but she, envious of her son and Psyche's happiness, colludes with her sons Eros and Anteros to destroy Psyche. Anteros, in a snake's skin, enter Psyche's part of the garden. He is described in Spenser-like diction: "In borrow'd gear, th'exulting losel glides" (stanza 21) to a rose bush and sits on a thorn. Milton, Spenser, and mythology are jointly instrumental in the quite effective temptation scene that follows. In stanza 38, Psyche "gusts" for the rose and takes hold of it, whereupon "Full many a thorn her tender body rent" (stanza 39). Immediately she mourns her lost innocence, feels shame, then despairs.

Like Milton's *Paradise Lost* book 10, postlapsarian nature is affected and effected: birds silent, sun gone, thunder and earthquakes working woe. Cupid convinces Venus to permit Psyche to live because a "greater good" will come thereby, that is, the defeat of Anteros, whose name is a transparency. In an interesting conjoining of Milton's punishment for Adam, Eve and Satan, the poet makes Psyche deformed and diminished. Nature (the garden), too, is altered. Winter, work, thorns, bellicose creatures, floods are the change. In a nice declension, Psyche thins and fades; then, appropriately in an alexandrine, metamorphoses into a caterpillar: "She creeping crawls, and drags a loathsome length about" (stanza 50). Finally, in summary fashion, Dodsley's readers are told of Cupid's fight with and conquest of Anteros and of Psyche's recovery and "crown."

Such a close account shows how two great native writers and mythology contribute to a successful, typical midcentury imitation. And readers of Wordsworth, Coleridge, Keats, and Shelley will see how in subject matter, treatment, and *models* Ridley's 1747 poem is like their later work. One's awareness of the romanticism in "Psyche" is heightened by the environment of like poems in Dodsley's volumes, whether the many explicit imitations of Milton and Spenser, poems on mythological topics and personified abstractions presented in simple allegories, or pieces clearly romantic in subject and manner such as the poems of Collins, Gray, and Joseph Warton. Yet another Dodsley-collection imitation of 1747, Robert Bedingfield's "Education of Achilles," like "The Choice of Hercules" and "Psyche," has all these characteristics as well. It is a Spenserian imitation in 14 Spenserian stanzas, it treats a mythological topic, it presents personified abstractions (Temperance, Fidelity, Benevolence) in an emblematic, woodcut, "simple" allegorical fashion.

Volume 3 holds one final poem fitting in this context. William Mason's macaronic Spenser imitation "Musaeus" is an elegy (ca. 1744) on Pope (who died in 1744) which uses some details from Pope, and also an imitation of Milton and Spenser's stanzas and diction. In the second stanza Mason catches himself: "But why do I descant this toyish rhyme / And fancies light in simple guise pourtray" when the subject is so mournful? What does this say about the use of Spenserian stanzas in elegies? Or the easy yoking of authors and their materials? Is tone hurt, is attention drawn to the writer instead of his subject, is this the joyance of a youthful writer misapplied on a solemn occasion? Mason's poem and those already noted indicate at least the variety of Dodsley's third volume, which offers much by way of Spenser, Spenserians, and midcentury poetry.

The final volumes get at some characteristics and trends not seen in those earlier. Volume 4 (1755), part of *A Collection of Poems in Four Volumes*, begins with two poems by Thomas Gray, "Elegy" and "Hymn to Adversity," followed by Gilbert West's first canto (of two) of "Education," which dramatizes the need to free the exclusively classical curriculum of the schools of his day. His poem's motto from Seneca anticipates the cogent argument for change: *Unum studium vere liberale est, quod liberum facit.* Although West's subject is necessary change in education, his particulars could also be applied to poetic models, and maybe even poetic practice and *telos.* A clever allegorical satire of his day's schooling, "Education" calls for liberty through learning and wisdom, both of which are correctives to custom's sway which has put England in thrall. The proper end of the enterprise is the "knowledge of the world and man's great business there" (stanza 87), abetted and aided by duty and religion. This remark could serve as the motto over the gates of every dissenting academy in England. While it indeed is an eighteenth century poem in matter and texture, "Education" has its Spenserian moments in diction, fable, descriptions, personifications, and similes. West has a Spenserian insight into custom, a giant in the poem who becomes less frightening "when known and practised than at a distance seen" (stanza 43). The motto-argument to canto 1 tells all:

> The Knight, as to Paedia's [Education's] house
> He his young Son conveys,
> Is staid [pun?] by Custom; with him fights,
> And his vain pride dismays.

Not without humorous possibilities, stanza 1 begins with "A Gentle Knight there was," a retiree with a loving wife and many children. A Palmer (educational reformer John Locke) educated them and now, with his squire, takes the children to Education who "On a wide mount had fix'd her rural Seat, / 'Mid flowery gardens placed, untrod by vulgar feet" (stanza 9). One wants to read the *topos* as meaning the lofty, classical, impractical curriculum, all figured in the trees, which were "But aliens to the clime [England], and brought of old / From *Latian* plains, and *Grecian* Helicon" (stanza 20). Later, some of what the Ancients have to offer is called "rubbish" (stanza 23).

The other major Spenser imitation of volume 4 is Moses Mendez's (ca. 1751) "Squire of Dames" (121–55). Referential to *The Faerie Queene*'s Legend of Chastity (3.7), where the Squire seeks virtuous women, are the two cantos from Mendez's poem in Dodsley. Referential as well is the self-conscious diction ("muchel scath" is one term); not so the stanza, which is only technically like Spenser's. The Squire's story (told to Satyrane) concerns misadventures in finding faithful women, a commission given him by his love Columbel. He recounts infidelities and in doing so satirizes women of convents, palaces, countrysides, theaters (certainly not a Spenserian detail), and married life: "Man throws the wimble [i. e. vacillating] bait, and greedy woman bites" (stanza 27). Disappointed, exhausted, the Squire sleeps and dreams of a beautiful woman named Chastity who tells him to search for a pure woman in fairyland (England), the place "Dan Spenser" sang about (stanza 32). His quest is to find 300 good women or abandon that sex forever, including his Columbel (stanza 33).

The second canto has the Squire in England at a fair pastoral castle described in terms echoing Chaucer's: "And all was bright, and all was passing gay, / You would have sworn it was the month of May" (stanza 8). The cheery doorman l'Allegro who advises him to "shun all dreryhed" (stanza 11) is part of a pleasant idyll, but the high point of the canto is Bon-vivant whose welcome (stanzas 13–15) charms and whose warning against the Blatant Beast (envy and distraction, according to the poem's glossary) chills; indeed it is the Beast who makes finding virtuous women so difficult. So the Squire sets off to slay him the next morning. A shepherd leads him to Merlin's gloomy cave, which is well presented in stanzas 31–33. The magician invites him to use all he owns except the magic mirror behind the door. When Merlin wings away on a dragon, the Squire at once runs to look into the mirror where, like Redcross's viewing of the false Una early in book 1 of *The Faerie Queene*, he sees his Columbel lasciviously at play with a naked youth. Dismayed, the Squire commits an unspeakable imitation of a Spenserian ejaculation: "O losel loose, O impious Columbel" (stanza 41). With even more temerity, in the final stanza the poet announces that he will leave the story there because he is fatigued! Aside from such lapses, the tale is not poor as a poem or as a Spenser imitation, particularly in locale passages, although with so much antique diction the glossary of 20 words could well be much longer.

Volume 4 also has three poems by Joseph Warton that reflect

earlier tastes and anticipate new poetic directions and tonalities. "Verses Written at Montauban in France, 1750" is a standard treatment of liberty but with some new turns on that theme, a favorite of romantic poets of course, particularly when they were young men. "The Revenge of America" in octosyllabic couplets inveighs against avarice but avarice presented in a fresh setting, as is his unsentimental blank-verse presentation of "The Dying Indian" talking to his son: Tell my mother

> I ne'er have worship'd
> With those that eat their God [Christians] and when disease
> Preys on her languid limbs, then kindly stab her
> With thine own hands, nor suffer her to linger,
> Like christian cowards, in a life of pain.
>
> (210)[6]

The subjects treated by Warton will more frequently be turned to by other writers, including Americans. A difference in them will be the tone and treatment: more sentimentality and more idealization—this the case at least up to the time of the early film treatments of this century.

Thomas Warton's blank-verse "Pleasures of Melancholy" (1745) is included in Dodsley's fourth volume, where poems in blank verse mirror the times's growing fondness for the form. Even though the poem is not a Spenser imitation, it is evocative of him, including his fancy when evoking night:

> . . . as Spenser saw,
> When thro' bewild'ring Fancy's maze,
> To the fell house of Busyrane, he led
> Th'unshaken Britomart.
>
> (219–20)

After two lines on Pope's "Attic page," Warton is transported by "magic Spenser's wildly-warbled song" wherein he sees "deserted Una wander wide / Thro' wasteful solitudes, and lurid heaths." Since Warton's subject is the pleasure deriving from melancholy, the Spenserian Una is more satisfying than Pope's

(*Rape of the Lock*) Belinda whose "gay description palls upon the sense, / And coldly strikes the mind with feeble bliss" (220). Once more, then, Pope and Spenser are treated together, this time with Pope losing out to his elder, for "all the lustre of [his Belinda's] brocade, / Amid the splendors of the laughing Sun" cannot give the pleasure and longevity of Una's melancholy, since the latter leads to contemplation and "deep-felt joys" (225). This attitude and presentation are not at all different from Milton's in "Il Penseroso" and not far from that expressed in many of Wordsworth's poems.

The fourth volume also offers numerous nature poems which had not as yet divested themselves of the usual stanzaic and couplet dress; but some are in blank verse. Dodsley's fifth volume (1758) opens with exclusively pastoral subjects treated in the newer fashion by Spenserian William Shenstone—none of them direct imitations of Spenser. These midcentury poems could well be from a collection of Wordsworth's poetry for they carry such titles as "Rural Elegance," "Inscription near a Sheep-cote," "Nancy of the Vale. A Ballad," and "Ode to Indolence." The first 48 pages of volume 5 are on similar subjects and in similar diction. The volume, however, is the least important for measurable Spenserian material. Some pieces such as Mr. Iago's puerile "Hamlet's Soliloquy, Imitated" ("Thus critics do make cowards of us all") manage to bring a smile. The sole distant relative to a Spenser imitation is Thomas Denton's monody "Immortality: or, the Consolation of Human Life" in 31 Prior stanzas. It is perhaps the most wretched Spenser imitation ever penned with its first-person moaning ("Come sighing elegy"); supernally generalized, unfathomable content; chaotic hyphenations; impossible diction ("Galileo's tube," stanza 21), and on it goes. The really poor imitations are consistently about abstractions such as Denton's, and many are in Prior stanzas, as is Denton's.

The volume's only other poem to be mentioned is the anonymous "Country Parson" in 12 stanzas of seven lines each, *ababbcC*. Unlike the realistic, clear-eyed "Dying Indian" of Joseph Warton, this portrait is sentimental, roseate, generalized, but pleasant. Its rural scene directly anticipates the popular Spenser imitation "Cotter's Saturday Night" and its several brethren: the "sturdy oak" parson who accepts his death "unfear'd and unresisted" (stanza 12); the simple, neat, solid wife, son, and daughter (stanza 5); the welcoming country setting, cot, and homey fireplace. Indeed, "tho' seasons change no sense of change they know" (stanza 7).

The series of Dodsley anthologies closes with the sixth volume's (1758) bad poetry and no life beyond its covers. In the later Dodsley volumes there are many fewer imitations of both the Ancients and Moderns. Volume 6 includes numbers of poems from the 1730s, as though the anthologist were padding his final book. Only one piece draws comment here,[7] Dodsley's postscript, which he says surveys the poetry of the past half century "thrown into the world, and carelessly left to perish" (333). He judges that he has preserved "the best," and this is mostly true regarding the earlier volumes. His collections taken together are harbingers and shapers of poetic preferences. They are auguries of poetic directions and samplings of the multivalent, charged atmosphere of differing poetic topics, tonal and dictional registers, and models, especially Spenser.[8]

A splendid final example of a midcentury Spenser imitation that blends poetic models and attitudes is Rev. Robert Potter's 1749 "Farewell Hymne to the Country. Attempted in the Manner of Spenser's Epithalamium" in 19 substantial, irregular stanzas.[9] The imitation is in places similar to Spenser's rural details, sensuous particularity, antique spelling and diction, personifications, generalizations, and moralizing. Blended are neoclassical diction and romantic notions of physical nature as teacher of virtue. An imitation of Spenser it is, but it is also an adaptation of Spenser and the epithalamion subgenre itself. For example, Potter's poem is not a wedding song; rather it is a celebratory lyric about the instructive aspects of nature.

A paean to country life, Potter's poem has the refrain "The hills, the dales, the woods, the fountaines ring" or a slight variation in the manner of Spenser's "Epithalamion." And it is a successful imitation of that poem. After a stanza given over to swans, dawn, sunset, rural walks, night, and sun-hot day, stanza nine begins

> ye lordings great, that in prowde citties wonne,
> Which gently-cooling breezes never blesse;
> In gorgeous palaces with heat fordonne,
> Come here and envy at my littlenesse.

Nature and the education and virtue only it can offer are celebrated in stanzas 10–13, where "an academic leisure here I find." Spenser, "lov'd Spenser of trewe verse the well-spring sweet," is the subject of the next stanza; Spenser, "the footing of whose feet / I, painefull follower, assay to trace." While strongly echoing the "Epithalamion," Potter calls Spenser what so many have, "Prince of poets." A green world and palace of art of sorts, this innocent, moralized country place, *locus amoenus*, must be abandoned because one must be up and doing, the latter commonly a Spenserian imperative, both explicit and implicit in *The Faerie Queene* and his shorter works. Thus Spenser's imitator bids "Farewell, sweet shade" (stanza 17) and "sweet poplar shade, farewell" (stanza 19).

The Potter lyric is both forward-pointing as a rumination in the manner of the romantic poets as well as an imitation of an Elizabethan poet. Sacramental nature and experience anticipatory of Wordsworth's attitude—as well as perhaps reflective of Potter's being a cleric—are seen in lines such as "'Tis sacred thus to tread the dewy Glade," an assertion and sentiment that continues:

> In the calme Solitude of that still towre
> To Nature's God the grateful Soul to powre
> Or in the silvery Shine, or doubtful Shade

By quiv'ring Branches made:
Rapt with the aweful Thought I cease to sing;
Nor Hills, nor Dales, nor Woods, nor Fountaines ring.

The stanzaic refrain pays obeisance to Potter's Spenserian model, but it also is of its time in such diction as *dewy* and *silvery*. His bee who extracts honey is predictably "The Chemist Bee."

Twenty-eight when he published this poem in 1749, Potter finds solace and instruction in his walks in the Norwich hills, much like students at Cambridge and Oxford found in their walks with Spenser in hand and head:

An Academick Leisure here I find
With Learning's Lore to discipline my Youth;
By Virtue's wholesome Rules to form my Mind.

Dorothy and William Wordsworth wrote just such lines during or after their walks where Spenser was read and discussed. The nature-learning-virtue-formation paradigm is precisely the same as that for the Wordsworths. A valedictory (the title of the poem is after all "Farewell") to bucolic nature and not an epithalamion in its denotative and historical sense, Potter's little lyric is offered as a compliment to the great poet of marriage, Spenser. Potter will then appropriately

Bring fayrest Floweres, the purest Lillies bring,
With all the purple Pride of all the Spring;
And make great Store of Poses trim, to grace
The Prince of Poets' Race;
And Hymen, Hymen, io Hymen sing;
The Hills, the Dales, the Woods, the Fountaines ring.

The poem ends in a Spenser-like cosmic stanza about spheres, muses, graces, concord, science. All contribute to "nobler Aimes" as the rural retreat is abandoned by the youth, who now has the proper formation in nature's ways of "Cherub Innocence" and "Contemplation sage." Potter admittedly is a

minor poet, but his "Farewell Hymne," a good poem representative of its time of composition, serves as a revealing example of the employment of Spenser as philosophic and moral
inspiritor and model in the service of some of the romantic
emphases shown above. I am confident in saying that Potter's
Spenser becomes the Spenser of British poetry for at least the
next two generations.

A visual example of a midcentury work that similarly feels
the pull of earlier days is Thomas Birch's 1751 three-volume
illustrated quarto edition of *The Faerie Queene* ... with
Thirty-Two Copper Plates, for the Original Drawings of the
Late W. Kent.[10] The plates are boon companions to reading
Spenser's epic, and the text is beautifully printed and appointed
with generous margins. The plates alone are worthy of study
as a reflection of eighteenth century notions of the poem. Like
John Hughes's mixing of classical and contemporary costum-
ing and trappings in his illustrations for the 1715 edition (reprinted the year before Birch's edition), and like the black and
white pictures by Fourdrinier for the Spenser imitation *Calendarium Pastorale* (see bibliography C), Birch and Kent meld
the medieval, classical, biblical, Elizabethan (Duessa and Luci-
fera wear Elizabethan collars), and contemporary. The eighteenth century reader clearly had no problem understanding
and appreciating such visual anachronisms and marriages. The
twin masters of allegiance to the past and necessary experimentation are discernible in presentations of Spenser, in works
produced in the manner of the poet (imitations and adaptations, the concern of this chapter), and in works about the
poet and in versions of his works (criticism and editions, the
concern of the section to follow).

In the earliest part of the century, as we shall see, critics
concentrated on Spenser's diction, pictures, and stanza, with
his pastoral poetry the subgenre most admired. After Hughes's
discussion of allegory in his 1715 *Works, The Faerie Queene's*
fable, unity, morality, and allegory begin to receive serious,

consistent attention; and the Spenser imitations reflect these two major Spenser interests, pastoral and epic fabling. As the midcentury approaches, and Spenser more and more appears in poetry collections, critical attention emphasizes his imagination, fancy, and his moral-instructive powers along with his own learnedness. The effect seems to be the encouraging of his imitators and adaptors to exercise their own fancies and push beyond what had earlier been considered and attempted as "Spenserian."

In the middle years of the century, a burgeoning of imitations and of Spenserians of differing competencies attests to the experimentation that existed, but also to regard for earlier attempts, other imitators, and the original model himself. Often conflations of Spenser, Milton, Pope, and at times other writers, Spenser imitations such as those appearing in the Dodsley collections showcased Spenser and brought him more insistently to the attention of both scholarly and "popular" readers. Both groups were open to new appreciations and applications of the poet. The times were propitious for a continuance of the poetic directions already set in motion, now with Spenser solidly at the forefront of change.

THREE

"Soon Their Beams Attract the Diver's Eye"

ଽୄ

Spenser Remarked and Edited

A logical result of school or school-age experiences of Spenser were many imitations and adaptations, as we have seen. His prominence in anthologies, a natural consequence of such encounters with the poet, likewise contributed to his renown and progress toward becoming a leading literary model. The picture of Spenser in the early eighteenth century is further clarified by an examination of criticism and editions, these also of a piece with and largely redounding from the other Spenserian activities discussed to this point.

While most of the following names have already been introduced in differing Spenserian contexts, perhaps here, by the example of three Spenserians who engaged in activities germane to this chapter, I could return to how foundational youthful encounters with Spenser were: specifically, the early century's two best editors, doing their work on either end of the period 1706–1762, and a significant critic writing in the middle of that span. John Hughes (1677–1720), translator, poet, essayist, and dramatist, published the century's first important edition of Spenser's *Works* (1715). A schoolmate of Isaac Watts at the dissenting academy in Little Britain, London, Hughes studied under Thomas Rowe, who in the *Dictionary of National Biography* is called the first to forego traditional school textbooks for the "free philosophy" of Descartes and John Locke, whose curricular revisionism we have already noted. Hughes's early affection for literature—he wrote a play by age 19—encouraged by his teacher and dissenting school, which we recall did have Moderns as part of the timetables, included Spenser.

Seen in the next chapter, which is concerned with the 1750s, John Upton (1707–1760) was the century's greatest editor of *The Faerie Queene* (1758)—and no mean Shakespearean as his 1746 *Observations* show. He was early disposed to his scholarly endeavor (his edition, particularly its notes, is erudite; indeed it is the direct forerunner of the 1930s Johns Hopkins' Variorum edition) because of the instruction provided by his schoolmaster father James and, later, by Oxford University. The elder Upton was Assistant Master at Eton before accepting the headmastership of Taunton Grammar School in Somerset, called by the *DNB* the "largest provincial school in England" with over 200 boys attending. James Upton was a scholarly model for his son not only in word but deed, for he edited and anthologized classical writers. I have not been able to discern any direct instruction in Spenser by the elder Upton, but it would be interesting to find if he had any influence upon his son John's becoming a Spenser imitator, even if one who wrote in Prior stanzas.

My final example, John Jortin (1698–1770), both imitator and an important early critic of Spenser, was educated at Charterhouse and then Cambridge. He wrote essays on both

Spenser and Milton, but it is his 1734 *Remarks on Spenser* that I turn to below. While I do not know of Jortin's being explicitly instructed in Spenser at Charterhouse, he certainly met Spenser there. Students in that school would have had access to Spenser's 1590–1596 *The Faerie Queene*, 1591 *Complaints and Poems*, 1611 *Works*, and 1653 *Shepheardes Calender* (see my chapt. 1, note 33). I surmise that Spenser imitator and critic Jortin may well have first read Spenser in the Charterhouse library.

It is worth noticing that what was negatively criticized in Spenser's art before the mid-eighteenth century commonly becomes admired and emphasized as one of the poet's glories thereafter. In brief, a changed sensibility occurs which is in part traceable through a comparison between the remarks made about Spenser in anthologies, studies, editions, and the practice of his imitators and adaptors. By this juncture in my own account, there is no need for an explicit comment on each point of connectedness; one can readily see strong ties first between education and imitation and then both of these as efficient cause of a Spenserian environment for the criticism and editions, this chapter's concern.

What follows will not supersede the work of Jewel Wurtsbaugh, R. M. Cummings, and William R. Mueller;[1] rather, their treatments of Spenser scholarship, the critical heritage, and changing taste are both complimented and complemented by remarks on the poet from writers either omitted in their accounts or, if included, presented in brief or used in surroundings different from the one created in my earlier chapters. Like theirs, however, my approach is generally chronological. I linger in some texts and direct quotation since the tone, language, and setting of the Spenser remarks are often revealing in themselves and at times defy neat encapsulations; since some of the texts are rare and the Spenserian material therein unremarked before; and since some texts are important both for their line of argument as well as the subjects treated.

From his own day, Spenser's diction was troublesome to readers, even to those who otherwise admired and learned from him. But one notices that before the fashion for Spenser occurs most particularly in the 1740s, many commentators on the matter who are not Spenser enthusiasts in general are more likely to carp on this one issue, or closely related ones such as diction and stanza, above all others and less likely to grant Spenser many artistic concessions in other areas of his art. In truth, though, most treatments of the poet are mixed. A useful example in anticipation of the remarks of the early eighteenth century is the anonymous 1687 paraphrase of book 1 of *The Faerie Queene* in 4,600 heroic couplets, *Spencer Redivivus*. Even though a Spenser imitation-adaptation, the work's subtitle hurries to assure its readers that *His Obsolete Language and Manner of Verse* [are] *Totally Laid Aside*. The intensifying *totally* calms just what anxiety in the readership, one wonders. Ben Jonson's famous complaint in *Discoveries* that "Spencer, in affecting the Ancients, writ no Language" (Herford and Simpson *Works* vol. 8, 618) also heralds what will become an iterated concern of critics of the poet (principally of *The Faerie Queene*), whose poetic technique involves one of four critical matters surveyed by Mueller—the other three being structure, allegory, and effect—that is, whether mainly pictorial or moral (2).

Jonson's judgment early in the seventeenth century carries forward to this 1690 comparison of Waller to Spenser, one which resembles others made when the new century arrives: "'tis a surprizing Reflection, that between what *Spencer* wrote last, and *Waller* first, there should not be much above 20 years distance: and yet the one's Language, like the Money of that time, is as currant now as ever; whilst the other's words are like old Coyns, one must go to an Antiquary to understand their true meaning and value."[2] But not only Spenser's diction bothered the young Joseph Addison four years later. In "An Account of the Greatest English Poets,"[3] he concludes his section on Spenser:

> But now the Mystick Tale [*The Faerie Queene*], that pleased
>   of Yore,
> Can Charm an understanding Age no more;
> The long-spun Allegories, fulsom grow,
> While the dull Moral lies too plain below.
> We view well-pleas'd at distance all the sights
> Of Arms and Palfries, Castle's, Fields and Fights,
> And Damsels in Distress, and Courteous Knights.
> But when we look too near, the Shades decay,
> And all the pleasing Lan-skip fades away.
>
> (319)

Although most critics who commented on the poet did not share Addison's opinion of Spenser, he did manage to announce in these lines several topics that received critical attention: *The Faerie Queene*, fable, moral, allegory, and effect on a reader. In the least, Addison's superciliousness is evident when he calls his age "understanding" in contrast to earlier times; but the quote also shows that Pope's contention may well be true, that Addison, while no reader of Spenser, nonetheless felt quite comfortable criticizing him. "Long-spun" Spenser's allegories may be, but no serious reader of him ever "when we look too near" thought him too superficial to "Charm an understanding Age no more."

Another major critical topic in the century is Spenser's stanza, the discussion of which was, once again, anticipated in the late seventeenth century. In the preface to his 1675 *Theatrum Poetarum, or a Compleat Collection of the Poets,* Edward Phillips considers "Spencer's Stanza (which I take to be but an Improvement upon Tasso's Ottava Rima, or the Ottava Rima it self, used by many of our once esteemed Poets) is above the way either of Couplet or Alternation of four Verses only. I am persuaded, were it revived, would soon be acknowledg'd, and in like manner the Italian Sonnet and Canzon, above Pindaric Ode, which, whatever the name pretends, comes not so near in resemblance to the Odes of Pindar, as the Canzon" (3–4). The unremitting stanza, one after another, Addison and others at the time judged "fulsom grow" (and of course few really wanted *The Faerie Queene* to be longer), but the composition and pedigree of that stanza, particularly from "the Italians" and Chaucer, also interested critics. Academic discussion of such stanzaic matters faded as the decades passed; the romantics seem to have just used the stanza instead of anatomizing it. Wordsworth, after all, did warn that we murder to dissect.

While the listing of Spenser imitations in bibliography C is arranged alphabetically rather than by date, it is fairly easy to discern the chronology and composition of the imitations and adaptations and understand that the Spensersian stanza was often used in the first half of the eighteenth century as well as the second. Such an examination also shows that while some writers worried over Spenser's diction and distanced themselves from his obsolete language and "Manner" as did the author of *Spencer Redivivus*, many more, while imitating the poet, embraced that same language and manner. The redoubtable Spenserian Matthew Prior, in or around 1718, wrote 11 of his own stanzas which he called *Colin's Mistake, Written in Imitation of Spenser's Style*; the final four words are of interest here.

Often invoking Aristotle and Longinus, but using Milton as his main example, severe critic John Dennis takes Spenser to task in *The Grounds of Criticism in Poetry* (1704). After declaring Spenser a failure in sacred poetry, Dennis gives rules for "Employing Religion in Poetry." He finds Spenser wanting in rules one and three: "The First is, That the Religion ought to be one that the Poet may be mov'd by it, and that he may appear to be in earnest. And the not observing of the Rule, was one Reason why *Spencer* miscarried" (113). If this observation involves morality in the poem and poet and not only organized religion as treated in Spenser's ecclesiastical and historical allegories, then indeed Dennis's judgment here is idiosyncratic, for *Moral Spenser* was progressively a prominent epithet for him for fully two centuries after Dennis.

Dennis sees Spenser breaking rule three as well with its concern for "inequalities" of action in a poem. Of course the unity and structure of *The Faerie Queene* have ever since been quests for Spenserians. Dennis never speaks substantively about Spenser in *Grounds of Criticism* as he promises to do (113), but it is clear in what he does say that rule-bound classicists found richer soil in Milton than in Spenser. The ironies of this need not be pointed out. But Dennis's ethical and structural concerns in 1704 are not what commentators on the poet most often wrote about at that early date. Rather, language, stanza, powers of description, and pastoral were far more popular subjects.

Sir Edward Bysshe's 1702 *The Art of English Poetry* continues the discussion of Spenser's style as seen in Phillips's *Theatrum Poetarum*. Typical of early-century treatments of Spenser, Bysshe's few remarks begin with a comment on his antique language: "tho' some of the Antients, as *Chaucer*, *Spencer*, and others, have not been excell'd, perhaps not equall'd, by any that have succeeded them, either in Justness of Description, or in Propriety and Greatness of Thought; yet their Language is now become so antiquated and obsolete, that most Readers of our Age have no Ear for them" (Preface). In his discussion of "stanzas . . . of an odd Number of Verses" (section 6), Bysshe, using Spenser's *Ruines of Time* as his example (the *Ruines* of interest to Spenserians ever since the early seventeenth century), and once again comparing Spenser with Chaucer as Ancients, says that "The Stanzas of 7 Verses are frequent enough in our Poetry" and that he has "chosen to take notice of this Stanza because that Poet and *Chaucer* have made use of it in many of their poems, tho' they have not been follow'd in it by any of the Moderns" (31–32). While not quite accurate here, Bysshe's topics for discussion concerning Spenser are standard for his time.

Turning to the Spenserian stanza, Bysshe, like some of his fellows, criticizes the form, for it is "very difficult to maintain, and the unlucky Choice of it reduc'd him [Spenser] often to the Necessity of making use of many exploded [out of fashion] Words: Nor has he, I think, been follow'd in it by any of the Moderns, whose 6 first Verses of the Stanzas that consist of 9, are generally in Rhymes that follow one another, and the Three last a Triplet," as in a nine-line poem by Cowley whom he quotes (33). Writing in 1702, a few years before Samuel Croxall's proficient imitations of the Spenserian stanza, Bysshe is incorrect about the rhyme scheme of the Spenserian stanza but nearly correct when he surmises that his immediate contemporaries and predecessors did not often use it; but there were some in the seventeenth century who did and of course many were to follow as the new century progressed. Perhaps of minor interest is the consonance Bysshe sees between Spenser's choice of the nine-line stanza and his antique diction, the former necessitating the latter. I believe that observation to be unique.

Spenser's language continues as a subject for critics throughout the earliest years of the eighteenth century, particularly his descriptive power to raise low subjects to a kind of sublimity, a word the romantics favored in describing Spenser. But this description of him is employed at least as early as 1712, when Leonard Welsted gives an appreciation of Spenser's transformative power in *The Works of Dionysius Longinus, On the Sublime*. While not pleased with Spenser's nauseous descriptions—such as that of Duessa in book 1 of *The Faerie Queene*[4]—Welsted finds that "*Spencer's* Description of his Dragon's Fight . . . seems to be conceiv'd with great Strength of Thought" (155). When not too ornamented, says Welsted, Spenser's verses can elevate mean thoughts in a "certain Appearance of Nobleness" (180).

Welsted offers quotes from Spenser to show that "What with
Ostentation of Language, what with Harmony of Sound, Pomp
of Epithet, and the agreeable Turn he gives it . . . Verses of this
sort . . . ["Tempestuous Fortune hath spent all its Spight, / And
thrilling Sorrow thrown his utmost Dart"] are like those Faces
which, if you consider each Feature distinctly, have nothing
agreeable, but discover variety of Graces when survey'd at once
in the Symmetry of the whole: The several Parts fall asunder
with disadvantage, but unite in a profussion [sic] of Charms."
Welsted is willing to wink at individual stylistic unhappinesses
in Spenser, if they are in the service of the harmony of the
whole. Even the "Iambick Foot" can work as synecdoche to
command the audience's attention and to create "Gravity or
Awe" and give the reader "somewhat of Composure." There
is a nice mix of classical concerns for form and the effect of
the art on its audience as well as romantic transcendental
uplift. The latter is based upon the particulars of the fiction
itself, which taken together allow a sublime elevation. Much
of this in Welsted seems to come directly from Longinus,
Welsted's main interest and easily the most important literary theorist for eighteenth and early nineteenth century
Spenserians.

Another writer aware of sublimity but no friend to "Tyran-
nick Rhyme, that cramps to equal Chime, / The gay, the soft,
the florid, and sublime," the minor critic Edmund Smith offers this on the comparative influence of Spenser and John
Philips, the popular early eighteenth century lyricist and pastoralist, in "A Poem to the Memory of Mr. John Philips. To a
Friend":[5]

> Our *Spencer*, first by *Pisan* Poets taught,
> To us their Tales, their Style, and Numbers brought.[6]
> To follow ours now *Tuscan* Bards descend,
> From *Philips* borrow, tho' to *Spencer* lend,
> Like *Philips* too the Yoke of Rhyme disdain;

They first on *English* Bards impos'd the Chain,
First by an *English* Bard from Rhyme their Freedom gain.
(154–55)

Smith's interesting passage presents additional critical concerns that become discussion points: (1) that Spenser is of the patrimony of such writers as Virgil, Ovid, Ariosto, Tasso and perhaps Boiardo; that he assimilated and disseminated their themes and manner; (2) that contemporary Italians now imitate English writers like Philips, who, while indebted to Spenser, disavows that master's rhyming verse in favor of blank verse, that is, Miltonic blank verse. And as the anthologies clearly show, blank verse will in another generation become increasingly popular until it will dominate. Spenserian rhymes, however, are certainly not abandoned.

The early eighteenth century not only credited Spenser with teaching the tales, style, and numbers of Italian poets but also with extending the allegorical possibilities of the Ancients. In a statement that reflects much contemporary thought on the matter, and a bit to the side of Addison, Thomas Parnell, in the preface to his 1713 *Essay on the Different Stiles of Poetry*, extols the efficacy and educative value of allegory and imitation:

> We are much beholden to Antiquity for those excellent Compositions by which Writers at present form their Minds; but it is not so much require'd of us to adhere meerly to their Fables, as to observe their Manner.[7] For if we preclude our own Invention, Poetry will consist only in Expression, or Simile, or the Application of old Stories; and the utmost Character to which a Genius can arrive, will depend on Imitation, or a borrowing from others, which we must agree together not to call stealing, because we take only from the Ancients. There have been Poets amongst our selves, such as Spencer and Milton, who

have successfully ventur'd further.[8] These Instances may let us see that Invention is not bounded by what has been done before, they may open our Imaginations, and be one Method of preserving us from Writing without Schemes. (3–4)

What is said here about imitation of the ancients is the practice of those who imitated and adapted Spenser—and not much of a departure from Johnson's and Young's imitation theory and caveats treated later.

The year before Parnell's *Essay,* the author of "On a Miscellany of Poems. To Bernard Lintott" in the 1712 *Miscellaneous Poems* hits on precisely the nature of Matthew Prior's chief borrowing from Spenser when he speaks of that imitator's *Hans Carvel*: "*Prior* th'admiring Reader entertains, / With *Chaucer's* Humour, and with *Spencer's* Strains" (172). Another imitator of Spenser, John Gay, humorously details his adaptation of Spenser's pastoral eclogues by building on what the Elizabethan did. ("Modernizing" Elizabethans is seen in writers other than Spenser, for a Mrs. Stanley updated Sir Philip Sidney's *Arcadia* in four books and 511 folio pages.) Gay's humor lies in the modernizing of what by his day was the "standard." In "The Proeme to the Courteous Reader" for his 1714 *The Shepherd's Week. In Six Pastorals,* Gay announces that he has hit upon the true "Eclogs": his purpose is "to [realistically not idealistically] set before thee, as it were a Picture, or rather a lively Land-scape of their own Country, just as thou mightest see it, didest thou take a Walk into the Fields at the proper Season."

Unlike Spenser's denizens of the fields in *The Shepheardes Calender,* "Thou wilt not find my Shepherdesses idly piping on oaten Reeds, but milking the Kine, tying up the Sheaves, or if the Hogs are astray driving them to their Styes. My Shepherd gathereth none other Nosegays but what are the growth of our own Fields, he sleepeth not under Myrtle shades, but under a Hedge, nor doth he vigilantly defend his Flocks from Wolves, because there are none, as Maister Spencer well observeth" (4–5). Such clear-eyed, desmystification of Spenser's pastoral trappings—themselves borrowings by Spenser from an ancient bucolic tradition—is one strain in early eighteenth century satiric poetry indebted to Spenser, verse which is always affectionate in its treatment of the poet. One can offer the example of Thomas Purney's Cubbin, Paplet, and Soflin in his 1717 *Pastorals*. There are more poems to present in evidence than just Pope's 1706 antipastoral "The Alley" and the anonymous 1713 couplet imitation of *The Shepheardes Calender* called *A Protestant Memorial*, but they may serve. The playful but strong antipastoral realism of the early eighteenth century is, of course, best seen in Jonathan Swift's 1709 "Description of the Morning" and his 1710 "Description of a City Shower," the latter of which is as well an imitation of Virgil's *Georgics*.

Gay continues with an appraisal of Spenser's beauties and faults, a way of writing about writers popular in (but not wholly invented by) the eighteenth century: "I must acknowledge him a Bard of sweetest Memorial. Yet hath his Shepherds Boy at some times raised his rustick Reed to Rhimes more rumbling than rural." The "rumbling" rhymes by Spenser reveal the disjunction Gay sees between the appropriate realistic diction and verse called for in a description of simple country life and Spenser's archaic, "resounding," "rambling" verse (both *OED* usages of "rumbling"). Similar charges, as we have seen, were made against Spenser's "rhymes" by other critics of the age. Richard Steele's exactly contemporary use of "rumbling" (*Tatler* 137) may also fit Gay's intention: "A few rumbling Words and Consonants clapped together, without any Sense" (*OED*). Gay and many of his contemporaries had the highest admiration and affection for Spenser but did not see him or present him as flawless in all his artistic decisions.

Gay next tells of his specific indebtedness to Spenser: "What liketh me best are his Names, indeed right simple and meet for the Country . . . some of which I have made bold to borrow," along with Spenser's calendaric eclogue approach figuring forth in Gay as days of the week rather than months of the year. Gay's practice is wittily put: "I have chosen . . . to name mine by the Days of the Week, omitting Sunday or the Sabbath, Ours being supposed to be Christian Shepherds, and to be then at Church worship." Such a line is no surprise from this member of the Scriblerus Club and the future author of *The Beggar's Opera*. Gay's debt to Spenser's *Shepheardes Calender* is palpable, early, and up to his day third in importance after Dryden's and Pope's indebtedness in their pastorals.

The 1714 *Guardian* 22 author gives two plausible reasons for the attraction of pastoral to practitioners such as Gay. Pastorals are liked "because all Mankind loves ease" (131) and we have a "secret approbation of Innocence and Simplicity"; no wonder, then, that the Ancients' pastorals are Englished and modernized (No. 30). In 1729, the year following the fourth edition of Gay's *Shepherd's Week*, the taste for pastoral was so strong that the dramatist Colley Cibber subtitles his *Love in a Riddle* a "Pastoral." As his 1720 two-volume *Poems on Several Occasions* reveals, Gay is also smitten with the traditions of pastoral,[9] whether the type is pastoral elegy, pastoral drama, or town eclogue. Gay of course knew firsthand the pastoralists among the Ancients, but Spenser among the Moderns was unambiguously an equal influence on his art.[10] Spenser's pastoralism, rather than any single Spenserian text, is imitated by Gay and other early eighteenth century writers. Some poets, of course, make title page proclamations that they are imitating Spenser. Title pages are often fascinating for what they reveal about indebtedness, for example that of William Mason's 1744 *Musaeus*. The title goes on to announce the piece as "in Imitation of Milton's *Lycidas*," celebrating "the Memory of Mr. Pope." The olio is compounded since *Musaeus* is as well a Spenser imitation—in which the opening stanzas copy Colin Clout's speech from *The Shepheardes Calender*'s first eclogue, and the remainder is given in Spenserian stanzas.

Mixing authors, types, and registers is not unique in the age and is seen also in music: one example is the 1746 *New Occasional Oratorio . . . the Words taken from Milton, Spenser, Etc. and Set to Musik by Mr. Handel*. In fact, the association between Spenser and music has always been intimate, not only seen in the sonorous verse he wrote (see Hughes below), a major reason for calling him the "poet's poet," but also his likenesses otherwise to the great Sister Art. George Sewell, ca. 1710, sees the latter correspondence in his couplet "The Force of Musick: A Fragment after the Manner of Spenser." And a few years thereafter, Colin Clout, the most frequent character in early eighteenth century imitations of Spenser, has his own madrigal, "Being the Anniversary of Her Majesty's Birthday," the 1728 *Colin Clout's Madrigal*. Of some interest also is the earlier Henry Purcell's six songs from *The Faerie Queene* and "An Epithalamium" and "A Dialogue in the Fairy Queen," sung by Mr. Reading and Mrs. Ayliff: in the 1702 *Orpheus Britannicus*.

Some "Fairy Queen" music (for example, Settle's *The Faery Queen: an Opera*, 1692) is based upon Shakespeare's *A Midsummer Night's Dream* and not Spenser's epic. Spenser's *Amoretti* receives musical treatment in 1739 in solo voice and figured bass accompaniment by the prolific composer Maurice Greene. Later in the century appear two editions of the Greene-Spenser *Amoretti* collaboration (sonnets 1–6) in the (rare) *Lady's Magazine* for October 1794 and January–May 1795, one sonnet for each issue. Spenser's pastorals are talked of in several numbers of the 1714 *Guardian*. By far the most famous is No. 40 where Pope ironically praises his rival pastoralist Ambrose Philips as "the eldest Born of *Spencer*, and our only true *Arcadian*," the latter term layered in its sarcasm. In No. 30 Philips is again coupled with Spenser, both of whom "have copied and improved the Beauties of the Ancients. . . . As far as our Language would allow them, they formed a Pastoral Stile according to the *Doric* of *Theocritus*"

(178).[11] *Guardian* 32 has Spenser and Philips together once
more with the following declension: Theocritus to Virgil to
Spenser, "and *Spencer*," Pope overstates, "was succeeded by
his eldest-born *Philips*" (190). Not only Spenser's pastorals
were admired in the early part of the century; his great epic
was, too. Matthew Pilkington's "Phoibo-Bathos: or the Poet's
Well" in the 1731 *Poems on Several Occasions* has him in
bayes for the epic, not the pastorals: "Sweet laurel'd *Spencer*
next was seen, / Immortal in his *Fairy-Queen*" (101).

Number 152 of the second volume of the 1714 *Guardian* is
of some note as one example of the eighteenth century's problems with Spenser, his allegory; that is, understanding it and
writing in the manner of it. But, then, all centuries have had
that problem. The author of No. 152 allows that "our Countryman *Spencer* is the last Writer of Note who has applied
himself to it with Success," then goes on to highlight some
general attributes of good allegory with emphasis on the instructive values the mode offers. As we shall see, the following
year John Hughes will return to this crucial subject with vigor.
He, in fact, will shape the Spenserian discussions after him.

The usual way of reading the poet at that time was as pictorialist and, increasingly, as "moral Spenser."[12] The rub comes
when the *Guardian* author himself tries his hand at a poem in
the manner of Spenser: "I was once thinking to have written a
whole *Canto* in the Spirit of *Spencer*, and in order to it con-
trived a Fable of imaginary Persons and Characters. I raised it
on that common Dispute between the comparative Perfec-
tions and Pre-eminence of the two Sexes, each of which have
had their Advocates among the Men of Letters" (368–69). After all this promising, though, the writer gives only the "naked Fable, reserving the Embellishments of Verse and Poetry
to another Opportunity." This absence is a blessing surely, for
the naked fable is a sketch of dismal abstractions interacting.
A versified fleshing out of this skeleton would have been in-
tolerable. Some imitators, as we have seen, did manage to write

worthwhile copies that were also competent demonstrations of sound criticism of Spenser.

The Hughes Edition of Spenser's Works

A major event for Spenser's reputation in the early eighteenth century is the publication of John Hughes's 1715 six-volume edition of *The Works of Mr. Edmund Spenser.*[13] Although not the first collection of Spenser's works since the Elizabethan period, Hughes's is a decided advance over earlier editions, a thesis demonstrated in chapter 2 of Jewel Wurtsbaugh's *Two Centuries of Spenserian Scholarship.* The old bugbear of Spenser's archaic words is faced immediately in part of the *Works'* very title, *With a Glossary Explaining the Old and Obscure Words.* The edition made Spenser more accessible to readers in the early eighteenth century and served as a pattern for editions that followed, not in the least in providing ways of talking about Spenser's works.

As indicated earlier, the illustrations for the edition are a conglomerate of mythological figures, a vestige of the emblem tradition, Roman and medieval and rustic and contemporary aristocratic personages which seem to embroider in a semi-allegorical manner rather than speak to the texts they accompany. To borrow a twentieth century locution, one might say they are decorative to the texts rather than organic, something akin to the relationship between Restoration and eighteenth century prologues and epilogues and the dramatic texts for which they serve as bookends. Hughes's edition has no notes and Spenser's works, volumes 2 through 5, have no accompanying commentary. The latter is included mostly in the first volume, which has as its center a Life of Spenser, "An Essay on Allegorical Poetry," and "Remarks on the Shepherd's Calendar," the final two essays of which were highly original and, once more, fundamental for criticism on Spenser for much of the remainder of the century. The final volume includes Theodore Bathurst's translation of *The Shepheardes Calender* and *Britain's Ida*, the last a work Hughes does not asĉribe to Spenser, although he includes it.

In his dedication to John Lord Sommers, Hughes speaks of his task in a manner not very different in its intention from remarks made by editors today: "An Editor of the Works of a dead Author ought to consider himself as a kind of Executor of his Will; which he should endeavour to perform with the same Care, and, in every Circumstance, after the same manner he believes the Author himself wou'd have done, if living" (2–3). Not at all different from the practice of contemporary editors such as Pope (of Shakespeare), Hughes's "Life of Mr. *Edmund Spenser*" is a disappointing account in method and execution: overly generalized everywhere, erroneous in spots, (curiously) indifferent to *The Faerie Queene*, and too much concerned with the erroneous monumental inscription dates: 1510 for Spenser's birth and 1596 for his death.[14] Of course, anecdotes about Spenser are savored.[15]

The heart of Hughes's criticism is his 32-page essay on allegorical poetry "With Remarks on the Writings of Mr. Edmund Spenser." The essay's subheadings could serve as an index of critical concerns in Spenser's art from his day in 1715 forward, especially in the first six decades of the century, when criticism of Spenser was more frequent and various than any time since the early seventeenth century—or would be again until the the nineteenth century. As expected, Spenser and Chaucer are compared: Spenser is granted the ascendancy in his descriptions, Chaucer in his characters. The essence of Spenser's descriptive powers is the happy blend of a "serious Turn, . . . an exalted and elegant Mind, a warm and boundless Fancy." The poet's main talent, however, is as "Imager of Vertues and Vices." "Moral Spenser" is largely the creation of the eighteenth century and heavily owing to Hughes. As I have already suggested, that particular emphasis does not disappear as the next century turns, if Wordsworth, Hunt, and others are admitted as evidence.

Hughes attributes to him unique status in description, the most arresting aspect of his writing to most readers then and now, especially young readers. Spenser has thus "been the Father of more Poets among us, than any other of our Writers; Poetry being first kindled in the Imagination, which *Spenser* writes to, more than any one, and the Season of Youth being the most susceptible of the Impression" (27). This statement by Hughes, echoed a few years later by anthologist Cooper as we have seen, is an accurate appraisal of Spenser and his effect as well as a fair statement for a goodly part of my study herein. Not minor, too, are Hughes's positive statements about Fancy and Imagination, faculties more often under suspicion in Hughes's day than they are apotheosized. Hughes had in mind examples of those taken with Spenser in their Season of Youth, namely, Cowley, Milton, Dryden, and the other writers I have already discussed.

The same talents Spenser owns in description stand him fair as an allegorist in *The Faerie Queene*, wherein, says Hughes, "Every Book . . . is fruitful of these visionary Beings, which are invented and drawn with a surprizing strength of Imagination" (43).[16] Hughes's presentation of allegory is otherwise standard neoclassical fare, short on particularization and long on generalities: Hughes would not have been accepted by Greenlaw as a contributor to the Spenser *Variorum* two centuries later. He ends his discussion of allegory expressing pleasure over the revival of talk about and practice of allegory by his contemporaries in the pages of the *Tatler*, *Spectator*, and *Guardian*, even though he would certainly have known that Addison—involved with each—was no rhapsode for Spenser or his way of allegorizing.

In his "Remarks on the Fairy Queen" (58 ff.), Hughes's theme is that Spenser's epic is brilliant in *inventio* yet flawed in *executio*, including the work's unity. Hughes's method is to give the "principal beauties" of each book of *The Faerie Queene*, which unshamefacedly results in impressionistic criticism. It is instructive to attend to Hughes's progress through the poem since his remarks are pattern-setting. Emblematist Spenser is examined in *The Faerie Queene* episodes and personages. Like other early eighteenth century critics and imitators of book 1, Hughes treats Duessa's address to Night (canto 5), the House of Pride and Holiness allegories, Spenser's employment and characterization of Prince Arthur, and so on. Hughes muses that Spenser is at his best when *not* the poet of miniaturization.[17]

He says, "as *Spenser* abounds with such Thoughts as are truly sublime, so he is almost every where free from the Mixture of little Conceits, and that low Affectation of Wit which so much infected both our Verse and Prose afterwards; and from which scarce any Writer of his own Time, besides himself, was free" (77). Many years before the appearance of those writers who bore the new sensibility called romanticism, Hughes recognized Spenser's sublimity. The accurate reader of Hughes would understand him as a product of the classical education of his age who would hold that the sublimity should arise from the general and enduring truths of the subjects and situations presented rather than the particularized "streaks of the tulip," to borrow the famous image from Dr. Johnson's *Rasselas.*

Hughes thus does not like Spenser's description of the House of Temperance "in which the Allegory seems to be debas'd by a Mixture of too many low Images, as *Diet, Concoction, Digestion,* and the like"; but he does favor the more "Allegorical Description" of Memory which he calls "very good" (82). Book 2 is in fact a "most Poetical" book in its recommendation of "worthy Sentiments" in such *topoi* as Idleness and the House of Mammon. The poetry of book 3 also has his approval, particularly the variety there: he finds "amusing"— by which he seems to mean that readers are able to deceive themselves into fancying involvement in the action depicted— Marinell's story as well as the account of the birth of Amoret and Belphoebe.

At one with all Spenser readers, he admires the Garden of Adonis episode, "Which is vary'd from the Bower of Bliss [canto 12] in the former Book, by an agreeable Mixture of Philosophical Fable. The Figure of Time walking in this Garden, spoiling the Beauty of it, and cutting down the Flowers, is a very fine and significant Allegory," he says (86), but of what precisely one is not sure. Of course he finds appealing the personifications, whether of Night, Morpheus, or Time. While he welcomes variety, Hughes does not like passages which "favour too much of the coarse and comick Mixtures in *Ariosto* as in the story of the Squire of Dames and Paridel" (86). Thus the ornamentation of the Masque of Cupid is judged "one of the chief Embellishments of this Book" (87).

Book 4 receives only a page or two by Hughes. What he does say about it echoes his comments on earlier books, but he compliments Spenser's treatment of sources, in this case Chaucer and Lucretius. An eighteenth century critic with the taste of an Elizabethan for ritual and pageantry, Hughes reveals both dispositions in his remark on the *ceremony* of the marriage of the Thames and Medway, "all which are describ'd with a surprizing Variety, and with very agreeable Mixtures of Geography" (88). *Pictures, variety, mixtures* are words repeated in Hughes in diction harkening back two generations or so to the emphasis and taste of Milton's teacher at St. Paul's. These nouns are important as well to most of the Spenserians to come for several more generations, including editors, critics, anthologists, imitators, and adaptors. To consider only the efforts in two kinds of imitation, one sees pictures, variety, and imaginative mixtures in little in the epithalamia and pastorals in the manner of Spenser, almost all of them the province of the first half of the century.

The most allusive of the *Faerie Queene* books "to particular Actions and Persons," according to Hughes, book 5 in its depiction of Justice becomes a "kind of figurative Representation of Queen *Elizabeth's* reign" (89). The pictorial Spenser

is returned to in an appreciation of book 6, judged as different from other books in its pastoralism: "The picture which
Spencer has here given us of his Mistress, dancing among
the Graces, is a very agreeable one, and discovers [reveals] all
the Skill of the Painter, assisted by the Passion of the Lover."
Since allegory and sublimity in *The Faerie Queene* have been
Hughes's controlling interests in the poem—as they were not
for contemporary Sir Richard Blackmore who in his "Essay
upon Epick Poetry" says that Ariosto and Spenser "have ran
too far into allegory"—it is reasonable to find him most
appreciative of the mutability cantos, book 7, "the most
sublime and best-invented Allegory in the whole Work" (91).
In an *O, Altitudo* summation, Hughes judges Spenser's inventiveness as so good it matches Homer's. The student of
this topic will not overlook the final pronouncement on the
poem's conclusion as containing a "noble Moral" (93)—by
extension, that is, written by *moral* Spenser.

For his final consideration in *The Faerie Queene*, Hughes
turns to Spenser's gifts as versifier. In this, the editor finds the
poet greater than all his contemporaries most particularly
because of musicianship. While erring in his choice of the nine-
line stanza, Spenser was nonetheless harmonious within it,
according to Hughes. Repeating the old charge against the tire-
someness of the Spenserian stanza in a long narrative poem,
along with its full stop at the end of each stanza when the
sense demands flow, Hughes lauds Spenser's "well-sounding
Epithets" and "such elegant Turns on the Thought and Words,
that Dryden [Dedication to Juvenal, one should guess] himself owns he learn'd these Graces of Verse chiefly from our
Author; and does not scruple to say, that in this Particular
only Virgil *surpass'd him among the* Romans, and *only Mr.*
Waller among the English" (96). Here is Waller again and the
seemingly obligatory comparison with the Ancients; it is as
though a writer's *real* stature can be measured only if one or
more of them is part of the yardstick.

About Spenser's other writings, *The Shepheardes Calender* in particular, Hughes believes "there seems to be the same difference between the *Fairy Queen* and the *Shepherd's Calendar*, as between a Royal Palace and a little Country Seat. The first strikes the Eye with more Magnificence; but the latter may perhaps give the greatest Pleasure" (98), a locution anticipatory of Dr. Johnson's periods a few years later. The simplicity of the work is found to be appealing in its offer of love and the country life. One of the pleasures of pastoral poetry is its ability to transport the reader "out of modern Life" to a place where "we are apt to fancy our selves reinstated for a time in our first Innocence and Happiness" (101). As such, pastoral poetry is "amusing." Hughes is generally accepting of Spenser's antique language in the pastorals since in the fifth and eighth eclogues his intention was "Allegorical Satire" where a "more antiquated Dress" is appropriate. Perhaps Gay missed this intention by Spenser in his complaint of Spenser's "rumbling" lines.

At one with Hughes's dislike of Spenser's mixing of types, the poet's use of satire in his pastorals is judged as an imperfection. Acceptable, however, is *Mother Hubberds Tale* where "we have a Specimen of our Author's Genius in Satire, a Talent he very seldom exercis'd" (106). In the year Hughes's edition was published, an eight-page "Jacobite parody of Spenser's poem" appeared, *Mother Hubbards Tale of the Ape and the Fox, Abbreviated from Spenser* (commented on by me in discussing Swift earlier). The point here is that the octavo edition some 70 years later was advertised "with the obsolete words explained." Old words became no less murky the older they grew. Hughes passes over many shorter works with just a mention but, typically for his age, he comments with precision on the sonnets as a "Species of Poetry so entirely disus'd, that it seems to be scarce known among us at this time" (108). Perhaps Hughes's definition of sonnets as "little Odes" shows why they assuredly were out of fashion in the early eighteenth century. Thomas Edwards' revival of the form lies half a century away.

Last, Hughes lays out his conservative editorial policy and rationale for an old-spelling edition, so far as I know the fullest statement of its kind in the entire century up to Malone.

> Care has been taken not only to collect every thing of this Author which has appear'd before [he has even included the *Britain's Ida* and Bathhurst's translation], and to preserve the Text entire, but to follow likewise, for the most part, the old Spelling. This may be thought by some too strict and precise; yet there was a Necessity for it, not only to shew the true State of our Language, as Spenser wrote it, but to keep the exact Sense, which wou'd sometimes be chang'd by the Variation of a Syllable or a Letter. It must be own'd however that *Spenser* himself is irregular in this, and often writes the same Word differently, especially at the end of a line; where, according to the Practice of that Age, he frequently alters the Spelling for the sake of the Rhime, and even sometimes only to make the Rhime appear more exact to the Eye of the Reader. In this, the old Editions are not every where follow'd; but when the Sense is render'd obscure by such Alterations, the Words are restor'd to their proper Orthography. (92)

Serving as a kind of note on the "Glossary Explaining the Old and Obscure Words in Spenser's Works" (115–40) is Hughes's explanation of how Spenser's words have changed in meaning, something of their derivation, and the influence of Chaucer. In diction, Hughes says, Spenser has taken great liberties and "Poetical Licenses"; yet, "his Diction is, for the most part, strong, significant and harmonious; and much more sublime and beautiful than that of any *English* Poet, who had written before him." It is noteworthy that Hughes is cautious in not saying that Spenser is greater than Milton or Dryden when he qualifies his statement with "English Poet" and "before him." Such prudence encourages Hughes's reader to find his other statements and judgments more credible. One contemporary found him so. In the 1716 edition of *Essays upon Several Subjects,* Sir Richard Blackmore, in his preface to "An Essay upon Epick Poetry," calls Hughes's edition "accurate" and the writer "ingenious" (6).

In contrast to Hughes's belief in the positive values of such pastorals as those by Spenser, the writer of the 1717 *Love and Resentment: A Pastoral* dislikes the form. In a vague, self-important essay "To the Reader," the author takes to task pastoral writers who "affect a Clownish (not to say British) Manner, in a mean uncleanly Stile" (2). He would rather have a writer who steered between the rusticity of Theocritus and the "cleanly Diction" of Virgil, although his pastorals, while "very natural and entertaining," are a "little over-season'd with some antiquated Words and Phrases" (3). The anonymous author does not name his ideal pastoralist or any of the Moderns such as Philips or Pope but does find fault with a "third sort of Writers, who have of late puzzled their few Readers with . . . a senseless Jargon," those who "run Mad in a fondness for Obscurity."

Does he mean Spenser's imitators such as Prior and Croxall? He, however, unlike the bad poets he sees all around him, endeavors to "distinguish betwixt the Countryman and the Clown; and to make my Swains speak of Things obvious to every Man of plain Sense and good natural Parts, with such Passions and Sentiments as are common to Mankind; and for their Stile, I think it much better they shou'd use Words familiar to all our People, than to be so very arch at the obsolete." He mirrors Gay, then, albeit boorishly. After all this, one would expect to find *Love and Resentment* a much better poem than it is. Yet, in this cranky, distant cousin to Gay, we understand wherein Spenser's old-fashioned pastorals hit a nerve with some readers in the early eighteenth century. But Alexander Pope was not one of them.

In the "Discourse on Pastoral Poetry" in his 1717 *Works,* Pope speaks about Theocritus and Virgil then turns to Spenser:

"Among the moderns, their success has been greatest who have most endeavour'd to make these ancients their pattern. The most considerable Genius appears in the famous *Tasso*, and our *Spenser*" (7). In the standard manner of plus and minus, beauties then faults, Pope, following Dryden's lead, evaluates *The Shepheardes Calender* as the "most complete work of this kind which any Nation has produc'd ever since the time of *Virgil*"—but not perfectly so in all points. Pope judges Spenser's eclogues as "somewhat too long, if we compare them with the ancients. He is sometimes too allegorical, and treats of matters of religion in a pastoral style as *Mantuan* had done before him. He has employ'd the Lyric measure, which is contrary to the practice of the old Poets. His Stanza is not still [always] the same, nor always well chosen." Pope would favor the tighter presentation of couplets (8).[18]

It is not unexpected in Pope's day that a Modern's faults are most visible when measured against the achievements of the Ancients. And it is reasonable that when Spenser himself becomes the model against whom writers are evaluated as the century wears on, he will occupy the exalted position that the Ancients held for Pope and his contemporaries. While ranking Spenser's "manners, thoughts, and characters" with those of Theocritus, Pope finds his countryman "inferior in his Dialect" to the great Greek pastoralist. Continuing with his critique of *The Shepheardes Calender*, Pope finds that the "addition he has made of a Calendar to his Eclogues is very beautiful" since this device "compares human Life to the several Seasons, and at once exposes to his readers a view of the great and little worlds, in their various changes and aspects" (9). Pope is critical, however, that the calendar "has not that variety in it to furnish every month with a particular description, as it may every season" (9). Thus Pope will use the seasonal approach in his own *Pastorals*, which nonetheless owe allegiance to Spenser, for they have as much "variety of description, in respect of the several seasons, as *Spenser's*." In a

formulaic gesture at modesty, Pope confesses that if his seasonal pastorals have "any merit, it is to be attributed to some
good old Authors, whose works as I had leisure to study, so I
hope I have not wanted care to *imitate* [my emphasis]." Along
with the Ancients, then, Spenser made his mark on Pope as
his *Pastorals*, his youthful imitation "The Alley," and his
poetry otherwise attest.

Unlike Bysshe's *Art of English Poetry* at the beginning of
the century, from which Spenser is conspicuously absent,
Charles Gildon in 1718 makes Spenser, along with Shakespeare, central to his discussion of *The Complete Art of Poetry*. At the end of volume 1, Gildon presents a collection of
Shakespeare's poetry as a corrective to his exclusion by "some
Modern Collectors [Bysshe] for his Obsolete Language" (304),
much the rationale for including Spenser also. Volume 2 is a
468-page anthology of poetry along with "Philosophers and
Criticks." For the first time Spenser is anthologized (for more
discussion on this subject, see chapter 2). That he is anthologized is quite important for the advancement of his reputation in the century, for Gildon, although often a literary
hack, was much read. Spenser appears in no section exclusively his; rather, he appears *passim* since the anthology is in
alphabetical arrangement by topic, not author: for example,
"Abbot" then "Abby" then "Absence" then "Adonis' Garden,"
under which five stanzas of Spenser's *Faerie Queene* are offered.
In this manner, Spenser is heavily presented throughout the
volume.

The second volume is described by Gildon as "A Collection of the most beautiful Descriptions, Similes, Allusions,
etc. from *Spenser*, and our best *English* Poets" (title page). In
his helpful Preface, Gildon takes Bysshe to task since his book
is purportedly the same sort of *omnium gatherum* as his own:
"He (tho' he calls his Book the Art of *English Poetry*) aims
only at giving Rules for the *Structure* of an *English* Verse, in
Rime, and the like. And thus in his Collection [the anthology

part], he aims at settleing [sic] a sort of Dictionary of Epithets and Synonymous Words" (6). In contrast to Bysshe, Gildon's plan is to "give the Reader the great *Images* that are to be found in those of our Poets, who are truly great, as well as their Topics and Moral Reflections. And for this Reason I have been pretty large in my Quotations from *Spenser*, whom he has rejected, and have gone through *Shakespear*, whom he seems willing to exclude. . . . And since *Milton* and *Waller* were made Poets by *Spenser*, I do suppose the same Cause may in all Probability have the same Effect [i. e., since they would be known as a matter of course by anyone interested in poetry].[19] When I say that *Spenser* made those two great Men *Poets*, I mean only that the true Ethereal Fire that they found in him, rous'd that Genius, which each of them had by Nature, into Act" (6). Gildon and not Bysshe is the model for anthologies that were to follow.

The first five parts of Gildon's work are set up as "Dialogues" in the manner of Dryden's *Essay of Dramatick Poesy*. Herein, Crites is Dennis, whom Gildon admired. There is high praise of Ambrose Philips as a pastoralist (156–62) in the third dialogue; this praise of him is common in the early decades of the eighteenth century, when he inexplicably rivalled Pope as a writer of pastoral poetry. Of more interest, one dialogist compares Spenser and Philips: "The great *Spenser* fell into an Error in the Stile, which Mr. *Philips* has admirably avoided; for imitating the Greek *Doric*, he gives us a Northern Dialect, which renders his Pastorals unintelligible, without the help of *Spelman*, or some other Glossarist" (160–61). The criticism of *The Sheapheardes Calender*, whether Gildon would have personally agreed with it or not, does represent the judgment of some of the era's commentators on Spenser's pastoral; yet that very work was one of the early eighteenth century's favorite models for imitation.

Matthew Prior, needless to say, had a prominent influence on Spenser's reputation. In 1718, Prior published *Poems on*

Several Occasions, a large-paper subscription volume with illustrations beautifully printed by John Watts. Prior's 1706 "Ode" is included with its much-copied stanzaic adaptation of the Spenserian stanza. There are no new Spenser imitations in the volume, prepared under his own eye for the reason given in his Preface: "a Collection of Poems has lately appeared under my Name, tho' without my Knowledge, in which the Publisher has given Me the Honor of some Things that did not belong to Me; and has Transcribed others so imperfectly, that I hardly knew them to be Mine."[20] Prior calls his volume "an indifferent Collection of Poems," composed "for fear of being thought the Author of a worse." Except for the one Spenser imitation, Prior's poems are in ballad stanzas, the six-line *ababcc* stanza, seven-line pentameters, and the eight- and ten-line couplet stanza. In a variation on the stanza used in his "Ode," he has some ten-line stanzas with an alexandrine as the final line, but the rhyme is couplet and not that of the "Ode."

In his practice as an imitator of Spenser, Prior, had he not predated Edward Young, would have taken Young's advice on imitation found in the latter's essay "On Lyrick Poetry": *Ocean. An Ode* (1728). Young, anticipating by a generation Dr. Johnson's warning pronouncements on imitation and verbalizing the limitations of all imitations (caveats that Prior and all good Spenser imitators well knew), holds that "*Originals* only have true Life, and differ as much from the best *Imitations,* as *Men* from the most animated *Pictures* of them. Nor is what I say at all inconsistent with a due *deference* for the great Standards of Antiquity." Like a good classicist, Young wants the imitation to be of "their example in the general *motives,* and fundamental *methods* of their working, than in their *Works* themselves." He wants the imitator to capture something of the "original spirit" and manner of the host or model who is imitated.

Young would probably conclude that the lesser Spenser imitators of that age are those who merely use old words as

Spenser did, or use the stanza he used, or borrow some proper names or incidents from the poet. One can only agree with Young's opinion that "This is a distinction, I think, not hitherto made, and a distinction of consequence." Proper imitation, which Young calls "the first of these Prizes," is judged "not so readily taken by the *Moderns*" for "Valuables too massy for easy carriage are not so liable to the Theif" (27–28).²¹ Young's observations are fairly standard for theorists and critics of his day, as I try to make clear in the chapter to follow, and John Jortin's remarks are representative of the age's scholars. Published monthly beginning in 1731, Jortin's edition of *Miscellaneous Observations upon Authors, Ancient and Modern* is a serviceable example of the scholar's part and also a foretaste of his treatment of Spenser in his 1734 *Remarks on Spenser's Poems.*

In his *Remarks*, which includes an interesting section on Milton (171–86), Jortin gives extended commentary on passages from Spenser, especially citations from the Ancients that Spenser may have used. By modern critical standards, Jortin's work is in some ways disappointing, but it is always and justly mentioned by the few twentieth century critics who have written about Spenser in the eighteenth century, probably because Jortin's is among the first "remarks" based upon a close scrutiny of Spenser's texts. In his behalf also one must grant that he has compared the Hughes's edition and the 1679 folio editions, pointing to "Many false prints in Hughes," including errors in logic, diction (as well as glossary anomalies), and grammar.²²

Indeed Jortin is confident enough in his understanding of Spenser to instruct his reader thusly: "I would read . . ." this passage this way and not that way. Yet he is humble enough when facing book 2 stanza 31 of *The Faerie Queene* to admit "it is not easy to know what *Spenser* had in mind here" (53). Jortin seems most comfortable when addressing scholarly matters in Spenser's works; and his remarks are scholarly by any age's standards as he easily moves through Latin, Greek, and French sources, analogues, analogies, and commentaries. In fact, Jortin would have been more pleased had Spenser himself acted more the scholar, particularly in his use of sources. As we shall see, Jortin's scholarly successor John Upton decides that Spenser is "learned" and an "authority," in his 1748 *Observations on Shakespeare*.

Jortin did not consider Spenser's works as sacred texts and is not loath to criticize the poet for placing the lilies of the field stanza where he did (*Faerie Queene* 2.16): "The Poet ought not to have placed them where he has" (54); and Spenser could be imagined as smarting under Jortin's charge that he displays a "confused idea" of Cicero and that "*Jupiter* slew *Prometheus* is a fiction of our Poet" (68). But Jortin seems almost relieved to say that certain lines are fine and "would not suffer by being compar'd with any thing that *Milton* has said upon this subject" (61).

In temperament and method, Jortin is the first of the direct forerunners of the Spenser *Variorum* editors and their manner of doing scholarship and writing about writers. John Upton is next, followed by Edmond Malone late in the century. Indeed, Jortin's appraisal of his own *Remarks* sounds much like those made by *Variorum* editor Edwin Greenlaw on the seminar papers of his Seminary C students (including Charles Lemmi, Ray Hefner, Charles G. Smith, W. G. Friedrich, and Jewel Wurtsbaugh) at Johns Hopkins University in the early 1920s. Jortin calls his *Remarks* an "Essay, or rough draught of a Commentary, deficient indeed in many points, yet in some measure useful and entertaining to a poetical reader of *Spenser*. Much more might be done, particularly towards settling the text, by a careful collation of Editions, and by comparing the Author with himself" (168).

Jortin's casual remark on energy ("that [collation] required more time and application than I was willing to bestow") and available texts ("I had only two Editions to consult," 168–69) would not have been relevant in Seminary C: the former attitude unthinkable, the latter not a problem since the Tudor-Stuart Room in Gilman Hall, through the good offices of William Osler and his son, had every edition and relevant document by and about Spenser. *Properly* preserving and presenting Spenser are given a boost by Jortin, whose serious work in the poet's corpus is certainly a forward step for the several scholarly and critical treatments that were to follow, most importantly in the years in and around the midcentury, when a variety of Spenserian activities were exponentially increased. Included among these activities are naturally Spenser imitations, editions, and a remarkable display of criticism of the poet from all the major writers of the sixth decade, who had much to say about imitation theory as well. Indeed 40 years of imitating Spenser passed before a body of imitation theory was written in the 1750s. I believe that the burst of Spenser editions, his widening popularity, and the fashion for imitating him directly encouraged some of the best authors to write their considerations of the poet, which often were within discussions of imitation theory. The 12 years between 1750 and 1762 were the most crucial for modelmaking and for shaping the Spenser we know today.

FOUR

Spenser Among New Voices

è.

Decade Six and Beyond

Perhaps Dr. Johnson's involvement with Spenser and Spenserians in the first half of the 1750s is as good a single focus as one who wishes to understand Spenser in that decade can expect. We have already examined his reaction to the incursion of Spenser imitations at the midcentury, for example in his *Rambler* pieces and 25 years later in his biographical sketch of Gilbert West in the *Lives of the Poets*. But his and Edward Young's pronouncements—that imitations at best are lesser forms of literary life than are the original productions of genius—did not at all dissuade young poets from having their go at Spenser, as the enormous popularity of the Dodsley *Collections* attests (and as my listing in bibliography C shows).[1] Spenser's nine-line stanza continued to be employed along with its truncated *ababcC* form in the 1750s, but even though used,

121

Spenser's stanza continued to be attacked as "labour'd," not "agreeable to those who love *ease* in reading," even as "slavery" for critics such as the author of the 1751 *Monthly Review* 4 (520). Even such devoted Spenserians as Thomas Warton had misgivings over the stanza.

In the early years of the decade Johnson, who had not yet gained the wide celebrity his *Dictionary* would give him after 1755, was interested in the question or problem of imitation. The year before his 1751 *Rambler* 121 complaint about the proliferation of Spenser imitations (*O imitatores, servum pecus*, the motto from Horace for *Rambler* 121), he, as a foretaste perhaps of his *Rambler* position, wrote the preface and postscript to the first edition of William Lauder's provoking *Essay on Milton's Use and Imitation of the Moderns*. Lauder's book itself spawned rejoinders and vindications, including a dismal Spenser imitation by Robert Lloyd, *The Progress of Envy* (1751), in 30 altered Spenserian stanzas—the last of which features a triumphant Milton who sees "Envy and Lauder die."

Aside from imitation theory and practice, Johnson, years after the event, remarked on an important Spenserian publication of 1750, a small-format, six-volume edition of John Hughes's *Works of Mr. Edmund Spenser*, originally published in 1715, which I treated in detail earlier. In his Life of Hughes in the *Lives of the Poets*, Johnson credits the 1750 *Works* (which offered no new features or information over the 1715 first edition; Hughes died in 1720) with being an integral part of the Spenser revival which was fully mobile by the mid-century. In character, Johnson balances his praise with a complaint about Hughes's philological innocence of Spenserian English. In his personal library Johnson displayed several texts of Spenser's works: including of course the 1750 Hughes *Works*, which was also part of fellow Club member Oliver Goldsmith's library;[2] the three-volume quarto 1751 *Faerie Queene*, featuring a Spenser biography by Thomas Birch and William Kent's engravings; and John Upton's 1758 large-format *Faerie Queene*.

In addition to these editions, Johnson owned three books by his friend and fellow Oxonian Thomas Warton: the two-volume 1754 *Observations on The Faerie Queene of Spenser*, as well as the 1772 *Life of Sir Thomas Pope* (founder of Warton's beloved Trinity College, Oxford) and the seminal *History of English Poetry*.[3]

One at first may wonder over the absence of Spenser from Johnson's *Lives of the Poets* in the 1770s. How could John Hughes be included and not Hughes's better? In chapter 2, I suggest that Spenser's absence is not to be construed as the result of Johnson's disaffection. The omission simply is the result of the publishers of Johnson's *Lives* declaring that they had no room for Spenser. And even if commissioned to do Spenser's Life, which was strongly urged upon him by King George III, Hannah More, and others, Johnson, by his own admission, would hesitate to attempt a life so major with so little new biographical information, particularly after Thomas Warton's thorough work in the *Observations*.[4] Several well-known contemporary testimonies speak to Spenser's absence in Johnson's book. The most familiar is undoubtedly Hannah More's anecdote: "Johnson told me he had been with the king that morning, who enjoined him to add Spencer to his Lives of the Poets. I seconded the motion; he promised to think of it, but said the bookseller's [publishers] had not included him in their list of the poets."[5]

That Johnson was indifferent or antagonistic to Spenser or other sixteenth century native writers is disproved by such information as that provided by Alvin Kernan, who notes that the 1755 *Dictionary* is packed with literary examples of writers from as early as the 1580s and Sidney, including Johnson's "great predecessors, Spenser, Shakespeare, Milton, and Pope."[6] And, too, the famous Preface to the *Dictionary* claims that Spenser and Sidney gave life to the language of poetry and fable. So far as Spenser's presence *in* Johnson's works is concerned, the surface of them does not suggest a direct influence.

Nevertheless, judging from the *Dictionary* examples and his remarks elsewhere, one is confident that Johnson intimately knew Spenser's writing and not just about it, knew even such minor works as *Ruines of Rome.*

Certainly Spenser the pastoralist had no salutary effect whatsoever. Johnson was not a sonneteer, not a friend to the Spenserian stanza or his characters' gothic peregrinations, and no eclogist. He did, though, as did his age and its allegorical Spenserian imitators, write "plain," generalized allegories in some *Rambler* pieces (e. g., Nos. 3, 22, 30, 32, 91, 96), in *Rasselas,* and in the *Vision of Theodore* (Johnson's favorite allegory) that may distantly owe something to Spenser's *Faerie Queene* journeys and a few of the *loci* therein (e. g., the Bower of Bliss and several Happy Valleys). But the didactic "characters" of Theophrastus are more to Johnson's taste and strength, as Bernard L. Einbond convincingly suggests.[7]

An old but still valuable study of Spenser-Johnson linkages, Percy Hazen Houston's 1923 *Doctor Johnson A Study in Eighteenth-Century Humanism* helps with this commonsensical appraisal: "Against the imitation of Spenser, then, as against the imitation of the ballads, of antiquity, and of the pastoral in general, Johnson revealed a consistent hostility," but not toward Spenser (136). Although Spenser's gothic flavor, so to speak, did not appeal to Johnson, he found attractive Spenser's role as "the grave and moral teacher whose mission it was to delight and instruct mankind" (138).[8] Also, Houston reminds us that Johnson wanted to hold to "cherished humanistic standards," expressed in the surety of uniform verse forms and versification, and eschew the "nascent romanticism" embodied in his age's fondness for Gray's odes, Spenser imitations, Ossianic poems, medieval literature, blank verse, sonnets, and "'our Pindarick madness,'" the latter manifesting itself in poetic irregularities (210).

Houston's paired listing is precisely the dialectic of poetic practices and tensions in the sixth decade, and not only involving Samuel Johnson. That he was open to newness, although typically cautious, is part of a testimony to his greatness as an important literary and cultural voice. The still-held notion of Dr. Johnson as the rigid, dour "last" neoclassicist (comparable to Milton as the Last Elizabethan in older literary histories) is unfair and not in keeping with evidence. And Johnson's remarks about Spenser show his own balance; for example, while he did not support Spenser imitations in general, he did praise individual imitators. The same balance is brought to his friend Warton's great project.[9]

Johnson generously encouraged Warton to move along with his book of Spenser criticism. An enemy to Spenser would not have been so vigorous and approving, even for a friend and fellow Oxonian. Johnson's 1754 letters to Warton show the very best face of friendship, wanting a friend to succeed; but they show as well Johnson's high estimation of Spenser. In his 16 July letter to Warton at Trinity College, Oxford, Johnson thanks his friend for a copy of the *Observations* and for "the advancement of the literature of our native Country. . . . The Reason why the authours which are yet read of the sixteenth Century are so little understood is that they are read alone, and no help is borrowed from those who lived with them or before them."[10] This suggestion that older writers should be studied in their contemporary literary environment will be revisited below.

Also, Johnson urges Warton to push ahead with a volume on Spenser's works other than *The Faerie Queene*. In a 28 November 1754 letter, Johnson prods his friend not to let such matters as "taking pupils" get in the way of this project. "I would not have it delayed," he urges. He then gives good practical counsel on how to get it done, saying "Three hours a day stolen from sleep and amusement will produce it." Johnson's own dilatory behavior in "projects" (at least *he* thought he was a procrastinator) stops him not at all from giving such advice. And "dictionary Johnson" comes through in his very next clause. When he tells Warton to "let a servitour transcribe the quotations and interleave them with references to save time" (No. 55, *Letters*, 58), Johnson gives precisely his own practice at that very time in preparing his great *Dictionary*.

Johnson's next bit of encouragement to Warton comes seven months later when he forewarns he will soon visit his friend at Oxford, when "I shall expect to see Spenser finished, and many other things begun" (No. 72, 10 June 1755, *Letters*, 73). With the Hughes 1750 *Works*, the Birch-Kent 1751 *The Faerie Queene*, the John Upton 1758 *The Faerie Queene* and the imitations, of course, Warton's 1754 *Observations* was *the* major critical contribution to the Spenserian package of the 1750s. In his way, Samuel Johnson advanced Spenser's renown.

There was no substantial discussion of Spenserian allegory and structure before the eighteenth century. As we have seen, the Spenser critics in the first half of the century had problems with allegory and structure, the two sometimes collapsed into one. They found fault with them in terms of clarity, unity, probability, and *telos*, all hallmarks of classical training, attitudes, and criticism. Joseph Spence in 1747 adds in his *Polymetis*, particularly its nineteenth dialogue, his severe appraisal of Spenser's allegory and moral as measured against the structural practices of classical epic writers. His judgment on Spenser comes to this, that he did not follow Nature, was literally unnatural, and therefore the opposite of Homer and Virgil. We have seen that Hughes in his 1715 edition also was a classical critic but importantly insightful in his observations that Spenser's epic is built and intended differently from classicists' notions of how an epic ought to be built and intended. He recognizes of course that along with the Ancients "the Italians" were major influences upon Spenser, especially Ariosto whose comic romance *Orlando Furioso* had a "gothick" structure, a term Hughes used 40 years before Warton, then Hurd, admitted it to the critical lexicon.

Hughes, more than any other critic before the midcentury, anticipates Thomas Warton's 1754 *Observations on The Faerie Queene* and its 1762 enlargement which includes remarks on Gothic architecture. The year 1762 is also the publication date of Richard Hurd's *Letters on Chivalric Romance,* which makes the claim of Gothic elements in Spenser much as did Hughes and Warton earlier. The year is also my study's *terminus* date since all the major theses are by then committed, and romantic attitudes struck. It would not be until the late nineteenth century and Edward Dowden's essay on "Spenser, the Poet and Teacher" in Grosart's edition[11] that the very real qualities that Warton and Upton and Hurd recognized in Spenser would be subsumed under rubrics such as moral, professorial, philosophical, ethical. Dowden's main candidate for a Spenserian model was Sidney's *Apologie.* The romantic, picture-making Spenser enthused over by James Russell Lowell, in his long 1875 essay on the poet in the *North American Review* and the Spenser of the romantic poets in the 120 years since the days of Warton, is muted in Dowden's less belletristic portrayal. Of course the Spenser of Lowell and the Spenser of Dowden are reflected, even if not exclusively, in twentieth century critics even to this day, albeit the dress is different.

Thomas Warton's *Observations* argues that *The Faerie Queene* has discrete unity, that is, unity within books but not so obviously between and among books. Echoing Hughes and anticipating Hurd, Warton sees in Spenser's epic a "gothick" manner and organization, not bound by classical "rules." Warton avers that

> it is absurd to think of judging either Ariosto or Spenser by precepts which they did not attend to. . . . Spenser . . . did not live in an age of planning. His poetry is the careless exuberance of a warm imagination and a strong sensibility. It was his business to engage the fancy, and to interest the attention by bold and striking images. . . . The various and the marvellous

were the chief sources of delight. Hence we find our author
ransacking alike the regions of reality and romance, of truth
and fiction, to find the proper decorations and furniture of his
fairy structure. (sect. 1, 1762)

Thus, the stuff of Warton's interpretation is, as David Fairer
succinctly puts it in his *Spenser Encyclopedia* piece on Warton,
"the romance motifs, fairy legends, ancient traditions, Arthurian and chivalric tales—those many fictions that so stirred
Spenser's imagination and his own." Warton's presentation is
itself at times Gothic in its variousness and arrangements,
but his aim is clearly historical. He is concerned to present
the native writers and folk art which helped to shape Spenser's
art rather than offer the influences of antiquity and Renaissance
Italy. In doing so, Warton offered a good example, to the poets
and critics who were to follow him, of where they might want
to look for their own traditions, examples, and inspiration.

Warton's major gift to scholars is, I believe, his historical
method, which includes a consideration of the books that
Spenser used; but for his contemporaries and the major romantic writers just on the horizon—Warton actually calls
Spenser "Romantic"—his contribution is new vocabulary, new
influences, new topics, and, as his title intimates, new insights
into the poem. In preparing his *Observations* it seems as
though Warton was at one with his friend Johnson's opinion
about the efficacy, in such studies as his own, of recreating
the milieu of one's subject, particularly the native setting
which included the influence of Mallory. He states once again,
"The Reason why the authours which are yet read of the sixteenth Century are so little understood is that they are read
alone, and no help is borrowed from those who lived with
them or before them" (16 July 1754 letter to Warton). For historical scholarship, Warton in a stroke made his insights and
practices the standard.[12]

Spenser the poet of the imagination, with his habitual lean-
ing toward allegory, is Warton's emphasis rather than Spenser

the learned, the moral, the didactic poet of Jortin and to some degree, Upton. Warton's affection for and recommendation of Spenser are communicated well through the *Observations* and his own poetry. He wanted Spenser to be broadly appreciated and understood, and he certainly was pleased to have yet another edition of the poet's work, Upton's effort of 1758. His poem "Sent to Mr Upton, on His Edition of the Faerie Queene" lucidly gives what Spenser meant to him as he read the poet "reclined on Cherwell's shelving shore" where he let *The Faerie Queene* work its own magical fancy on him.

Very soon, many other poets would want that same magic for themselves. The Spenserian Gilbert West, who in 1739 published "A Canto of the Fairy Queen" and in 1751 brought out his *Education* imitation, became, because he enjoined Upton to undertake a Spenser edition, the addressee of *A Letter Concerning A New Edition of Spenser's Faerie Queene* (1751) written by John Upton. This 39-page letter was a sketch of the greatest eighteenth century edition of any Elizabethan writer's work, the 1758 *The Faerie Queene*, which superseded all previous editions for scholarship even if not for carrying convenience. The Hughes 1750 better fit into a student's pocket.

The Rev. John Upton (1707–1760) gave notice that he could execute such a learned project as he envisioned the Spenser edition to be, for in 1739–1741 he published a distinguished edition of Flavius Arrianus's *Epictetus*. As noted earlier, he was splendidly trained by his father James, who was Assistant Master at Eton, and by Merton College, Oxford, where he proceeded M.A. in 1732. His letter to West explains that he planned to attempt the edition only because the scholar John Jortin was not going to do so. Restating his previous observations in *Critical Observations on Shakespeare* (1746, 1748), Upton says something important about editing Spenser, which he seven years thereafter will practice: "Methinks every reader would require that the last editor should consult every former edition, and that he should faithfully and fairly exhibit all the various readings of even the least authority; he would require, too, that an editor of *Spenser* should be master of *Spenser's* learning: for otherwise how could he know his allusions and various beauties? [Warton would agree with this.] When and in what manner to omit them, or to lay them before his readers?" (1–2).

Most of the letter is naturally about *The Faerie Queene*, on which Upton demonstrates his own learning, which would be abundantly communicated in his edition's magnificent notes; and the letter includes a "Specimen" of his proposed edition. This first critical edition of *The Faerie Queene* would be a mighty influence on Edmond Malone in his own century and the prototype of the twentieth century *Variorum* in its attempts to give historical identification of Spenser's characters; for example, Arthur as Sidney or the Earl of Leicester, Timias as Raleigh, the identification of the bloody babe in book 2, and so on. Upton uses Spenser's other writings (such as the *Vewe of Ireland*) to explain *Faerie Queene* allusions, and impressively musters some of Spenser's important sources: Chaucer, Ovid, Tasso, Ariosto, and many of the Ancients. A product of his age, Upton points out Spenser's idiosyncrasies and faults—his stanza foremost among them—but also his greatest strength, his imagination: "Milton saw and avoided the rock [the overuse of the stanza] that *Spenser's* split on: in other respects *Spenser's* imagination was greater" (27).

Aside from his historical criticism of *The Faerie Queene*, a poem "hitherto very little understood" (20), Upton's edition is intended as a corrective to earlier critics such as Dryden and especially Hughes, who was not only philologically wanting but incorrect in seeing the poem as disunified. Often without descending to transitions, Upton argues for Spenser's unity of action, seeing a *gestalt* in the elements of quest, beginning-middle-end, simplicity of design (!), and great and important actions. Thus, the poem's epic character. Upton advances the discussion of fable in the poem by calling it "probable"; that is, the allegory is unified and expectations are satisfied if one will but make sense of Spenser's fabulist manner, which gives "historical events under concealed names" and allegorically disguises physical and moral sciences, truths, virtues, and vices (26). He adds, "though in one sense you are in Fairy land, yet in another you may be in the British dominions" (27).

After the manner of Jortin, Upton is in all places the scholar and not only the appreciator of Spenser. His section on diction is short, and his impatience with Spenser's nine-line stanza is captured in the phrase "jingling sound" of rhyme (33), which is remindful of Gay's charge against Spenser's "rumbling" verse. Much of his temperament is communicated by his judgment on the 1611, 1617, and 1619 "frequently consulted" editions: they are of "very little authority," a phrase common to today's readers but fresh to Upton's.[13]

Since Upton considers Hughes's glossary to be applicable mainly to Spenser's pastorals and not *The Faerie Queene,* and since the earlier editor gives "misleading" and "unscholarlike" explanations, Upton presents a first-rate glossary, the best up to his time, intended "to serve both for an index and dictionary" (41). One expects and finds that the entries are provisioned with information on etymologies, sources, usages (in Spenser as well as Chaucer, Ariosto, Shakespeare, Gower, Fairfax, Milton), and definitions. This edition's masterful notes have always been recognized as Upton's greatest contribution to Spenser studies. His "Notes on the Fairy Queen" take up fully half of the second volume. They are impressive in their range, depth, learning, completeness, even boldnesss. Unlike some notes, Upton's really do help the reader to understand the poem's text and context. He shows just how learned Spenser was, and his edition of the poet's epic has served as a model for his age's serious readers and those editors of later ages who were to be in his debt: Rev. Todd in 1805, the Hopkins

Variorum editors in the 1920–30s, and several in between and since.

The years between Upton's plan and its execution in the 1758 edition of *The Faerie Queene* held other Spenserian presentments that helped to establish even more firmly his reputation. Imitations naturally were an important spur to the substantive and traceable outpouring of Spenserianism in the 1750s. Along with the previously treated Spenser imitations (part of the several Dodsley *Collections* of the sixth decade) appeared pieces separately published or variously gathered as disparate in subject, tone, form, and faithfulness to Spenser as Warton's bucolic "Morning," Pitt's parodic "An Imitation of Spenser" (1750); West's satirical-allegorical *Education*, Mendez's quite able dictional exercise "The Seasons," and the anonymous and monumentally oxymoronic pastoral-industrial "Industry and Genius," a poem about the city of Birmingham of 1751. And so it went for the remainder of the decade.

Although of first importance, Dodsley's anthologies were not the only worthy ones at the midcentury. A 1753 miscellany collected by Thomas Warton called *The Union* was a popular collection different from the Dodsley efforts in that Scots and English poems are mixed. Dodsley's miscellany is praised, however, in the preface as "The best miscellany of this day extant in our language, and the first complete one of the kind which we have seen . . ., which boasts the greatest names of the present age among its contributors."[14] Ten of the 38 poems in *The Union* are by or about Spenserians, and one is a Spenser imitation. Such prominence would have been unlikely earlier in the century, when the forces described in this study were only gathering. By the 1750s, the Spenserian ubiquity seems quite natural to the modern student once the elements which gave it rise are understood.

As in the Dodsley collections, the Spenserians Collins, Gray, Shenstone, Akenside, and the Wartons appear in the pages of *The Union*, along with the numerous Spenser references typical of the period. Only a few examples from the miscellany are needed to show the consonance *The Union's* pieces had with Dodsley's. In "Ode on the Approach of Summer. By a Gentleman of the University of Aberdeen" (Warton), the season's heat is escaped. Through Spenser's works, "By Spenser's lavish pencil drawn," one can fly through the poet's fancy to "Some more romantic scene . . . / Or fairy bank, or magic lawn" (89–90). Warton includes his own light "A Pastoral in the Manner of Spenser" (six stanzas *ababcC*), a pleasant poem notwithstanding such diction as *askaunce, yblent, besprent, whilom, eyne, deemen, depeinten,* and *despight*. Also easy to accept is the first of "Four Elegies," on "Morning," which has this stanza, so reminiscent of others on Spenser, who is ever a good companion when one is out and about in nature:

> Oft Spencer too, Eliza's blythest swain,
> With her [morning] in dalliance has the hours beguil'd,
> From oaten reed oft pip'd the artless strain
> To moral fiction, fancy's loveliest child.
>
> (108)

One of course does not overlook the last line's reference to Spenser as a moral teacher, a belief about him, with highs and lows, held by attentive readers well into the twentieth century.[15] The year 1753 also saw the publication of a seemingly unpromising work for our purposes, except that its editor is Bishop Richard Hurd, who figures importantly in Spenser's progress a few years thereafter. What Hurd does in *Q. Horatii Flacci Epistolae ad Pisones* is give the best and longest discourse on imitation in an essay—that prefigures his 1762 remarks on chivalry and romantic mimetic theory. Without addressing Spenser imitators specifically, Hurd nonetheless fashions the clearest theoretical frame for them. Writing at a time when imitation theory is at its zenith, Hurd at least puts the imitators at ease in his claim, against Johnson's and Young's, that imitation can itself be high art. For my own study, what Hurd has to say about imitation's tie to education could not be more assuring.

After the first volume's "Epistle to the Pisos" by Horace comes the "Epistle to Augustus" in volume 2, which has also "A Discourse Concerning Poetical Imitation." The 100-page essay (117–231) speaks of "painting" or "portraitures" in poetry, especially Shakespeare's (134). As a cleric and a good classicist, Hurd would naturally see "moral parallelisms" as well, including imitations of the Ancients. Unlike some imitation theorists at midcentury, Hurd does not agree that all resemblances are thefts (157). While speaking of imitating form, manners, passions, and the like, he makes analogies to sculpture and painting, thereby recalling Hughes's openness to the sister arts, as well as presaging Sir Joshua Reynolds's comparativist practice within the next few years.

Hurd goes against the orthodoxy on the issue of imitation, by calmly stating that the "common end of poetry" is "to please by imitation." In addition to the fable, three other parts of a poetical work are affected by artistic imitation: episodes, descriptions, and similes (187 ff.), exemplified best by the work of Milton. On the expression of poetry, that is, style, phrase, and diction, Hurd once again extends the discussion with his contention that "The expression of two writers may be similar, and sometimes even identical, and yet be original in both," for resemblance is not the same as imitation (208). Johnson would have found this troublesome.

Making it clear that he speaks of the "professed imitators" and, similar to Johnson, not hacks "who creep servilely after the sense of some other" (211), Hurd accounts for the popularity and naturalness of imitation by emphasizing the crucial role of early education: "The most universal cause, inducing imitation in great writers is, the force of early discipline and education" (211). Exactly. Milton at St. Paul's School under Dr. Gill and many other Spenserians support Hurd's assertion, which I encountered many years after I conceived of the idea of looking to the schools for some accounting of Spenser's advent in the eighteenth century. Hurd goes on, to my mind with the greatest accuracy, to characterize the mechanics of education in the training of imitators: "We are habituated to a survey of this secondary and derivative nature, as presented in the admired works of art, thro' the intire course of our education. The writings of the best poets are put into our hands, to instruct us in the knowledge of men and things, as soon as we are capable of apprehending them. Nay, we are taught to lisp their very words, in our tenderest infancy" (212).

Thus, model authors are "mirrors, which are the constant furniture of our schools and closets" (212). Since almost all have this common experience, the habit and custom of imitation necessarily leads to "resemblances" between and among writers. Is this manner of learning harmful to the true poet? Hurd asks. No, he answers; therefore, his advice to modern poets is to be at ease, to imitate the *best* models, and not to hope for "originality." Hurd makes his reader wonder if Spenser himself had such assurances about his own imitations when he was a schoolboy at Merchant Taylors' under Richard Mulcaster.

Undoubtedly the major literary event of 1755 was the publication of Johnson's *Dictionary of the English Language*, whose preface cites Sidney and Spenser as formative examples of the "dialect of poetry and fiction." The year also offered a handful of short Spenser imitations—by Bagot, Emily, Percy, Rider, Stone—which displayed a spread of topics and forms.[16] One different sort of imitation, Cornelius Arnold's *The Mirror*, cleverly satirized the fashions and vanities of the day in 44 Spenserian stanzas.

The poem's target is the prodigiously gifted and vain actor-playwright-director David Garrick, the dedicatee of the piece since he is "the great Master of the Mirror" (dedication title). Not a fine imitation, *The Mirror* nevertheless deserves mention for the uses it makes of Spenser. While almost all his Spenserian brethren were serious, Arnold is playful and ironic in keeping to "some few of the obsolete words of *Spenser's*, and . . . the Simplicity of the Diction . . . at the End of most of the Stanzas, to give it more the Air of that great Original" (1). He continues wryly with a defense of the Spenserian stanza, since it is "generally, if not universally allowed, the most suitable for Works of this Kind" (2). Had Spenser not been esteemed, the statement would not have succeeded, of course. Given the satiric butt (Garrick), the poem appropriately utilizes theater conventions such as characternyms like Sir Thrifty Gripe and Sir Politic and "manners" situations, with everyone gathered at the Lord Mayor's procession, including Garrick and Death. A moderately successful social satire of things and types constituting the *beau monde, The Mirror* turns dark when Death kills off nearly everyone in sight; and the poem disappoints utimately in its unconvincing, preachy conclusion: since only virtue will survive, "be humble" and "resigned."

The second half of the decade produced, in addition to Upton's *The Faerie Queene* edition, an unremarkable and largely unremarked "new edition" of that poem in 1757 (but appearing in 1758) by Ralph Church in four volumes. The edition excited little critical reaction.[17] But Warton's *Observations* was regularly cited. For example, the writer of *The Connoisseur* 16 (6 May 1754) uses Warton's work as the authority to settle a dispute over the source of the Shylock-Antonio scene in Shakespeare's *The Merchant of Venice:* "I should perhaps have acquiesced in this notion [that the source is from the story of Paul Secchi], if I had not seen a note in the 'Observations on *Spenser's* Faerie Queen, by Mr. T. Warton of

Trinity College', where he seems to have discovered the real source . . . [,] an old ballad" (123–24).[18] The *Observations* drew negative notice as well. Two years after its first appearance in 1754, William Huggins, an Ariosto editor who disagreed with Warton's treatment of his author, published a severe pamphlet critique of Warton's honesty and methodology in a work whose full title tells much: *The Observer Observ'd. Or, Remarks on a Certain Curious Tract. Intitled Observations on the Faiere Queene by Spencer, by T. Warton.* But throughout history, the memory and judgment of many decidedly favor Warton over Huggins.

A critical work on Alexander Pope's writings seems on the face of things unpromising for Spenser commentary. Yet the evidence we have already examined presents Spenser and Pope often paired in the early eighteenth century in both criticism and imitations. There are many references and analogies to Spenser in Joseph Warton's 1756 *An Essay on the Genius and Writings of Pope* and cogent remarks on imitation. The school experience and the fact of so many Spenser imitations trained that interest, a *general* interest, or the topic would not be treated in popular collections of essays such as *The Rambler, The Bee, The Adventurer, The Connoisseur,* and their like. Joseph Warton can be certain, then, that his remarks on imitation and imitators were widely of interest and relevant, for Spenser imitation in the 1750s was for the first time in the century, the literary fashion.

Like the other Wartons, Joseph admired Spenser's "pathetic" powers (citing *Faerie Queene* 1.9.36) and seriousness of intention. He did not take kindly to burlesques of the poet such as Pope's "Alley" (1706), which he named a willful corruption and a "kind of travesty" of the "sweet and amiable allegorical poet" (93). He refers to like-minded critics such as his brother Thomas, Hurd, and Hume[19] for his position and for his (accurate) appraisal of the aping times: "It has been fashionable of late to imitate Spenser, but the likeness of most of

these copies, hath consisted rather in using a few of his ancient expressions, than in catching his real manner." As with
the critics he names, and Dr. Johnson himself, Warton considers some Spenser imitators able personators since they write
"with attention to that simplicity, that tenderness of sentiment, and those little touches of nature, that constitute
Spenser's character" (99–100). Warton particularly favors "The
School-Mistress" and "The Education of Achilles," which he
read in Dodsley's *Miscellanies*—significant evidence of the
utility and significance of Dodsley's collections.[20]

Other Forums, Other Voices

What one may consider a revisionist anthology appeared in
1757, the anonymous two-volume *Beauties of Poetry Display'd*, which seems to be an attempt to open up the choices
for models worthy of imitation. Indistinguishable from other
anthologies in giving authors' passages (the "Beauties" of the
title) under various topics, this collection differs in several
regards: the topics are oddments often, and the authors chosen for emulation are not the usual generous representation
from Milton, Shakespeare, and Spenser. Rather, the model
writers are Moderns and a mixed group (age, sex, renown) of
lesser and greater lights: Behn (playwright, novelist, feminist),
Broome (hack, translator), and Garth (satirist of physicians
in *The Dispensary*) are there by the side of (much of) Pope.
As close as the anthologist deigns to come toward Spenser
are his imitators such as Akinside, Prior, Blacklock, Leapor,
Thomson, and West.[21]

That the collection includes women (Behn and Leapor,
namely) and minor writers unheralded elsewhere can be seen
as broadly paralleling, albeit in a minor collection that nonetheless is exciting, the progressively vigorous movement to
air out the schools's curricula; to be more sympathetic to the
downtrodden, minorities, children, animals, and all sorts of

"unfortunates"; to be less xenophobic and insular in social and political matters; to be alive to new literary subjects, modalities, and forms; to write about the values and beauties of physical nature as the occasion of transcendental experience and new epistemologies—to name a few of the movements astir in the sixth decade and immediately thereafter. As if written to demonstrate some of these elements at the end of the 1750s, William Vernon's (1758) "The Parish Clerk," in 28 *ababcc* stanzas, recalls the simple, value-laden "School-Mistress" of Shenstone.

Vernon invokes that poet in his tale of the humble clerk of Barton-Dean, a poor and good man with flowing silver hair and rural staff, who knows the accounts of old England and the ways of topographical and human nature. On Sundays he is to be found seated beneath the curate at church, eager for instruction in moral things, which he practices in his kind and conscientious treatment of others. He is the eighteenth century *good* person in contrast to the *great* person, a comparison dating back at least as far as Chaucer's parson and as close to Vernon as the fiction of Fielding and some of the plays presented then. An untutored fellow himself, Vernon captures the homey part of country life in simple lines at times vaguely reminiscent of Spenser. Probably the description of a rural wedding is the most affecting part of the poem. But marriages speak of youth, and the remainder of the piece presents an old, somewhat deaf clerk who still welcomes the opportunity to tell his visitors, including the poem's narrator, of former days when he was an athlete. When death approaches, he forthrightly speaks of it. Even though Vernon presents a modest poem about a modest man, important things are communicated about a well-lived life. He is a minor link in the tradition of this sort of portraiture, leading directly to Wordsworth's picturings within a very few years.

One voice from that time not heard as yet is that of Oliver Goldsmith. One may not expect him, an important although often untamed member of Johnson's conservative club, to consider Spenser as "our old favorite" who provides, now that the Church edition, in his estimation, tricks out Spenser so smartly, the opportunity to "tread the regions of fancy without interruption and expatiate on fairy wilds, such as our great magician [Spenser] has been pleased to present them." This is much closer, one might suppose, to the enthusiasms of Warton and Hurd than it is to Johnson. But to say this is to speak of the "old" Johnson, presented in some literary textbooks as a sort of taxidermal specimen, a Johnson who never actually was, and a Johnson different from the man who was friendly to and admiring of Spenser. Goldsmith notes that Spenser has the transporting power to make his readers "leave the ways of the present world" and greet "all the ages of primeval innocence and happiness" (241).[22]

He does fault Spenser for not using Virgil's *Aeneid* as his model but then writes a remarkably insightful evaluation of Spenser and elevates his reputation by calling him the first poet of the imagination who had much to do with the formation of other poets:

> However, with all his faults, no poet enlarges the imagination more than Spenser. [Abraham] Cowley was formed into poetry by reading him; and many of our modern writers, such as Gray, Akenside, and others, seem to have studied his manner with the utmost attention: from him their compounded epithets, and solemn flow of numbers, seem evidently borrowed; and the verses of Spenser may, perhaps, one day be considered the standard of English poetry. It were happy, indeed, if his beauties were the only objects of modern imitation; but many of his words, justly fallen into disuse among his successors, have been of late revived, and a language, already too copious, has been augmented by an unnecessary reenforcement. . . . This at least is certain, that posterity will perceive a strong similitude between the poets of the sixteenth and those of the latter end of the eighteenth century. (242)

Goldsmith's understanding of what Spenser's influence was and would continue to be is set against the backdrop of the imitation debate of the century's sixth decade.

Goldsmith sees in chapter 6 of his 1759 *Enquiry into the Present State of Polite Learning* a "parallel between the rise and decline of ancient and modern learning," that is in "polite" learning and letters, caused by critics and the "affectation in some popular writers leading others into vicious imitation" (287–90).[23] About imitation, Goldsmith, with his usual clarity and particularity, writes a piece he calls "The Characteristics of Greatness" in *The Bee* 4, 27 Oct. 1759, disagreeing with the common wisdom that writers of "the last age" (Elizabethans) are the "properest models" for imitation.

Yet here and in his pieces in the 1757 *Monthly Review* and 1759 *Critical Review*, Goldsmith holds that imitation is better than precept (compare this with Spenser's Letter to Raleigh and "ensample rather then rule"), feelings better than rules, but originality prized above the practice of the "herd of imitations" (chapter 12 of the *Enquiry*, wherein he scorns the fad for using the "tuneless flow" of blank verse on trivial subjects,[24] preferring rhyme). He finds distasteful the trend toward "didactic stiffness of wisdom" in trivial poems and hits at the "affected obscurity" of odes such as those by Thomas Gray. He shows himself to be a close reader even of the decade's poorer imitations, noticing their "pompous epithet, laboured diction, and every other deviation from common sense," which, he scornfully adds, "procures the poet the applause of the connoisseur; he is praised by all [not quite], read by a few, and soon forgotten"—all this the fault of the critics ("Enquiry," Friedman, *Works*, 317–18).

In *The Bee*'s "Characteristics of Greatness," the Irish Goldsmith proposes that the tradition-bound conservatism of the English temperament keeps them from being daring and innovative enough, a trait seen in their choices for models to imitate, especially the Elizabethans (unnamed). They thus have settled into predictability, he says, mediocrity and boredom: "In a word, the little mind who loves itself, will write and think with the vulgar, but the great mind will be bravely eccentric, and scorn the beaten road, from universal benevolence (*Works*, 430).[25] Goldsmith would of course include himself among the great minds.

All in all, Goldsmith is realist enough to recognize and accept his age's disposition toward imitation and the fact that some imitations of older models succeed admirably. For example, in his 1767 compilation *The Beauties of English Poesy* he calls Johnson's imitation of Juvenal's Third Satire, "London," the "best imitation of the original." He provocatively suggests that "Imitation gives us a much truer idea of the ancients than even translation could do" (*Works*, 330). And one imitation of "the last age," rather than of an Ancient, comes in for special notice, William Shenstone's Spenser imitation, "The School-Mistress." Goldsmith considers this to be Shenstone's finest poem and "a happiness"; and "though I dislike the imitations of our old English poets in general, yet, on this minute subject, the antiquity of the style produces a very ludicrous solemnity" (320–21).[26]

Like his fellow club member Johnson, Goldsmith at times sends differing signals about Spenser. He is commonly described as solidly in the tradition of Dryden and Pope, as though being so would automatically and naturally make him averse to the excitement, originality, and imagination of such works as Spenser's. But the spuriousness of such compartmentalization has already been shown in that Dryden and Pope are properly seen as Spenserians themselves.[27] Goldsmith's biographer Lytton Sells, in the 1974 *Oliver Goldsmith His Life and Works*, notices some of his subject's positive leanings toward Spenser. Also, relying on Goldsmith's words in the *Critical Review*, Sells presents this summation of the matter: "It may seem surprising therefore [contrary to Goldsmith's negativism about Gray's Spenserian *Odes*] that he should admire Spenser's *Faerie*

Queene. He in fact warmly commends Ralph Church for establishing the original text of 'this ancient poet.' The pleasure inspired by allegory he regards as 'of a subordinate nature'; and yet, 'with all his faults, no poet enlarges the imagination more than Spenser.' In reading him, 'all the ages of primeval innocence and happiness rise to our view. Virgil, and even Homer, seem to be modern, upon the comparison'" (205). Thus, Spenser's prodigious evocative powers were significant to Goldsmith.

If the sixth decade of the century has one encompassing theme, it is imitation. Imitators copied originals both ancient and modern as well as other imitators.[28] Editors imitated other editors. Critics imitated other critics. Most striking, though, is the number of serious commentaries on the nature and execution of imitation. The 1750s were indeed the most prolific ten-year period of the century for this topic. No critic of imitation serves better as a capstone example than "Night Thoughts" poet Edward Young. Coming as it does at the very end of the decade, *Conjectures on Original Composition. In a Letter to the Author of Sir Charles Grandison* (Samuel Richardson's 1754 novel) has epigrammatic periods on imitation, discernments which themselves demand attention and suggest authority as well as some closure on the matter. The subject is original versus imitative writing, a matter taken seriously at the midcentury. Echoes of Johnson, Goldsmith, and the decade's other essayists are heard in Young. Even though Spenserian imitation is not explicitly treated, all that Young says is perfectly applicable to Spenser and to this decade so solicitous in his behalf.

Since Young is a moralist here writing near the end of his life (he died in 1765), and since Samuel Richardson is the addressee of the *Conjectures*, there is sentimentality in the essay, especially in its second half's talk of heart, feelings, goodness, virtue, perfectibility, and piety—a litany of the very sentiments measurably part of the fabric of Richardson's epistolary novel

Clarissa (1748). Refuting some critics who groused about the printing presses being "overcharged," Young takes the position of "the more [good] composition the better" (5). But within good submissions to presses, "*Originals* are the fairest flowers: *Imitations* are of quicker growth, but fainter bloom." Johnson said much the same thing earlier.

In the most sophisticated, centered discussion of imitation up to his time, Young distinguishes two kinds of imitation: of nature (originals) and of authors (imitations). As his book's title denotes, Young sides with originals, for "they *extend* [my emphasis] the republic of letters" while imitators "only give us a sort of duplicate of what we had, possibly much better, before" (10). It is as though Young is following Francis Bacon, who many years earlier held that learning could not be *advanced* by pursuing the methods of Scholasticism and deductive reasoning, which is tantamount to imitating already postulated generalizations. Posing the question of why there are so few originals, Young answers, "because illustrious examples *engross, prejudice,* and *intimidate*" (17). And, concurring with nearly all the decade's commentators on imitation, Young agrees that copying the Ancients is well and good, "but imitate aright." He may take the matter further than anyone had in his advice to "imitate not the *Composition* but the *Man*" (21), but in writing this he was not the clearest among the commentators.

Along with Pope, who regarded the progress of dullness a clarion of a dark age, Young, less dramatically, sees serious ill effects from imitation: namely, that the liberal arts will decay by its proliferation. I suppose this is so because learning will be stifled since originality will not be practiced, nature's design will be thwarted, and too many will thus "think little and write much" (42–44). Sighing that imitation is the lot of most writers, he, quoting Shakespeare and Milton and chiding Swift, uses balance and antithesis to deliver something of a sermon on imitation, with stylistic echoes of Polonius, Pope, and Poor Richard. "Imitation is inferiority confessed; emulation is superiority contested, or denied; imitation is servile, emulation generous; that fetters, this fires; that may give a name; this, a name immortal."[29] As an end on the decade's imitation theory and practice, Young is memorable here; but notwithstanding his discriminations, imitations proliferated, including those of Spenser.[30] The discussion of imitation continued also, even if less gnomically.

Immediately after the next decade begins, in 1762, the final years I consider, Spenser imitation and the sister arts are the concern of Spenserian James Beattie, in *An Essay on Poetry and Musick. As They Affect the Mind*.[31] Not only an adroit theorist of the imagination, Beattie favors an imagination such as Spenser's and Ariosto's more than "the fashion" of his day which is "to imitate great performers' art," especially "ornamental" and "mechanical" rules (157). Not an enemy to imitation, Beattie would, in chapter 2, have young writers hone their poetical invention by "an intimate acquaintance with the best descriptive poets, Spenser, Milton and Thomson," joined with "some practice in the art of drawing" which will "promote this amiable sensibility in early years; for then the face of nature has novelty superadded to its other charms, the passions are not preengaged, the heart is free from care, and the imagination warm and romantick." Like music, poetry imitates nature, says Beattie, who, unlike Johnson and Young, refuses to see such a falling off of all originality in the act of imitation since "that which is properly termed *imitation* has always in it something which is not in the original" (189–90).

Beattie's central statement on Spenser imitations occurs in the section of his "Essay on Poetry and Music" called "Of Poetical Language, considered as Significant" (vol. 6, part 2, chap. 1). He begins the way most critics of the subject begin, with obsolete diction self-consciously employed. Beattie considers words such as *transmew, moil, losel, albe, thews, couthful* and the like to be ruinous of the "pathos of modern language." Why are such old words more attractive in Spenser, who himself purposively employed such diction, than in his imitators, Beattie wonders. He then answers "because in him they seem . . . natural" whereas in the "mixed dialect of these imitators" the diction is "artificial" and rings false (43).

He believes that Spenser's own obscurant diction had the "same bad effect that words now obsolete have in his imitators" (44). Beattie would agree with Ben Jonson that better dictional models than Spenser are available; for Beattie, good authorities for the "use of a poetical word" include Milton, Dryden, and Pope (45). Antique diction, then, is not crucial to poetry even if in prose one may admit its use on occasion, if the aim is to "confer dignity upon a sublime subject" or to "heighten the ludicrous quality of a mean one" (46). These are reasons not far from Pope's advice on alexandrines.

Shock is not the effect, therefore, when one reads Beattie's long, cogent essay against the fashion of modernizing school curricula while defending a classical education in grammar schools, *Remarks on the Utility of Classical Learning. Written in the Year 1769* (*Works*, 6, 305–76). That he shapes his defense in terms of imitation is to be noted. In conclusion, he considers the use of Moderns as models for imitation. Granting Milton's, Dryden's, and Pope's greatness, Beattie asks, why copy a copy? Since these authors are themselves accomplished, close imitators of classical writers, Beattie argues, why not go to the sources themselves for models? They are unchanging— Beattie does call, however, for better translations—worthwhile, and enduring.[32]

This author of *The Minstrel*, a thoughtful Spenser imitation containing many of the elements of the "new" sensibility we have been attending to, was at the same time a classicist and educational conservative. In fact, most of the writers considered on these pages have the same dual attitudes, which we know are not necessarily conflicting attitudes. The age's capacity to be open to old and new allegiances and behaviors, literary and otherwise, seems to me not different from, say, the face the *Beowulf* poet offers in his poem, which reflects an amalgamation of nascent Christianity (although only Old Testament references are made, with no explicit Christian eschatology in evidence) and Germanic-Roman paganism (reflective of a culture described in Tacitus's *Germania* and local lore). They seem to be not at all in tension but rather coexist easily even if strangely, with one element or energy not having a decided ascendancy over the others.

Only two works remain to be examined. One is fairly well known; the other is unknown. Richard Hurd's extremely popular (a dozen editions by the century's end) and influential 120-page *Letters on Chivalry and Romance* (1762) is fully anticipated by its predecessors. It is true that Hurd's *Letters* does recommend an important strain in Spenser's history and does surely point the direction to be taken in the continuance of that history. But, competent as he was, Hurd did not prophesy from a wilderness; Hughes, Thomas Warton, essayists, a number of imitators, and Upton, contributed to his remarks.

Turning around a lasting complaint that Spenser, along with Milton, Ariosto, and Tasso, was "seduced" by the "barbarities" of chivalry and Gothic romance, Hurd, in the first letter, commends these very influences, judging them compatible with genius and the "ends of poetry." He accuses "philosophic moderns" of excess in "their perpetual ridicule and contempt" of the barbarities (4). Of course *The Faerie Queene* serves as Hurd's great example of gestes, knights, chivalry, romance, giants, paynims, savages, Gothic trappings, and the like. Identifying Spenser as "our great Poet" (31), Hurd, using him and Milton as exemplars rivaling Homer, argues persuasively that the Gothic and heroic ages resemble each other closely.

Thus when he makes statements such as *the more Gothic the more poetical*, he means at the same time *the more Gothic the more heroic.* And, as he says in letter 7, *The Faerie Queene* is more properly understood as a Gothic poem with Gothic structure, yet one not unattentive to classical structural concerns and unity, than as a fully classical poem. The latter phrase he would reserve for *Paradise Lost.* Hurd's notion of *The Faerie Queene* as a Gothic composition appears in his longest letter, the eighth, which recalls Hughes and Warton, where the poem is not given the classical structure of a central hero's single action but rather a unity of "design." The center of that design is Gloriana's feast where commissions for knightly adventures are given. Yet the knights have anything but univocal experiences. Therefore, Hurd advises, consider the poem for what it is, and do not fault its author for what he did not write or intend.

In letters 11 and 12, Hurd turns briefly to Spenser imitations but more importantly makes some of the period's most insightful observations about Spenser and his history since the time of Queen Elizabeth, who outlived the poet by four years.[33] Since the appraisal is so germane to our study and to the direction Spenserianism is to take in the final decades of the eighteenth century and first decades of the next, I follow Hurd closely here. Yet I am not sure of just what he means by saying that the "noble" *Faerie Queene* "is fallen into so general a neglect, that all the zeal of its commentators is esteemed officious and impertinent, and will never restore it to those honours which it has, once for all, irrecoverably lost" (letter 11, 111). Does he mean that Spenser is lost to the common reader forever and has become exclusively the property of the learned? Does he, writing in 1762, have in mind specific Spenserian "events" or critics now lost to us? Is he covertly referring to the academic Spenserians of the previous decade, namely Warton and Upton? Or does he, like so many of his contemporary critics, see the tide of mediocre Spenser imitators supplanting the model itself, or at least diluting the poet's work severely?

Hurd helps somewhat, certainly in tone even if not much otherwise, in this wistful utterance: "Poor Spenser then . . . must, for ought I can see, be left to the admiration of a few lettered and curious men" who love his moral and marvellousness" (111–12). That he would identify Spenser's morality and inventiveness among all the poet's gifts as the major interests of the learned is interesting indeed and borne out by the remarks of others writing then. They also fit the interests of the next two generations of Spenserians, but not only of the learned, as is shown in the imitations and criticism of the romantic writers.

The final letter, the twelfth, traces the decline of taste, a sign of which is the ignoring of Spenser. Yet, says Hurd, Spenser's own time was not much better since his readers and critics were not at first enamored of his fanciful manner, forcing the poet "to hide his faery fancies under the mystic cover of moral allegory" (116). In the seventeenth and eighteenth centuries, likewise, fanciful writing was subsumed under works of "strict truth" (119). But despite the protean ways of literary fashion, Hurd concludes that "*Faery* Spenser still ranks highest among the Poets; I mean with all those who are either come of that house, or have any kindness for it" (129). Perhaps too close to the matter, Hurd ends on a needlessly pessimistic note: "What we have lost [by this revolution in taste] is a world of fine fabling" (120). Spenser already was triumphant as the greatest of imaginative poets and a leading model for imitation.

In a study such as mine, so much helped by the evidence of poetical and essay collections, it is probably right to conclude with yet another anthology, this one, though, quite different in that it is also what we would today call an "introduction to poetry" text. The advertisement says that the anthologist-publisher John Newberry "has endeavoured to introduce ["young pupils"] to the Arts and Sciences."[34] As is so often the case with eighteenth century books, the full title assists in understanding the nature of the work: *The Art of Poetry On a New Plan: Illustrated with a great Variety of Examples from the best English Poets; and of Translations from the Ancients: Together with such Reflections and critical Remarks as may tend to form in our Youth an elegant Taste* (1762, first ed. 1741). In a sense, then, we are returned to where we started, native and classical models in education.

Newberry's is a two-volume selection of literary examples intended for the education of young boys and girls in *belles lettres*. Newberry, a name still associated with children's literature, remained consistent in his interest in the education of youths for he earlier wrote children's books, "little Books . . . to lead the young pupil to a Love of Knowledge" (7). There is no search for Spenser in Newberry's pages, as was often the case with the earliest collections; the poet is everywhere, and lessons on how to read him, what to like in him, and reasons for reading his works appear in *print*. There has been a long distance traveled, then, from the century's earliest anthologies where Spenser, and Shakespeare as well, needed to be rescued, introduced, or recommended to readers.

How Spenser is presented of course interests us most. Newberry's first volume has literary excerpts organized into sections headed by the editor's (often superficial) headnote "precepts"; for instance, the "precept for the pastoral with occasional remarks" is followed by pastoral selections, including *The Shepheardes Calender*'s fifth eclogue. The second volume, dated 1761, begins with precepts for allegory, served by 20 pages of *Faerie Queene* passages and two pages from the *Castle of Indolence*.[35] The instruction for the *Faerie Queene* section (chapter 17) at the outset of volume 2 reveals quite tidily the common midcentury appreciation of Spenser as an allegorical writer "who had a bold and boundless fancy, and was a most admirable painter, or imager, of the virtues and vices. His descriptions are indeed rich and luxuriant; if I mistake not, it is principally owing to his just and beautiful *allegories* (the creatures of his own fancy) that he has been deem'd the father of *English* poetry, and led more young minds into the study of this bewitching art than any other poet" (2–3).

Although not a profound statement, it is accurate, full, and has within it the voices of many of the Spenserians presented throughout my pages. Also, Newberry carries us back to where we began: Spenser as influential model, Spenser and education, and Spenser and the young. In the latter regard, the gulf between Newberry's day and ours is shown in the editor's recommendation of *The Faerie Queene*'s Cantos of Mutabilitie to his young readers "as worthy of the young students' repeated perusal" (2. 18). These cantos today would not be the popular choices for first readers of Spenser, but perhaps they should be.

We hear the voices of Warton and Hurd as well in Newberry's argument against *The Faerie Queene*'s being read and judged strictly in terms of classical epic and its demand for unity of action. Rather, the poem should be recognized for its Gothic, chivalric, and romantic content, which fit well with the Elizabethan age (9). Newberry then instructs his readers that Spenser's great triumph is not so much in his fabling acumen but rather in the "justness and moral tendency of his allegories, the sublimity of his thought, the variety and harmony of his numbers (which are great, nothwithstanding the ill choice of his stanza) and in that exhaustless invention and richness of imagery or painting, with which every part of his work is replete" (10). Once again, Newberry captures some of the significant ways in which Spenser had been discussed through the century's first six decades, and, except perhaps for allegory and structure, the ways the Spenserians among the British romantic writers would appreciate him.[36] One almost has the impression that this later group of writers found the "doing" of Spenser more congenial and fruitful than the talking about him.

Spenser's history in the remainder of the century differs little in the subjects attempted from the account I have provided for the first six decades. As bibliography C shows, imitations continued to be varied in topics and verse (and even prose) forms. Noticeable, however, are the increased length and frequency of the imitations; but the imitations' quality and faithfulness to the model are not strikingly improved or different from the first half of the century: Mendez, Mickle, Beattie, Blake, Wordsworth, and Coleridge may overall be more gifted poets than Croxall, Shenstone, and Thomson, but their Spenser imitations as imitation are not much superior. The anthologists and essayists—editors do not enter the picture again until the turn of the next century—say basically the same sorts of things that were said earlier, but one difference is the easy prominence of Spenser, because the model had been fashioned and the taste for him acquired. The pupa stage of the poet's emergence and celebrity had been gone through, and the butterfly's beauty was admired and imitated by fresh youths, adventurous men and women writers, who engrafted the poet anew and passed him on to new lovers—even to today.[37]

Notes

1. Such evidence would extend from anecdotes such as Lord Somers's request that Sir Godfrey Kneller paint him "with a Spenser in his hand" to Spenser's influence on Gothic garden design: for both, see Joseph Warton's *Essay on Pope* 2:182–89, 36n. Warton herein also mentions Spenser's influence on gardening. He was not of the first tier of influence as were Milton and Pope, Warton reminds; after all, Spenser "has an artificial fountain in the midst of his bowre of bliss."

2. These descriptors are headings under which numerous epithets for Spenser, or judgments on his works, might be placed. See Bishop Hall's "misty moral types" or Drayton's "Grave moral Spenser" or Gray's "Truth severe, by fairy fiction drest" or Milton's "sage serious Spenser" (quoted in Thomas Warton the Younger, *Observations on Fairy Queen*, 2nd ed., "Corrected and Enlarged" 2:115).

3. Whether or not Thomas Warton Sr.'s 1706 "Philander" (not published until 1748) or Alexander Pope's juvenile imitation "The Alley" (ca. 1706, in 6 Spenserian stanzas) was the first of the century's Spenser imitations, Matthew Prior's 1706 *Ode to the Queen* (35 "Prior stanzas") was certainly one of the century's most influential. Its 10-line adaptation (*ababcdcdeE*, the capital an alexandrine) of Spenser's stanza was often used by other imitators for the period under consideration, notably its first half. One may go so far as to say that Prior re-sparked the fashion of imitating Spenser. Indeed the Whigs who read his 1706 *Ode* declared it an imitation of "an obsolete form of verse" (see Charles Eves's *Prior*, 194). For sheer weight even if not literary value, the most noteworthy imitation, appearing at century's end, is Sir James Bland Burges's (significantly, a Westminster School alumnus) *Richard the First* in 1,849 Spenserian

stanzas. For a severe appraisal of Pope's "The Alley," see Joseph Warton's *Essay on Pope* (2:30–41).

Notes to Chapter One

1. The nature of "creative" *imitatio*, the sort encouraged in the schools, is explored by Gordon Campbell, "Imitation in *Epitaphium Damonis*" (165–77); for *aemulatio*, see Howard D. Weinbrot, "'An Ambition to Excell': The Aesthetics of Emulation" (121–39). For emulation of Milton in the eighteenth century, see Dustin Griffin, *Regaining Paradise*, especially Griffin's "Afterword: Notes Toward an Eighteenth-Century Theory of Literary Influence" (229–38). R. S. Crane's essay, treated in my text proper, although old now, still is of considerable importance for imitation theory.

2. The four other noteworthy women imitators of Spenser are Elizabeth Thomas, Miss Hunt, Mary Robinson, and Elizabeth Smith. The poems of the nine imitators appear in bibliography C. The subject and composition date of each imitation are consonant with the general run of poetry respectively, whether written by men or women.

3. Based solely upon allusions to Spenser in the seventeenth century, the facts are somewhat different in that *Fowre Hymnes, Mother Hubberds Tale,* and *The Ruines of Time* are frequently alluded to, with *The Faerie Queene* and *The Shepheardes Calender* of course leading in frequency. This is not the case with eighteenth century imitations of the minor works, although each of the three above was imitated at least once. For seventeenth century allusions, see William Wells's index to part 2 of *Spenser Allusions*. Spenserian characters most often alluded to are Colin (by far) and Braggadochio. *The Faerie Queene* is the most frequently alluded to, and of that work book 1 has highest count (216)—and of that book 1, canto 1 most often (47) and canto 12 least often (3). Did readers finish a *Faerie Queene* book less often than they started one?

Book 2 is next in frequency (134); book 7 is least often alluded to (8). After *The Faerie Queene* comes *The Shepheardes Calender*, with all months therein rather evenly treated—May has 20—except for March (5). Some of these facts hold true for the eighteenth century imitations as well. For representative playful nineteenth and early twentieth century imitations of these Spenser works, see the "Spenser Parodies" file in Lilly Library, Indiana University (listed in bibliography C).

4. One is grateful for evidence such as that for Alfred Lord Tennyson's home education by his father the Rev. George Tennyson, who taught his son languages in preparation for his Cambridge studies. We know that Tennyson wrote exercises imitating the manner of

Milton, the Elizabethan playwrights, and most likely Spenser and his imitator James Thomson. Certainly Tennyson carefully read both of the latter poets when a young man, for the early "Lotus-Eaters" is heavily indebted to *Faerie Queene*, book 2, and *The Castle of Indolence*.

5. Chatterton's mother operated a Dame school (his father was a schoolmaster), and we know that he began to write poems in his preteenage years at Colston's Hospital, a Bristol charity school. Chatterton's private reading in the town's circulating library contributed to his Rowley poems, dating from 1765 when the boy was 13. As we will note, two Spenser imitators who were importantly responsible for publishing ventures involving the poet were anthologist Robert Dodsley and editor-critic John Upton. Both had a school-teacher parent.

6. Joseph Warton can report that "Spenser and Waller were [Pope's] great favourites, as he told Mr. [Joseph] Spence, . . . in his early reading" (*Essay on Pope*, 2.39n).

7. Quoted by Dennis G. Donovan from Edwards' 1751 letter to the novelist Samuel Richardson in *The Sonnets of Thomas Edwards* (8). University experiences with Spenser are treated below. Suffice it here to say that Spenser was imitated at university as shown by poems in *The Student* (1750–51), where one piece is by the ardent Spenserian Thomas Warton the Younger. Several prizewinning compositions were Spenser imitations, including a 1755 effort by Lewis Bagot in *Gratulatio Academia Cantabrigiensis*. There were also five Cambridge Prize poems published in *Musae Seatonionae* soon after the turn of the next century. There is an "exercise" quality to most of these prize poems, suggesting that the imitation lessons of the schools were indelible. Spenser's own university did not forget him, then; but there is a curious paucity of evidence of Spenser in his own Merchant Taylors' School.

Indeed, F. W. M. Draper's opinion in his 1962 history of *Merchant Taylors' School* is that the poet's "education at the School was completely forgotten until 1877, when the Townley Hall MSS in two volumes were published by the Rev. A. B. Grosart," in which Spenser's name appears passingly three times (31–32). Spenser's anonymity in terms of the school is also indicated by the following, recorded by Draper. At the opening of a new School on 6 April 1875, with the Prince of Wales presiding, the clerk, while giving a litany of distinguished alumni, announces Spenser's name, "'the fact of whose education at the School has only become known during the last years by the research of the Historical Manuscripts Commission among some papers in possession of the Townley family'" (185). Two other significant dates Draper mentions are 1921, when a "house system, so often advocated, was established, the four houses taking their names from the founders of the School and St. John's, Hilles and White, and from Spenser and Clive, our great poet and our great proconsul" (207); and 1948, when "the School formed a valuable alliance with a Cambridge college [Pembroke] with which it already had a long connexion from the days of Edmund Spenser and Lancelot Andrewes, both Pembroke men" (231). Spenser's dilatory recognition by his own school in later times is not at one with his being highly regarded in the eighteenth century, for, Draper notes, Spenser's stone inscription in Westminster Abbey has this last sentence: "'Restored by private subscription 1778.'"

8. See Thomas Warton the Elder's 1706 "Philander: An Imitation of Spencer" in *Poems on Several Occasions* (63–75, in 20 six-line stanzas, *ababcC*). Recent scholarship shows that some of the more romantic poems in this volume were actually written by sons Joseph and Thomas, the latter his father's student at Basingstoke Grammar School. That the younger Thomas was early taken with Spenser is indicated by David Fairer in "The Origins of Warton's *History of English Poetry*" (37–63): "Warton's interest in Elizabethan poetry can be traced to his earliest undergraduate days. In 1744, the year of his matriculation at Trinity as a 16-year-old, he became the proud possessor of the 1617 folio edition of Spenser's *Works* [also the edition that Ben Jonson annotated], and inscribed his own name and the date inside the cover. This volume, now in the British Library, had been given him by his grandfather (the name of Joseph Richardson occurs alongside his own). During the next ten years the book was obviously a catalyst for his reading in earlier poetry—the margins of the book became crowded with annotations, later to be used in the *Observations on the Faerie Queene*, but it is evident that originally the young man was planning an edition of Spenser" (45). The unwieldy notes and crowding analogues resulted in the *Observations* rather than the contemplated edition of Spenser. See, too, Fairer's *Spenser Encyclopedia* piece on this Warton.

9. Wordsworth, like Keats, was a reader of the eighteenth century imitators, proved by his 1802 "Stanzas written in my Pocket-copy of Thomson's 'Castle of Indolence.'"

10. Apparent from her *Journals*, Dorothy Wordsworth was a sensitive, regular reader of Spenser, privately as well as aloud to her brother William as part of their many walks. They both admired Spenser's marriage poems and the "terrain" of *The Faerie Queene*. Also, Wordsworth's wife Mary read Spenser to him in the evening. For an exemplary study of evidence of Spenser in Wordsworth, see Samuel E. Schulman's "The Spenserian Enchantments of Wordsworth's 'Resolution and Independence,'" (24–44).

11. Herbert E. Cory's 1910 Harvard dissertation "The Influence of Spenser on English Poetry" quotes the preface to the anonymous end-of-century "The Village Sunday": the poem combines the influence of Shenstone, Burns, and Spenser, and in that order.

12. Almost certainly, Burns's often-anthologized Spenser imitation "The Cotter's Saturday Night" (1786, in 21 Spenserian stanzas) issued forth without benefit of Burns's direct experience of Spenser. The poem is actually not very Spenserian: even the stanza is indebted to Shenstone and Beattie, the scheme to Robert Fergusson's "The Farmer's Ingle" (1773); and there are some touches from Thomson's *The Castle of Indolence.*

13. Thomson and Shenstone are the century's master imitators of Spenser's nine-line stanza with its concluding alexandrine. James Beattie and Samuel Croxall would constitute the second level of imitators, in my estimation.

14. *The Complete Poetical Works of Keats* (345).

15. *Gentleman's Magazine*, 6 (Sept.–Nov., 1736): 447, 611, 679. The author says in a footnote, "This was wrote at the time of the Siege of Gibraltar" (i. e., 1704).

16. See Pope's portrait of Busby in *Dunciad* (4.139 ff.).

17. A distinguished Latinist who became Headmaster of Westminster School in 1712, Freind wrote Matthew Prior's epitaph. For Freind at that School, see Lawrence E. Tanner's 1934 history of *Westminster School.*

18. While there was not a large gathering of Spenser imitators at Charterhouse or at Harrow, there were some. These schools, like the others, had an entirely classical curriculum, where in the lower two of the under school's three forms, the main activity was translation of Latin writers into English. Like Westminster, Charterhouse emphasized in its third form "make[ing] Latin or English themes." One might well suppose, given this fact and the difficulty of Spenser's verse, no rendering of Spenser would have been attempted before that time in a schoolboy's career. In Jonson's *Discoveries*, Spenser is encouraged as a model for content even if not for language, especially for beginning students: "For the mind, and memory are more sharply exercis'd in comprehending an other mans things, then our owne; and such as accustome themselves, and are familiar with the best Authors, shall ever and anon find somewhat of them in themselves, and in the expression of their minds, even when they feele it not, be able to utter something like theirs, which hath an Authority above their owne," quoted in James A. Riddell and Stanley Stewart's 1995 *Jonson's Spenser.* By way of interpretation, they go on to say that Jonson would want the most open and the clearest of the "best Authors" taught first. And since Spenser is not the clearest, even

though he is among the best, he is not to be offered as a first model because of his language; but he is to be offered early for his content. Gill's emphasis at St. Paul's was both language and content, especially the former.

19. Thomas Warton the Elder, early in the eighteenth century, combines the Bible and Chaucer in his "Paraphrase on the Holie Book entituled Leviticus Chap. XI. Vers. 13, &c. Fashioned after the Maniere of Maister Geoffrey Chaucer in his Assemblie of Foules" (*Poems on Several Occasions*, 30–33). For sample treatments of Dryden and Milton, see Matthew Prior's *The Hind and the Panther Transvers'd* (1687); John Hopkins' *Milton's Paradise Lost imitated in rhyme* (1699) and "In Imitation of Milton" in the anon. 1701 *Collection of Poems* (393–400). A flood of Milton imitations began in 1701. A few ephemeral imitations of Butler's *Hudibras* and Defoe's early works were published soon after their initial appearance in the Restoration period, and a few more early in the next century.

20. For the Restoration period there are few imitations of Spenser, but mention can be made of a "pure" imitation and an adaptation: Samuel Woodford's 1679 *Epodē. The Legend of Love* in 189 Spenserian stanzas, and the 1687 (anon.) *Spencer Redivivus Containing the First Book of the Fairy Queen . . . Delivered in Heroic Numbers*, nearly 5,000 of them. This period was, however, rich in Spenserian activities: the second edition of William Winstanley's *England's Worthies* with its *Life* of Spenser (1684), and a 1679 edition of Spenser's *Works*. For an account of how Spenser editions figure in the work of late eighteenth century imitator William Blake, see Robert F. Gleckner's 1985 *Blake and Spenser*. On Blake's "An Imitation of Spencer," Gleckner argues that since the poem may be as early as 1771 (not printed until *Poetical Sketches*, 1783) when Blake was 14, Blake read Spenser early and "much in the spirit of other eighteenth century imitators who found Spenser a poet to emulate for his diction, mellifluousness, and his 'Gothic' stanza." Gleckner shows that other poems in *Sketches*—"To the Evening Star," "To Morning," and "To the Muses"—prove that Blake read Spenser "extensively and with considerable care," and that he knew "Epithalamion," "Teares of the Muses," *The Faerie Queene, Amoretti*, and "Prothalamion," wherein Blake admired Spenser's "vision."

Richard Helgerson helps with the term "Gothic" as used to describe *The Faerie Queene* by eighteenth century critics: "they referred to its departure from classical epic design and decorum, to its multiple plotting and its fabulous knight-errantry: precisely those features that sixteenth century Italian critics had already blamed in [Ariosto's] *Orlando Furioso*," objections, Helgerson adds, that Tasso's *Jerusalem Delivered* was "designed to answer . . . not by eliminating Ariosto's romance but rather by subordinating it to epic" (154): "Tasso on Spenser: The Politics of Chivalric Romance" (153–67). Henry Pemberton's 1738 *Observations on Poetry* passes over Spenser while naming Homer, Virgil, and Milton the greatest epic poets in terms of sublimity (Longinus is Pemberton's authority). Praised are Milton's harmonious numbers, Virgil's characters, and Homer's "sublimity of Sentiment." That same year, another epic was brought out, one of Spenser's main sources, Torquato Tasso's *Jerusalem Delivered* (books 1–3 only), translated by Henry Brooke and published by Spenserian Robert Dodsley as *Tasso's Jerusalem, an Epic Poem.* The market for epic remained good, for the next year (1739). Elizabeth Singer Rowe translated from Tasso's *Jerusalem* in several pieces in *Miscellaneous Works.*

21. The full title is *John Milton at St. Paul's School: A Study of Ancient Rhetoric in English Renaissance Education.* In addition to valuable details of the curriculum at St. Paul's, form by form, even day by day at times, Clark offers theoretical remarks on the nature of imitation, especially adaptations of the *Methodus* of Petrus Ramus, that are quite similar to imitation theory in the eighteenth century, including remarks in prefaces, introductions, and notes by Spenser imitators. One pertinent excerpt in Clark is from Charles Butler's statement on imitation, *Oratoriae Libri Duo* (1629). "Exercise consists in Genesis and Analysis. It is Genesis when we compose our own orations according to the precepts of Art and in imitation of the Orators. It is Analysis when we take apart [*resolvimus*] the orations of others, observing in them what rules of Art are followed and what virtues of the authors are worthy of imitation. It is imitation when we copy the method [*rationem*] of speaking of another. There are two rules in Imitation: that we should imitate those who are excellent and those qualities in them which are excellent" (152, but also see 158).

22. One rhetoric that Milton would have known, Charles Butler's abridgement of Talaeus's *Rhetorica*, titled *Rhetoricae Libri Duo* (4th edn., 1618), differed from the original in that Butler, according to Clark (see n. 21 *supra*), "introduces the innovation of illustrating *rhythmus* (accentual or nonquantitive verse) with two stanzas from Spenser's *Ruines of Time.*"

23. Joseph Warton's 1746 *Odes on Various Subjects*, in Richard Wendorf's 1979 Augustan Reprint Society facsimile edition, from which Warton's odes below are quoted.

24. Quoted by Wendorf, Warton's *Odes* (10). While I have not been able to find Laurel Bradley's 1979 "Eighteenth-Century Paintings and Illustrations of Spenser's *Faerie Queene*" (31–51), the *Spenser Newsletter's* Fall 1983 detailed review (13.3:60) shows it to be a

pertinent study. What Bradley finds about the pictorial tradition is consonant with much of the evidence presented here. She says, however, that during the eighteenth century "images from Spenser's *Faerie Queene* in the visual arts," notably illustrations of the Cave of Despair and the figure of Una, reflect a shift in critical opinion away from the Augustan poets' "admiration for the idealized naturalism of Spenser's landscape imagery and moral righteousness of his allegory" to a romantic concern with "terrible sublime episodes and richly imaginative imagery" (31). Is Spenser's landscape in reality so different from this romantic concern?

Bradley's remarks on visual treatments of Spenser's epic are useful. Pope's notion of the "picturesque" in nature and art is matched, we are told, by William Kent's illustrations for the 1751 *Faerie Queene* edition, illustrations which reflect the influence of the seventeenth century Italianate landscape as well as Kent's commitment to the concept of the "poetic garden." The later emphasis of Spenser's "Gothic invention" by Thomas Warton and Richard Hurd anticipates a "new fantastic interpretation of *The Faerie Queene* . . . in the visual arts around 1770" (37), exemplified especially by Fuseli, who celebrates the work as "sublime." Blake excepted, by 1810, illustrations of the poem "show the strong narrative bias which becomes dominant in nineteenth century British art" (43), recalling Scott's preference for Spenser's characters "in their outward and exoteric sense" and Hazlitt's impatience with complex allegorical meaning. Nineteenth century illustrations generally neglect allegorical resonance in favor of melodrama; only the Pre-Raphaelite painters respond "in highly personal ways" to "dream and visionary sequences in the poem" (44). As Riddell and Stewart have shown in *Jonson's Spenser*, Ben Jonson, *not* the enemy of Spenser that he has been portrayed as historically, was influenced by Spenser's "pictures."

25. While speaking of Nicholas Rowe's (Westminster alumnus) play *Lady Jane Grey*, Joseph Warton points out "There are . . . some images . . . strong painted . . . worthy of Spenser": *An Essay on Pope* (1.272n). In this work, Warton considers Pope's satires ephemeral and judges that, since "Nature and passion are eternal," the best works by the great Augustan are "Eloisa to Abelard," *The Rape of the Lock*, and "Windsor-Forest." These are the very works that Warton would say do not moralize and that are full of invention and imagination (see Advertisement to *Odes* above). Warton puts Spenser in the forefront of "our only three sublime and pathetic poets." Shakespeare and Milton are the other two. Warton's skill as a reader of Spenser is demonstrated by his tracings of Pope's lines to Spenser.

26. A full account of the adherence to Warton's leanings by the Spenser imitators who were at Winchester under Warton is a subject

beyond this study; but that Moderns were used as models for imitation at Warton's school is indicated in his *Essay on Pope* (2, appendix 1). In defense of Matthew Prior, Warton praises some of his odes, including the Spenser imitation "Ode to the Queen" (1706). Warton grants the flaws of *Solomon A Poem* but liked individual passages. He also notes that the first book of his work was translated "classically" by Dobson when he was at Winchester "as a school exercise" (413). See bibliography C for Robert Lowth and William Whitehead, two Winchester alumni, who engaged in Spenser school exercises.

27. In "Colin's Mistakes," Prior says about himself, "And much he lov'd, and much by heart he said / What Father *Spenser* sung in *British* Verse. / Who reads that Bard desires like him to write, / Still fearful of Success, still tempted by Delight": quoted in Eves's *Matthew Prior*, 195. Eves also quotes from the Webeck Abbey Prior MSS on imitating Spenser: "No dangers daunt the Heart wch Venus has inspir'd / But when Thou bidst me Imitate Spenser I drop my pen / As well I might out with Arthur's Shield or Edward's Sword." Extremely popular, Prior, up to 1741, enjoyed at least six editions of his works and several imitations, including one by Henry Price, in his 1741 *Poems*.

28. Dryden seems to have been impressed by Busby during his Westminster days, as Matthew Prior was when he was Busby's charge. See Charles E. Ward's 1961 *Life of John Dryden* (8–13) for Dryden, Busby, and Westminster School. Instead of imitating Spenser in whole works, Dryden liberally borrowed from the earlier poet. For example, in Dryden's *King Arthur*, act 3, the character Genius is modelled upon Spenser's Orgoglio: see William R. Hill's 1981 "The Source for Dryden's *King Arthur*" (23–29). See chapter 2 for more on Spenser and Dryden as well as the other major early eighteenth century writers.

29. Perhaps something of the experience of Spenser imitators as schoolboys is found in the experience of the Milton imitator John Philips, who went to Winchester College after "he was well grounded in Grammar-Learning." At Winchester he became a capable imitator of classical writers; he first read Spenser and Chaucer at Christ Church, Oxford, however. In his "Life of Mr. John Philips," a preface to Philips's 1728 *Poems on Several Occasions*, fourth edition, (Spenser imitator), George Sewell says that Philips "made himself Master of the Latin and Greek Languages [at Winchester], and was soon distinguished for a happy Imitation of the Excellencies which he discovered in the best Classical Authors." By contrast, an unlettered reader of Milton, who nonetheless wrote imitations of Horace and Claudian, the thresher poet Stephen Duck tells of his impoverished education, but also of his serious reading in the preface to his

1736 *Poems on Several Occasions.* Duck's private reading of English authors was similar to the experience of several unschooled Spenser imitators: Robert Burns, the ploughboy poet; Mary Leapor, much admired by William Cowper; William Vernon; Alexander Wilson; and the Bard of Snowdon, Richard Llwyd. In the 1736 *Poems,* Joseph Spence writes "An Account of the Author" (Duck) in which he details at length Duck's private reading in a friend's library. This edition contains Duck's poem "To the Rev. Dr. Freind on his quitting Westminster School" (173–76; see n. 17 above).

30. John H. Jesse's *Memoirs of . . . Celebrated Etonians* (n.d., 1: 121).

31. Alumni of Harrow included William Sotheby and Lord Byron. Spenser imitators from St. Paul's include Thomas Dudley Fosbroke, John Huddleston Wynne, Samuel Woodford (very early), and William Rider, who was, from 1763 to 1783, Surmaster there. Cornelius Arnold was the fairest son that Merchant Taylors' could boast, as was Mark Akenside at the dissenting academies. The Scots imitators so far unmentioned—John Armstrong, Thomas Blacklock, Robert Fergusson, William Hamilton, Andrew Macdonald, Henry Mackenzie, James Macpherson, William Julius Mickle (a fine imitator of Spenser), John Ogilvie, William Reid, John Scott, William Wilkie, and Alexander Wilson—were schoolboys in Edinburgh; James Beattie in Aberdeen. For Scottish education in and about that time, see the Rev. M. Russel's 1813 *View of . . . Schools and Universities of Scotland* (see bibliography B).

The Irish imitators include Henry Boyd, Samuel Boyse, and Samuel Whyte, all of Dublin schools, and Thomas Dermody of Ennis. Samuel Whyte, 50 years a tutor in Dublin and editor of the thoroughly Spenserian *Shamrock,* taught Thomas Moore, biographer of the dramatist Richard Brinsley Sheridan. Moore says that he "owes to that excellent person [Whyte] all the instructions in English literature he has ever received" (*Memoirs of . . . Sheridan,* 1826, 1.2). It would be interesting to discover the Spenserian disposition of the teachers of the following, all Spenser imitators who were schoolchildren at schools not already mentioned: John Bidlake (Plymouth), Henry Francis Cary (Rugby), Samuel Taylor Coleridge, Leigh Hunt, and Charles Lamb (Christ's Hospital), Robert Dodsley (Sherwood Forest, returned to below), Hugh Downman, John Merivale (Exeter), John Gay (Barnstaple), Thomas Park, Christopher Smart (Durham), Ambrose Philips (Shrewsbury), Richard Polwhele (Truro), James Ralph (Philadelphia), James Scott (Bradford), William Shenstone (Hales-Owen), William Thompson (Appleby), and Mary Robinson (Bristol Dame School, operated by the sisters of Hannah More).

32. Writing masters appear to have been at first strictly calligraphers whose copybooks were engraved sheets of model "hands."

Ambrose Heal, in his 1931 study of *The English Writing Masters*, points out that not until the nineteenth century is space given in these books for the student's own writing. The other sense of writing master, a teacher of writing, is the subject of the anonymous 1732(?) *Case of the Writing-masters*, which takes to task teachers who themselves cannot write well.

33. Eighteenth century students in Charterhouse would have had access to Spenser's works, for a former pupil of the school, antiquary and book collector Daniel Wray, gave his library to the school in that century. *The Catalogue of the Library of Daniel Wray* (1790) lists under Spenser "*Faerie Queene.* 2 vols. 1590–1596; *Works* 1611; *Complaints and Poems* 1591, and *Shepherds Calendar* 1653." As William B. Hunter Jr., explains in the introduction to his 1977 edition of *The English Spenserians*, Spenser was model for a whole generation of imitators at the beginning of the seventeenth century because of the reprinting of his works: "the entire *Faerie Queene* with the added Mutabilitie Cantos in 1609, followed in 1611 by the publication of a full collection of his works which was so successful that a new edition was called for in 1617" (1). Immediately, imitations and adaptations followed. The pattern of textual stimulus and literary response serves for the following century as well.

34. Moore, *Memoirs of . . . Sheridan* (1.2–10). For Byron, Harrow, and Spenser, see Leslie A. Marchand's 1957 *Byron* (1.35, 84–85, 212; and 3.1014); for Byron and Spenser generally, see Marchand's 1973 edition of *Letters and Journals* (2.210; 3.168; 4. 13, 50).

35. This does not seem to be as true for Milton, who was nonetheless often and variously imitated (see John Hopkins's 1699 *Milton's Paradise Lost Imitated in Rhyme*). And one need not be reminded that by 1730 *Paradise Lost* was in its 14th edition. His proximity to the eighteenth century, his less antique diction, and his thematic material (such as the garden myth) made him more accessible to eighteenth century readers (this is not to say that Milton was ignored as imitation model in schools). For the garden myth and other reasons Milton was appropriated by imitators, see Griffin, *Regaining Paradise, passim*.

36. A matter addressed in my 1993 "Native School Models and the Beginning of the Profession of English Literature" (17–28), an essay I use freely below.

37. *Handbook of Research on Teaching the English Language Arts*, ed. James Flood (1991, 1–17).

38. J. W. Ashley Smith's 1954 *Birth of Modern Education* (221–22). See Herbert McLachlan's 1931 *English Education Under the Test Acts*. See also Foster Watson's 1909 *Beginnings of the Teaching of Modern Subjects in England*: "English triumphs after the Restoration. In the eighteenth century the real educational life and activity

was outside the Grammar Schools, and even outside the Universities, and is noticeably to be found better established in the Dissenting Academies. In all the *newer* [my emphasis] institutions, English had entirely triumphed" (573). Textbooks also were in English.

39. Anthony Ashley Cooper, Third Earl of Shaftesbury's 1716 *Several Letters* (letter 7, 5 May 1709). For the advice of a mother to her son, see Mary Barber's 1734 *Poems*. In a turnabout in having the addressee not at university but at Eton, Dr. Littleton presents a disgruntled Cambridge student complaining that he is "Wean'd from the sweets of poetry / To scraps of dry philosophy" (290). Cambridge studies are "tedious philosophic chapters" which "quite stifle my poetic raptures" (291), the latter judged as moribund since his Eton days. The jingle listing of the Cambridge courses communicates their nature, presentation, and reception: in "A Letter from Cambridge to a young Gentleman at Eton School," vol. 6 (1758) of Robert Dodsley's *Collection*, 290–94. For the education of "gentlemen," one aimed at a polished style and taste cultivated by a "reading of the most admired English poets and prose writers" (75) for preparation for public service, see George C. Brauer Jr.'s 1959 *Education of a Gentleman . . . 1660–1775*. See, too, Brauer's 1955 "Recommendations of the *Spectator* for Students During the Eighteenth Century" (207–08). For a delightful and substantial "Personal History A Lasting Impression" of the classics at modern-day Oxford, and at Christ's Hospital before that, see Oxford don Ved Mehta's 1991 *New Yorker* account (83–110).

Notes to Chapter Two

1. See Harriet Kramer Linkin's 1996 "Romanticism and Mary Tighe's *Psyche*."

2. For additional elements of Spenser's reputation in this period and beyond, see David Hill Radcliffe's helpful 1996 *Edmund Spenser A Reception History*. For a stimulating attempt to situate Spenser in the eighteenth century, see Jonathan Brody Kramnick's "Placing Spenser in the Eighteenth Century" (*ELH*, 1996).

3. Oldys discovered that Robert Allott was the *Parnassus* compiler (Thomas Warton owned Oldys's annotated copy). This influential miscellany which preserved Elizabethan verse, arranged alphabetically by subjects, quotes Spenser (one year dead when the book first appeared) 225 times, more than any other author (Shakespeare has 79, Jonson 13, Marlowe 33, but Daniell 115 and Drayton 163, according to the *DNB* under Allott). Oldys's considerable scholarly pursuits were influenced by the books he inherited from his father and grandfather's libraries (both men educated at Winchester College),

as well as by his open access to Robert Harley's important collection.

4. The Dodsley volumes reveal poetical changes in progress, for during the 11 years of their publication (1748–1758) there are more— but different from earlier—odes, short lyrics, simple verse forms, and subjects and treatments traditionally regarded as romantic. Dodsley's very choices of what to include insure the forward thrust to 1800 rather than back to 1700, although I do see his *Collections* as Janus-like. For the contributors to the Dodsley *Collections* and analysis of both, see W. P. Courtney's seven articles in *Notes & Queries* (Nov. 1906–June 1907). See Wallace Jackson's 1978 *The Probable and the Marvelous* for a demonstration of how midcentury English writers harkened back to earlier major poets such as Spenser. It should be noted that several of the Spenser imitations were published elsewhere before Dodsley, but this fact does not diminish the importance or impact of their appearance *together* in the Spenserian environment of Dodsley's collections (vols. 1–3, 1751, 3rd ed., read "in three volumes"; vol. 4, 1755 [1st ed.], read "in four volumes"; vols. 5–6, 1758 [1st ed.], read "in six volumes").

5. The poem excoriates England's treatment of Ireland: "Severe revenge on Britain in thy turn / And ample spoils the treach'rous waves obtain'd, / Which sunk one half of Spenser's deathless fame." Anglo-Irish relations were of course a concern of Spenser himself, as they were for Jonathan Swift and for Samuel Johnson to name only two writers on either end of this sonnet. There is an aptness, then, of the loss of this particular English treasure, both Spenser and his work, presented in terms of revenge on England for her treatment of Ireland.

6. Perhaps of some interest regarding the Native American topic is the attitude expressed on a sheet inserted in the Folger Shakespeare Library's "Commonplace book 1700–1725": "*California* was discovered anno 1577 by Sr. Francis Drake, but being a barren country it was left to ye Natives."

7. Although Dr. Littleton's "A Letter from Cambridge to a Young Gentleman at Eton School" has worthwhile things to say about schooling and studies then, with implications for seeing how Spenser was realized in the early eighteenth century.

8. For a persuasive treatment of miscellanies and canon formation, see Barbara M. Benedict's 1996 piece of that title; and for how anthologies create readers, see Benedict's 1996 *Making the Modern Reader*.

9. Potter's poem does not appear in Dodsley but it was anthologized later in Bell's *Fugitive Poetry* (1790, vol. 11, 105); and its popularity is attested to by its appearance in *The Gentleman's Magazine* 19 (Oct. 1749, 468). Under separate covers, it is reprinted in 1750

and 1775, the latter in Potter's *Poems*. The poem was still well-regarded as the new century arrived, and it enjoyed a reprise in volume 4 of the 1804 *Poetical Register*.

10. Birch will go on to write a Life of Milton in the *Works* of 1753. For the new Spenser edition, the 1590 and 1596 editions of the first three books of *The Faerie Queene* are collated and the last three books with the 1609 folio, he claims. Editing advances.

Notes to Chapter Three

1. Respectively, *Two Centuries of Spenserian Scholarship (1609–1805)* (1936); *Spenser the Critical Heritage* (1971); and *Spenser's Critics Changing Currents in Literary Taste* (1959).

2. Preface to *The Second Part of Mr. Waller's Poems*, appended to the fifth edition of Waller's poems (A4v). In "An Epistle to Mr. Southerne, from Mr. Fenton" in Thomas Southerne's 1721 *The Works of Mr. Thomas Southerne* (A5v), Fenton surveys native authors and places Waller at the end and top of a distinguished line (while providing me with a chapter title as well):

> *Chaucer* had all that Beauty cou'd inspire,
> And *Surry's* Numbers glow'd with warm Desire:
> But now are priz'd by few, unknown to most,
> Because the Thoughts are in the Language lost;
> Ev'n *Spencer's* Pearls in muddy Waters laye,
> Yet soon their Beams attract, the Diver's Eye.
> Rich was their Imag'ry, 'till Time defac'd
> The curious Works; but *Waller* came at last:
> *Waller* the Muse with Heav'nly Verse supplies,
> Smooth as the Fair, and sparkling as their Eyes.

3. In *The Annual Miscellany for the Year 1694*.

4. Compare the reaction to her in William King's *The Toast, an Epic Poem in Four Books* (Dublin, 1732), Bv.

5. In (William Wordsworth's copy, the Lilly Library of Indiana University) *Miscellaneous Poems and Translations*, 1712, wherein is Pope's two-canto version of *The Rape of the Lock*.

6. According to Walter Harte, "*Spenser's* thoughts in solemn numbers roll," in "To a Young Lady, with Mr. *Fenton's* Miscellany," in the 1727 *Poems on Several Occasions*, 94.

7. An antiquarian and philologist, Parnell translated into Latin part of the first canto of *The Rape of the Lock* "after the manner of the ancient Monks"; and he wrote "A Fairy Tale in *Ancient* English *Style*" (not a Spenserian imitation): see Thomas Parnell's 1722 *Poems on Several Occasions*, 32–45 and 113. Some indication of the obvious importance of antiquity for the literate can be gleaned from the

many extant catalogues of private libraries, for example that of John Bridges' 1725 *Bibliotheca Bridgesiana Catalogues,* sold 7 Feb. 1725/6, which lists over 4,000 books and manuscripts in "all languages, particularly in Classics and History." Most of the collection is comprised of Latin and Greek works with a generous representation of the Italian writers Dante, Tasso, Petrarch, and Ariosto. Strongly present, too, are antiquities and histories of Great Britain and Ireland. Native writers are more scarce than the Ancients, although Chaucer, Swift's 1709 *A Tale of a Tub,* and Prior's *Poems* of 1718 are there. As is the case in the seventeenth century, Homer, Horace, and Pindar are paraphrased, imitated, and translated by classicists such as William Congreve (see *Works,* 3rd ed., 2 vols., 1719). Spenser's works are more commonly listed in the "Books" sections of newspapers such as *The Flying-Post,* 1728–1730 (which also contains "The Consolation" in four Prior stanzas, in No. 41 for Sat. July 12, 1729); for example, for Saturday, 26 Apr. 1729, No. 30, the "Works of Spencer in Octavo" are listed in the Books section where the libraries of a lawyer and "another Gentleman" are announced to be sold.

8. The author of the preface to the 1732 *St. James's Miscellany,* in couplets in four parts, grants that Homer and Virgil are "the noblest *Patterns* of our *Imitations* [herein]"; yet the Morpheus and Despair sections appear to be indebted to Spenser's *Faerie Queene* book 1. There is a House of Sleep in part 2 and a Dungeon of Despair in part 4. In the century, many usages of Spenser names occur in non-imitations; Colin Clout and Gloriana are two of the most popular. A typical reference is Thomas D'urfey's calling Princess Anne "Gloriana" throughout his 1714 "The Poet's Vision. A Funeral Poem" in the 1720 *New Operas, with . . . Poems.* Duessa is another appropriated name, even in the English and Latin of William King's *The Toast* (see above). In the translator's preface, "The Picture of the witch *Duessa* in *Spencer* is scarce more shocking than the description of Scheffer's [he gave the Latin] Hermaphrodite."

9. Others were taken with Gay's *Shepherd's Week* as well. There was a fourth edition of the work in 1728 and a Dublin edition that same year, an *annus mirabilis* for Gay, for it was also the year of *The Beggar's Opera,* the eighteenth century's most popular play. Lady Mary Wortley Montague's 1747 *Six Town Eclogues* (pub. as *Town Eclogues* in 1716) are in the manner of Gay's Monday-through-Saturday approach but distant from Spenser, as Gay's were not. For the period's most famous discussion of pastorals, see *Guardian* No. 40 (below) and Samuel Johnson's *Rambler* Nos. 36–37 (Johnson however was not disturbed by allegory; see that same *Rambler* 37 and Nos. 3, 22, 30, 32, 91, 96). On the dangers of imitation, see No. 121. Spenser indeed influenced the period's pastorals (see bibliography C imitations particularly in the first half of the century)—commonly

poor poems: e. g. Isaac Thompson's 1731 *Collection of Poems*, where seven pastorals open the volume, in addition to "An Epithalamium," "Colin in Despair," and "A Pastoral Ode."

10. For an interesting defense of modernization and nationalism as well, see the Scot poet Allan Ramsay's 1721–28 *Poems*, where he gives an apologia for the Scottishness of his poems: "The *Scotticisms* which perhaps may offend some over-nice Ear give new Life and Grace to the Poetry, and become their Place as well as the *Doric* Dialect of *Theocritus*, so much admired by the best Judges [he apologizes for not knowing Theocritus directly]. A small Acquaintance with the Language, and our old *English* Poets will convince any man, that we spend too much Time in looking abroad for trifling Delicacies, when we may be treated at home with a more substantial, as well as a more elegant Entertainment" (7). At the end of the volume he has several imitations of Horace—in Scots, which he says "only snatch'd at his Thought and Method in gross, and dress'd them up in Scots . . . so that these are only to be reckoned a following of his Manner." This could well be said of most eighteenth century imitations in general, whether of Horace or Milton or Spenser. But for Spenser, certainly a few imitators caught more than the manner. Of interest here, too, is the early (1721)—but not the earliest—reaction against solely having the Ancients as models.

11. The high reputation of Ambrose Philips as pastoralist is somewhat understandable when "the times" are taken into account, but surely Matthew Prior nodded when judging Philips's blank verse as potentially the equal of Milton's had he lived long enough: see preface to "Solomon on the Vanity of the World. A Poem in Three Books" (vol. 2 of the 5th ed. of Prior's 1733 *Poems*, 139). Prior was one of many who took Philips's verse seriously. Earlier in the preface, Prior, after stating how Virgil, Tasso, and Ronsard copied their predecessors and in turn were themselves copied, asserts that Spenser is different: "In our Language Spenser has nor contented himself with this submissive Manner of Imitation: He lances [launches?] out into very flowery Paths, which still seem to conduct him into one great Road." Had he completed his epic, "the Whole would have been an Heroic Poem, but in another Cast and Figure than any that had ever been written before." It is interesting that Prior considers Spenser's epic unfinished. Compare with Herbert F. Tucker Jr.'s 1977 "Spenser's Eighteenth-Century Readers and the Question of Unity in *The Faerie Queene*," 322–41.

12. A moralist Spenserian imitator, Samuel Wesley has "Advice to One who was about to Write, To avoid the Immoralities of the Ancient and Modern Poets" in the 1743 *Poems on Several Occasions*, 186 (see his 1736 *Poems* for two imitations):

Since not loose Stories for the Nonce,
Where Mirth for Bawdry ill atones,
Nor long-tongu'd Wife of Bath, at once
   On Earth and Heaven jesting:
Nor, while the main at Virtue aims,
Insert, to sooth forbidden Flames,
In a chaste Work, a Squire of Dames,
   Or *Paridell* a feasting.

13. For a Life of Hughes, see "An Account of the Life and Writings of John Hughes Esq," volume 1 of the 1735 *Poems on Several Occasions*, 1–37. There is only a casual paragraph on his edition of Spenser, but included are some interesting biographical points that help us to understand Hughes's analogies between literature and the Sister Arts. Later in volume 1, Hughes's remarks on style, first written when a young man, are comparable to comments he is to make later for Spenser: see "Of Style. Written at the Request of a Friend, in the Year MDCXCVIII" (247–55), albeit mostly on the style of prose since poetic style was not as much to his youthful liking. When he does turn to poetry in volume 2 (329–33), "On Descriptions in Poetry," he warms to poetical description, as he will do in his edition of Spenser.

14. "'Tho' the tomb of *Spencer* has suffered greatly by time, and was erected in an age when taste was in its infancy in *England*, yet there is something in it venerably plain, and not absurdly ornamental. The materials were certainly very rich, and I don't recollect any of the same standing that deserve so little censure": James Ralph's 1734 *A Critical Review of the Publick Buildings*. The remark on the unlicked taste of the "last age" is not unusual for eighteenth century commentators on such matters (cf. Addison, e. g.). John Dart's 1742 *Westmonasterium* has the following just after a long section on Chaucer in "Westminster Abbey: A Poem": "With *Ivy* Crown immortal *Spencer's* Shrine, / And grace his Shade with Rites almost divine, / Whose heav'nly Muse describ'd in deathless Lays / *Eliza's* Reign and *Albion's* golden Days" (1.39). In "A View of the Monuments" (75), Spenser's tomb is described as the first one comes to upon entering the door of the South Cross.

15. And continued to be reported as the century wore on. A nice collection of anecdotes is *The Plain Dealer* of 1730 (In vol. 1 there is much of Milton including imitations of him.) In volume 2 Spenser is discussed as neglected in his own time. In Number 72 the story is retold of Queen Elizabeth's ordering Spenser a "Hundred marks for some Piece of his Poetry" and the interception by the Lord Treasurer. In Number 60 the persistent topic of Spenser's use of old words is revisited. Number 82 quotes two stanzas from *The Faerie Queene*

on friendship. Spenser was often ransacked for pithy stanzas on generalized topics such as friendship, a practice dating back at least as early as Dr. Gill at St. Paul's School and one which would become more frequent as the generations passed.

16. Hughes's "strength of Imagination" is not unlike Jonathan Richardson the Elder's analogy four years later regarding the imagination of a painter: "As the Poets, so the Painters have stor'd our Imaginations with Beings, and Actions that never were; they have given us the Finest Natural, and Historical Images, and that for the same End, to Please, whilst they Instruct, and make men Better" (22–23, vol. 2 of *Two Discourses* of 1719). In these essays on aesthetics, Richardson does not mention Spenser, but Spenser's artistic follower John Milton is generously quoted to buttress points about painting. Thus, very early in the eighteenth century, Hughes's and Richardson's remarks on the imagination go far in accurately describing an important facet of Spenser's art and go just as far in proving that "fancy" and "imagination," spoken of with approval, are not solely within the province and purview of preromanticism at just about that time or of "high" romanticism later in the century.

17. A considerable body of early eighteenth century music, however, would seem to argue that the art of miniaturization is a sign of excellence, if their musical practice is a measurement. Perhaps more indebted to Shakespeare than Spenser (compare Henry Purcell), elves and fairies are seen throughout the period. Musical pieces on fairies are typically—and oxymoronically—generalized and written for specific and "matching" instruments. An example is *The Faerie Queene*, an anonymous, sprightly tune in D major, the text in six-line couplet stanzas where the Fairy Queen, not Gloriana, addresses her elves, whose life and duties are described (vol. 2 of the 1729 *Musical Miscellany*, 22–2; in vol. 5, eight fairies speak in "The Fairies," 99–101). Something of the musical taste of the age, at least in short pieces, is reflected in the plethora of pastoral songs in these six volumes (1729–1731). Fairies also seem to be of interest outside poetry and music: one example is the Countess D'Anois' 1728 *Collection of Novels and Tales of the Fairies*.

18. In letter 17, 24 Nov. 1710, Pope, speaking of "Defects in Numbers of several of our Poets," advises the avoidance of the "too frequent use of *Alexandrines*, which are never graceful but when there is some Majesty added to the Verse by 'em, or when there cannot be found in 'em a Word but what is absolutely needful" ([Curll's] 1726 *Miscellanea*, vol. 1, 52). In this same volume appears a "Sonnet. By Spenser, Never before Printed" (138–39). For Spenser's alexandrines (and Milton's adaptation of them), see Kenneth Gross's "'Each Heav'nly Close': Mythologies and Metrics in Spenser and the Early Poetry of Milton" (21–36).

19. Giles Jacob, in "An Introductory Essay, on the Rise, Progress, Beauty, &c. of all Sorts of Poetry," also combines Spenser and Milton, but as equals rather than literary father-son: "we . . . Produc'd some few Poets which have preserv'd the Dignity of Poesy, and amongst these *Spenser* and *Milton* are the chief and deservedly esteem'd" (vol. 2 of the 1720 *Poetical Register*). For representative early eighteenth century appraisals of Milton, see Nos. 108, 113, 116, 118, 125 of *The Grub-Street Journal* of 1731–1733. (Both volumes of Jacob's *Register* are very scarce.) Also in volume 2 is a biographical sketch of Spenser along with the Spenserians Croxall and Prior. Although not a critic of high stature, Jacob, in this same "Introductory Essay," gives five useful "qualities" that poetic language should have. These are commonplace topics used by commentators on Spenser's language during the early eighteenth century: aptness, clarity, naturalness, splendor, "numerousness." Jacob says that the language of poetry "must be apt, so as to have nothing that is impure or barbarous; it must be clear, that it may be intelligible; it is to be natural according to the Rules of Decorum and good Sense . . .; it must be lofty and splendid, for the common and ordinary Terms are not proper for a Poet. And the Language is to be numerous to uphold that Greatness and Majesty, which ought to reign throughout in poetry" (21–22). These characteristics are needed for poetic harmony, and only after these are observed is poetic license allowed.

20. In Prior's 1720 *Poems on Several Occasions*, the writer of the "Letter sent to the Publisher of this new Edition," at the end of the book, after praising the economy of this small-format edition of Prior, says how much improved the book is over the earlier edition; then follows this highly unusual egalitarian comparison: "The generality of our English Writers have great need of such revision; because they are very inaccurate in their stile and diction. Our Neighbours the French are much more careful in this Matter" (Gg5v).

21. The writer of the 1730 *Plain Dealer* 109 handles the matter much less soberly than Young when he shows how imitators of Homer's catalogues of ships servilely follow him but how a *good* imitation of this Homeric device is a *short* one.

22. Like Hughes, Jortin emphasizes the early Books of *The Faerie Queene*; unlike Hughes, Jortin has very little of *The Shepheardes Calender*; he does like *Virgil's Gnat*, however. Had the pastoral fashion mostly passed by the time of Jortin's writing in the mid-thirties? No, if the evidence of the imitations and adaptations are considered. Jortin does not comment on poems that do not encourage "scholarly" treatment. A decade later, John Upton will show something of Jortin's spirit in his 1746 *Critical Observations on Shakespeare*; in the index under Spenser, this editor will note that he has "explained and corrected," a service he will also perform for Chaucer.

Notes to Chapter Four

1. David Hume has a slightly different appraisal of the parasite-host relationship in imitations: "'Several writers of late have amused themselves in copying the style of Spenser [as did Thomas Warton]; and no imitation has been so indifferent as not to bear a great resemblance to the original'": from Hume's *History of England*, quoted in *Johnsonian Miscellanies* (1.190).

2. John Forster's 1871 *The Life and Times of Oliver Goldsmith*.

3. See Donald Greene's 1975 *Samuel Johnson's Library*.

4. According to "Anecdotes of Literature," *European Magazine* 1 (Jan. 1782), 24, Johnson was to write a Spenser biography; see Thomas Tyler's remark in *Johnsonian Miscellanies* (2.373).

5. *Johnsonian Miscellanies* (2.192).

6. *Printing Technology, Letters and Samuel Johnson*, 1987, 195–202.

7. *Samuel Johnson's Allegory* (1971, 10, 63), where Johnson is said to be considered by eighteenth century contemporaries as the rival of Spenser, Bunyan, and Addison. Einbond grants that the allegory of *Rambler* 33 does have Spenserian details. For more of Spenser *in* Johnson's allegories, see Thomas M. Curley's *Samuel Johnson and the Age of Travel* (1976, 138, 140–41, 264), where the claim is that Homer's *Odyssey* and Spenser's *Faerie Queene* 2.12 (Bower of Bliss) allegories are given a Johnsonian "somber view of human frailty and self-defeating mortality." See also Leopold Dambrosch Jr.'s *The Uses of Johnson's Criticism* (1976), especially 80–83, for Johnson's negative attitudes about the Theocritan-Spenserian strain in pastorals. Johnson wrote a life of Ambrose Philips who composed pastorals in that tradition: by Petrarch's calling rural poems *Aeglogues*, says Johnson, "he meant to express the talk of goatherds, though it will mean only the talk of goats. This new name [eclogue] was adopted . . . by our Spenser."

8. Not all of Johnson's contemporaries saw Spenser that way. Some wanted him sanitized for tender ears: "Indeed so susceptible had the polite female of the period become that when in 1773 a Mr. Rishton read *The Faerie Queene* aloud to his wife and sister-in-law he won their approval by being 'extremely delicate, omitting whatever, to the poet's great disgrace, has crept in that is improper for a woman's ear,'" in *Johnson's England* (1933, 1.338). Isaac Watts, who championed a Dissenting education, agreed with such cleansing. In his "Discourse on the Education of Children and Youth," Watts wants "acquaintance with good verse" in the best authors, especially Milton, in order "to know and taste and feel a fine stanza, as well as hear it, and to treasure up some of the richest sentiments and

expressions," so long as they are morally anchored (*The Works of . . . Isaac Watts*, 1753, 6.380).

9. Classicists other than Johnson worried over maintaining the old ways and values, seeing the tide of romanticism as potentially having adverse cultural, ethical, and moral ramifications. Of course Pope and Swift felt similarly about advancing dullness and upstart enthusiasts, projectors, and "mechanicals" well before their deaths in 1744 and 1745 respectively. Writers in *The Adventurer* (1752–1754) saw danger in the "Paucity of original writers" (1753, No. 63, 142) and the rush-to-print by a tribe of would-be authors. The situation was dire enough to cause the writer of Number 115 (1753) sarcastically to name his day "The Age of Authors," both men and women (the latter called "Amazons of the pen"), who have the "itch of literary praise" and are bent on "the destruction of paper" (51).

10. Letter 53, *The Letters of Samuel Johnson* (1952, 1.52).

11. In *The Complete Works . . . of Edmund Spenser* (1.304–39).

12. For Thomas Percy's contribution to the 1762 enlargement and Warton's reciprocal help on Percy's *Reliques*, see the introduction to *The Percy Letters*, 1951.

13. The primacy of the text for Upton is communicated well by his remark on the Birch-Kent edition that appeared between the re-issue of the Hughes edition in 1750 and his own: "Some time after the printing of my letter to Mr. West concerning a new edition of Spenser's Fairy Queen, Mr. Kent's edition was published under the care of Mr. Birch: which came chiefly recommended by the designs and engravings, though its chief recommendation was Mr. Birch's name and care of it" (39). Still, Upton castigates Birch's picture of Redcross defeating Error, saying the Knight of Holiness is therein shown a coward and the figure Error presented idiosyncratically "from the painter's head without allusion or meaning" (40). Upton then details how the picture should have been done in terms of the *facts* of Spenser's first book. One can only imagine what he would have to say about the Zeigler *Faerie Queene* panels in the Enoch Pratt library in Baltimore (see my introduction).

14. Ralph Straus's 1910 *Robert Dodsley Poet, Publisher and Playwright* offers a full account of the Spenserians Dodsley published in his *Collection*, including his accommodating of Akenside, West, Shenstone, Gray, and others I treat elsewhere on these pages. Straus also gives an indication of the popularity of the *Collections* by unknotting the skein of its editions at and around the midcentury. See W. P. Courtney's seven *Notes and Queries* articles on the printing and contents of Dodsley's *Collections*.

15. One other piece from *The Union* is of some relevance within the manifold commentaries in the 1750s about mechanical imitation.

In doggerel, Spenserian Robert Lloyd writes "Epistolary Verses" to the dramatist and critic George Colman. Praising Matthew Prior's artless art, Lloyd attacks contemporary imitators: "Who but a madman would engage / A Poet in the present Age? / Write what we will, our works bespeak us / *Imitatores, servum Pecus* [Horace, earlier quoted by Dr. Johnson in the motto to *Rambler* 121 on imitation]. / Tale, Elegy, or lofty Ode, / We travel in the beaten road. / The proverb still sticks closely by us, / *Nil dictum, quod non dictum prius*" (127). Playful, too, is another poem in the miscellany, "The Child Birth. In the Manner of Gay," which has the swain Colin Clout lamented by fair Marian, the maid he impregnated (151–56).

16. That year and the next produced a curious work, or title at least, that students of modern advertising might benefit from. Only the period under consideration could seriously yoke Virgil and a pisspot (a jordan): *Poems by the Celebrated Translator of Virgil's Aneid. Together with the Jordan, a Poem: in Imitation of Spenser,* 1756. The decade's middle did see two ode imitations by Christopher Smart, two indebted sonnets by Thomas Percy, two anonymous efforts on "Westminster Abbey" and Greek history, and, the best of the lot, Moses Mendez's *The Squire of Dames,* in 82 Spenserian stanzas.

17. A distinguished exception is Oliver Goldsmith's positive review of Church's edition in *The Critical Review* 7 (Feb. 1759, 241): "In proportion as the number of editions of the 'Faerie Queene' have increased, the text has become more precarious. . . ."; Goldsmith praises Church as an "exact and cautious editor" who nonetheless writes notes that are "mostly imitations or various readings" (243).

18. *The Connoisseur* is a convenient single-work gathering of literary and education topics, some concerning Spenser directly, that interested readers in the sixth decade. See the four volumes of the 3rd edition (1757–60), even though the 140 weekly numbers are from the years (Jan. 31) 1754–(Sept. 30) 1756. The two main writers are George Colman (n. 15 *supra*) and Bonnell Thornton. The questions over education and imitation are the standard ones, spiritedly treated in the following numbers. Volume 1: Number 6 (1754) describes with humor a scribbler's school days; 22 (1754) compares satirically boys's and girls's education (compare Newberry, n. 34 below); 24 (1754) satirizes polite learning and gives a comic "catalogue of books" for the *beau monde* (190–93); volume 2: Number 42 (1754) takes to task modern practice, which is careless of the English language while advocating the study of English in the schools; a new note sounded is the attack on the two university presses for publishing so little in English; 67 (1755) laments the imitation frenzy, citing those modelled

on Prior, Swift, Milton (called the favorite model); advises "Write from your own imagination," not like the Spenser imitators described in these lines (248):

> Others, who aim at fancy, chuse
> To wooe the gentle *Spenser's* Muse.
> This poet fixes for his theme
> An allegory, or a dream;
> Fiction and truth together joins
> Through a long waste of flimzy lines;
> Fondly believes his fancy glows,
> And image upon image grows;
> Thinks his strong muse takes wond'rous flights
> Whene'er she sings of peerless wights,
> Of dens, of palfreys, spells, and knights:
> 'Till allegory, (*Spenser's* veil
> T'instruct and please in moral tale)
> With him's no veil the truth to shroud,
> But one impenetrable cloud.

Volume 3: Number 83 (1755) concerns fondness for alliteration (Spenser mentioned); volume 4: Number 120 (1756) attacks the Modern's "too correct a taste," saying one is without soul "who does not admire the fancy, the strength, and elegance of *Spenser*" who nevertheless has the "disagreeable habit his day dictated" (allegory? stanzas? "rumbling" lines?).

19. See Hume's 1757 "dissertation" called "Of the Standard of Taste."

20. Warton also loved "that exquisite piece of wild and romantic imagery, Thompson's Castle of Indolence; the first canto of which is marvellously pleasing, and the stanzas have a greater flow and freedom than his blank-verse" (100). Warton gives two disparate bits of information which support observations made earlier: that Addison never read Spenser (305n.) but nevertheless attacked him; and that Pope read *The Faerie Queene* at age 12 and again in his later years, a story repeated by Goldsmith in *The Critical Review* 7 (Feb. 1759), 241n. Another prominent writer, education reformer Thomas Sheridan, used Dodsley werein he discovered Spenser imitator Gilbert West's "Education" to be a "beautiful poem on that subject [i. e. education] . . . found in the 4th volume of Dodsley's Collection," *British Education*, 1756, 203; see also his book 3, chapter 6 remarks on the sister arts and imitation, and oratory's importance to them.

21. The amassing of Spenserians in *Beauties* was complemented by the (separate) publication in 1757 of imitations by Erskine, Dodsley, Gray, and especially William Thompson.

22. From Goldsmith's review of Ralph Church's 1757 edition, *The Critical Review* 7 (Feb. 1759) in *The Works of Oliver Goldsmith*, 1881 (4.240–44).

23. In *Collected Works of Oliver Goldsmith*, 1966 (1.259–69).

24. For example, an anonymous blank-verse rendering of both Spenser's and Sidney's pastorals had just appeared: *The Shepherds Calendar . . . Attempted in Blank Verse*, 1758.

25. Compare with *The Bee* 5 (3 Nov. 1759), where Goldsmith explains why imitations of the Ancients are so frequent: "When the writers of antiquity were sufficiently explained and known [in what he calls the European Renaissance], the learned set about imitating them" (452).

26. Two remarks further clarify Goldsmith's position on imitation. At the end of the preface to the posthumous (pub. 30 June 1774) *History of the Earth*, he concludes that the "best imitation of the ancients was to write from our own feelings, and to imitate nature" (355). Of more relevance to our concern, in his review of Gray's *Odes*, in *The Monthly Review* of Sept. 1757, Goldsmith harshly judges that the young Gray needs to be less abstruse and learned and less imitative of Pindar, one of his models. His advice is for more originality, a gift that Goldsmith brought to his own work, even if one is only to consider the several literary genres in which he wrote and excelled.

27. Conflicting Johnson reckonings of Spenser not already mentioned in my study are to be found in his works after the 1750s. On Spenser imitations, see Johnson's *Lives* of Gay, Collins, and Thomas Warton, for example. On Johnson's use of Spenser's authority and genuine appreciation of the poet, see the preface and notes to his edition of Shakespeare, particularly *A Midsummer Night's Dream*, *Much Ado about Nothing*, *The Tempest*, *Henry the Sixth (3)*, and *Timon of Athens*. For all these Johnson texts, see the volumes of the Yale edition of the *Works*.

28. Why not follow the lead of Spenser himself, a distinguished imitator in the best sense of the word? Thomas Warton recognized this practice in his *Observations*, which has a section "Of Spenser's Imitations from Old Romances." In "Memory and Imagination" (1783), James Beattie, citing Virgil, Tasso, and Pope, concludes "In fact all good poets imitate one another more or less" (231). Such a statement in all probability also applies to musicians and performers of the other sister arts.

29. Shakespeare is Young's great example of originality with Ben Jonson an imitator of his wide learning. Milton was an original, but had he "spared some of his learning, his muse would have gained more glory" (82). Among the Moderns, Addison is "brightest,"

"great," and, unlike Jonson and Dryden, full of heart (86–97). *Heart* is writ large in Young's *Conjectures*.

30. Mention might be made of two collections of 1761 that have imitations of Spenser employed in the service of congratulatory poems on the nuptials of King George III and Charlotte. Spenser is fittingly employed, for the eighteenth century well knew his great paean to royalty, *The Faerie Queene*, recognized the proper patronage he did not receive, and appreciated his gifts in *epithalamia*. These three matters are involved in the encomiums in the volumes that were offered as the two universities' wedding gifts: *Gratulatio Academiae Cantabrigiensis* and Oxford's present, *Epithalamia Oxoniensia*.

31. In *The Works of James Beattie* (1809, 5.157–377): "*Language* is the poet's instrument, as *sound* is the musician's, and *colour* the painter's" (6.1).

32. See Daniel Webb's 1762 *Remarks on the Beauties of Poetry* for originality in writers like Milton, Pope, and Shakespeare. Compare with the "Author's Apology" in *Poems by* [Spenser imitator] *Robert Lloyd*, 1762, for references to schooling; one good illustration is "Latin, I grant, shews college breeding, / And some school-common-place of reading. / But has in *Moderns* small pretention / To real wit or strong invention" (4). Seven years earlier, Lloyd wrote a poem on imitation, "To * * * * About to publish a volume of Miscellanies" (*Poems*, 23–27). "Let not your verse, as verse now [1755] goes," be a kind of prose in imitation of some writer: "For copies shew, howe'er exprest, / A barren genius at the best.—But Imitation's all the mode—/ Yet where one hits, ten miss the road" (23). Lloyd mentions the "easy" Prior imitations, the scurrilous imitations in the manner of Swift, and the vogue for Milton copying; "Others, who aim at fancy, chuse / To wooe the gentle Spenser's Muse" (26).

33. Donald G. Marshall's *Spenser Encyclopedia* article on Richard Hurd concludes that "Always a neoclassical rationalist, he became convinced that the feebleness of mid-eighteenth century poetry demanded renewed stress on feeling and imagination, precisely the qualities attributed in his era to Elizabethan literature."

34. Not formally credentialed but a prodigious reader, John Newberry had four years of life left to him when he published, with Oliver Goldsmith's aid, his revised and expanded *Art of Poetry* in 1762. But he was not an old man (b. 1713) or new to the subject of the education of youth. In 1748, he published an *Arithmetic* for "young gentlemen and ladies" and other instructional manuals. An entrepreneur, Newberry succeeded in collecting literary talent for his several periodicals, including Goldsmith, Johnson, Smart. The *Dictionary of National Biography* notes that he pioneered children's

literature. His *Juvenile Library* (miniatures) and *Lilliputian Magazine* are considered "classics of the nursery." It may appear odd to some that Johnson aided him in his children's publications, but Johnson was among the most versatile writers. And Johnson would remember him in his Jack Whirler portrait in the *Idler*. For his friendship with Goldsmith he won through to a small room in *The Vicar of Wakefield*.

35. The omnibus nature of the work as an instruction is indicated by sections in volume 1 on dieting and exercise and, in volume 2, "Improvement of Life. An Eastern Story" by Johnson (33); selections from Virgil, Milton, Tasso, Voltaire, and Shakespeare (318–50); and much from both the Ancients (Homer, Virgil) and Moderns (Pope, Gay, e. g.). The favorite models are Milton, Shakespeare, and Spenser among the English Renaissance writers. Unclear is the meaning of the title's "new plan" unless the loosely mixed scheme of "didactic," "descriptive," "epigram," and "allegory" are meant; or unless the phrase refers to the explicit teaching of youths by precept (instruction) and example (quotes). There is truth regarding the newness of each, if these indeed were Newberry's meanings.

36. It is of some note that Newberry uses the Hughes edition for his examples (some of which were Hughes's own examples). The long excerpts are the old chestnuts from *The Faerie Queene*, dating back to Gill's practice, although he saw beauties in other of Spenser's works as well: Duessa's soliciting Night, Duessa's simile (compared to a crocodile), description of Night, pageant of the Seven Deadly Sins, House of Pride, Spenser's several gardens, and Mutabilitie's description of Jupiter, for example. *The Faerie Queene* (2.7) Mammon episode is given as a vivid example of Spenser's "power in painting" with its images "not only bold and animated, but just and natural; and the figures [Contemplation, Jealousy, Truth] placed in such attitudes, and so distinguished by their proper emblems, as to strike the imagination in the most forcible manner" (2.18).

37. Spenser's progess in the century is as variegated as his own pictures (without the mock-heroics) in "Muiopotmos: or the Fate of the Butterflie," one of the poet's *Complaints* (1591). If the Spenser historian of the century's final four decades, just beyond the reach of my study, would continue with the examination of Spenser-yielding documents, she or he may well see Wordsworth's 1800 preface (and 1802 appendix) to the *Lyrical Ballads* as imbued with Spenser, who nonetheless is unmentioned in that work. That famous preface will remain a brilliant reflection of its young author and its time as well as continue to be seen as a ringing literary manifesto. Yet I suggest its content and spirit will be understood differently from what has been conventional readings among critics; for just before the Preface's

appearance at the beginning of the nineteenth century, Wordsworth, schooled in the eighteenth century in ways just like those I describe in chapter 1, imitated Spenser seriously and was avidly reading and talking about the poet with his sister Dorothy and their friend Coleridge, who himself had shortly before written his own imitation of Spenser.

Bibliography A

Seventeenth and Eighteenth Century Works Cited or Consulted

With few exceptions, the works listed below do not include the books and serial publications that contain eighteenth century imitations and adaptations, which are the subject of bibliography C. The two bibliographies together constitute a thorough listing of primary sources for my study's several topics.

Academiae Cantabrigiensis Luctus [mourning] *in Obitum Fredirici celsissimi Walliae Principis.* Cambridge, 1751.

An Account of Charity Schools . . . 9th edn. London, 1710.

Addison, Joseph. "An Account of the Greatest English Poets" in *The Annual Miscellany for the Year 1694. Being the Fourth Part of Miscellany Poems.* London, 1694.

———. *Miscellaneous Works, in Verse and Prose, Of the Late Right Honourable Joseph Addison, Esq;* . . . 3 vols. London, 1726.

———. *Spectator* (1711–1714), ed. Donald F. Bond. 5 vols. Oxford: Clarendon, 1965. See *Tatler* below.

The Adventurer. 4 vols. London, 1752–1754 (Hawkesworth, Johnson, Bathurst, Joseph Warton the major essayists therein).

Akenside, Mark. *The Pleasures of the Imagination. A Poem. In Three Books.* London, 1754.

Anderson, Robert. *The Works of the British Poets.* 14 vols. London, 1795.

"Anecdotes of Literature" in *European Magazine* 1 (Jan. 1782): 24. Mention of Dr. Johnson's undertaking a Spenser biography.

The Annual Anthology. Vols. 1–2. Bristol, 1799–1800.

The Annual Miscellany for the Year 1694. Being the Fourth Part of Miscellany Poems. London, 1694.

"Anti-Paedagogus." *The High Road to Parnassus, with the Flogger Flogged; or, the Paedagogue Lash'd in his Turn.* London, 1720; 2nd ed. 1730. With drawings.

Armstrong, John. *Imitations of Shakespeare and Spencer.* London, 1770.

Atterbury, Francis. *The Second Part of Mr. Waller's Poems.* London, 1690.

[Atwood, William]. *A Modern Inscription to the Duke of Marlborough's Fame. Occasion'd by an Antique, in Imitation of Spencer. With a Preface unveiling some of the beauties of the ode, which has pass'd for Mr. Prior's.* London, 1706.

Aylett, Robert. *Divine, And Moral Speculations in Metrical Numbers Upon Various Subjects, By Doctor R. Aylet . . .* London, 1654. Heavily Spenserian, including some imitations. See F. M. Padelford, "Robert Aylett" in *Huntington Library Bulletin* 10 (Oct. 1936): 1–48.

Bailey, Nathan. *English and Latin Exercises for School-boys.* London, 1706; 11th ed. 1744.

Barber, Mary. *Poems on Several Occasions.* London, 1734.

Beattie, James. *An Essay on Poetry and Musick. As They Affect the Mind* and *Remarks on the Utility of Classical Learning Written in the Year 1769* in *The Works of James Beattie, LL.D.* 10 vols. Philadelphia, 1809.

———. *Dissertations, Moral and Critical.* London, 1773.

———. *Essays.* Edinburgh, 1776.

Beaumont, Joseph. *Psyche, or Loves Mysterie. In XX Canto's Displaying the Intercourse Betwixt Christ, and the Soule.* London, 1748; 2nd ed. 1702 by Beaumont's son Charles. Heavily indebted to *The Faerie Queene.*

The Beauties of Poetry Display'd. 2 vols. London, 1757.

Bedell, William (?). *A Protestant Memorial, or The Shepherd's Tale of the Pouder-Plott. A Poem in Spenser's Style.* London, 1713. Earlier thought to be ca. 1605 and by Bishop Bedell.

The Bee, or Literary Weekly Intelligencer. Vols. 1–18. Edinburgh, 1790–93.

Bell, John (ed.). *Bell's Classical Arrangement of Fugitive Poetry.* 14 vols. London 1789–1790. Vols. 10 and 11 devoted exclusively to imitation of Spenser and Milton: the former getting 1 2/3 vols.

Biographia Britannia: Or, the Lives of the Most eminent Persons who have flourished in Great Britain and Ireland . . . 6 vols. London, 1747–1763.

Birch, Thomas (ed.). *The Faerie Queene, By Edmund Spenser, With an exact Collation of the Two Original Editions. Adorn'd with Thirty-Two Copper-Plates, for the Original Drawings of the Late W. Kent, Esq; Architect and Principal Painter to His Majesty.* 3 vols. London, 1751.

Blackmore, Sir Richard. *A Collection of Poems on Various Subjects.* London, 1718.

———. *Essays upon Several Subjects.* London. 1716.

Boswell, James. *The Life of Samuel Johnson.* 2 vols. London, 1791, ed. G. B. Hill; rev. L. F. Powell. 6 vols. Oxford, 1934–64.

Bowle, John. *Reflections on Originality in Authors: Being Remarks on A Letter to Mr. Mason on the Marks of Imitation. . . .* London, 1766.

Bridges, John. *Bibliotheca Bridgesiana Catalogues: or, a Catalogue of the Entire Library of John Bridges.* London, 1725.

The British Magazine and Review; or Universal Miscellany. Vols. 1–3. London, 1782–83.

Browne, Isaac Hawkins. *A Pipe of Tobacco. In Imitation of Six Several Authors.* 3rd ed. London, 1744.

Butler, Charles. *Oratoriae Libri Duo.* London, 1629.

Bysshe, Sir Edward. *The Art of English Poetry.* 2 vols. London, 1702. 4th ed. 1710; 5th ed. by 1714 wherein 2nd and 3rd parts pub. as *The British Parnassus; or a Compleat Common Place-book of English Poetry.* 2 vols.; reissued in 1718 with new titlepage; 7th corrected and enlarged ed. 1724; 8th 1737.

[Cambridge, Richard Owen]. *The Scribleriad: an Heroic Poem. In Six Books.* London, 1751.

Case of the Writing-masters, in and about the Cities of London and Westminster. London, 1732(?).

A Catalogue of School Books now in General Use. London, 1766.

Chalkhill, John. *Thealma and Clearchus. A Pastoral History, in Smooth and Easie Verse . . . by . . . An Acquaintant and Friend of Edmund Spenser*. London, 1683.

Chapone, Hester. *The Works of Mrs Chapone: containing letters on the improvement of the mind. . . .* 4 vols. London, 1773, 1807.

Church, Ralph (ed.). *The Faerie Queene*. 4 vols. London, 1758–59. Rev. by Oliver Goldsmith in *The Critical Review* 7 (Feb. 1759), 241–43.

Clarke, John. *An Essay upon the Education of Youth in Grammar-Schools*. London, 1720.

Clavall, Robert. *The General Catalogue of Books . . . And a Catalogue of School Books*. London, 1680.

Coleridge, Samuel Taylor. *Poems on Various Subjects*. London, 1796; ed. Ernest Hartley Coleridge. London: Oxford UP, 1912.

Colin Clout's Madrigal. London, 1728.

A Collection of Poems. London, 1701.

A Collection of Poems; consisting of Odes, Tales, &c. as well originals as translations. London, 1734.

A Collection of Poems, Mostly Original, by Several Hands. 3 vols. Dublin, 1789–1801.

Collins, William. *Odes on Several Descriptive and Allegorical Subjects*. London, 1747 (See *Poems of Gray, Collins, and Goldsmith*, ed. Roger Lonsdale. London: Longman, 1969.).

————. *Eclogues*. London, 1742; repr. 1757 as *Oriental Eclogues*; repr. 1768 in Pearch's *Collection of Poems*.

Commonplace Book 1700–1725. Folger Shakespeare Library ms. W.A.126.

Congreve, William. *Works*. 2 vols. 3rd ed. 1719.

The Connoisseur. By Mr. Town, Critic and Censor-General. 4 vols. 3rd ed. (Jan. 31 1754–Sept. 30 1756). London, 1757–60.

Cooper, Anthony Ashley, Third Earl of Shaftesbury. *Several Letters Written by a Noble Lord to a Young Man at the University*. London, 1716 (10 letters written 1707–1710).

————. *Characteristics of Men, Manners, Opinions, Times*. London 1711; revised 1713.

Cooper, Elizabeth (ed.). *The Muses Library; Or a Series of English Poetry, from the Saxons to the Reign of King Charles II*. London, 1737.

————. *The Historical and Poetical Medley: or Muses Library*. London, 1738.

Cowley, Abraham. *The Works of Abraham Cowley*. London, 1681.

The Critical Review. Vols. 1–70. London, 1756–1805.

[Curll, Edmund]. *Miscellanea. In Two Volumes. Never Before Published*. 2 vols. London, 1726.

D'Anois, the Countess. *Collection of Novels and Tales of the Faeries . . . in Three Volumes*. 2nd ed. London, 1728.

Dart, John. *Westmonasterium. Or the History and Antiquities of the Abbey Church of St. Peters Westminster . . . In 2 Vol. By Mr. John Dart. To which is added Westminster Abbey, a Poem, By the same Author*. London, 1742.

Davidson, Francis. *A Poetical Rapsody Containing Diuerse Sonnets, Odes, Elegies, Madrigalls and other Poesies, both in Rime, and Measured Verse*. London, 1602; 2nd ed. 1608.

Dennis, John. *The Grounds of Criticism in Poetry*. London, 1704. (see *Critical Works*, ed. Edward Niles Hooker. 2 vols. Baltimore: Johns Hopkins UP, 1939–43).

Digby, Sir Kenelm. *Observations on the 22. Stanza in the 9th Canto of the 2d. Book of Spencers Faery Queene*. London, 1643.

Dodsley, Robert (ed.). *Collection of Poems. By Several Hands. In Three Volumes*. London, 1748. 2nd ed. 1748. His 6-vol. *Collection* appeared 1751–58: vols. 1–3, 1751 3rd ed.; vol. 4, 1755 (1st ed. in 4 vols.); vols. 5–6, 1758 (1st ed. in 6 vols.); 1766; 1775.

————. *The Preceptor: Containing a General Course of Education*. 2 vols. London, 1748; 7 eds. by 1783.

Drayton, Michael. *The Works of Michael Drayton, Esq. . . .* London, 1748. 1st. collected ed.

Dryden, John. *Poetical Miscellanies: the fifth part*. London, 1704.

————. *Miscellany Poems*. 5th ed. 6 vols. London, 1727.

————. *Dryden: The Dramatic Works*, ed. Montague Summers. 6 vols. London, 1931–32.

————. *The William Andrews Clark Edition of Dryden's Works*, ed. E. N. Hooker, H. T. Swedenberg, Earl Miner *et al.* Berkeley and Los Angeles: Univ. California Press, 1956–. See Charles E. Ward, *The Life of John Dryden*. Chapel Hill: Univ. North Carolina Press, 1961; see especially James A. Winn's 1987 *John Dryden and His World*.

Duck, Stephen. *Poems on Several Occasions*. London, 1736.

D'Urfey, Thomas. *New Opera's, with . . . Poems . . . never before printed. . . .* London, 1721.

Edwards, Thomas. *The Sonnets of Thomas Edwards (1765, 1780)*, ed. Dennis Donovan. Augustan Reprint Society Pub. No. 164. Los Angeles: The William Andrews Clark Memorial Library, 1974.

Englands Helicon. London, 1600.

Epithalamion Oxoniensia, sine Gratulationes in Augustissimi Regis Georgii III. Et illustrissimae Principissae Sophiae Charlottae Nuptias Auspicatissimas. Oxford, 1761.

The European Magazine, and London Review. Vols. 1–39. London, 1782–1802.

The Examiner examin'd. In a letter to the Englishman: occasion'd by the Examiner of Dec. 18, 1713, upon the Canto of Spencer. 2nd ed. London, 1713.

The Faerie Leveller: or, King Charles his Leveller described and deciphered in Queene Elizabeth's dayes. By her Poet Laureat Edmond Spenser, in his unparaleld poeme, entituled, the Faerie Queene. A lively representation of our times. London, 1648.

Fairfax, Edward. *Godfrey of Bulloigne, or The Recouerie of Ierusalem Done into English Heroicall verse, translation of Tasso's Gerusalemme liberata*. London, 1600.

Fanshawe, Sir Richard. *Il Pastor Fido . . . with An Addition of divers other Poems*. 2nd ed. London, 1648.

Fawkes, Francis, and William Woty. *The Poetical Calendar*. 12 vols. London, 1763.

Felton, Henry. *A Dissertation on Reading the Classics and Forming a Just Style*. London, 1713 (written 1709); 2nd ed. 1715; 3rd ed. 1718, 1723; 4th 1730; 5th 1753.

Fenton, Elijah (ed.). *Oxford and Cambridge Miscellany Poems*. London, 1708.

————. "An Epistle to Mr. Southerne, from Mr. Fenton" in *The Works of Mr. Thomas Southerne. Volume the First*. 2 vols. London, 1721.

Fletcher, Giles. *Christs Victorie, and Triumph in Heauen, and Earth, over, and after death.* Cambridge, 1610. See next.

Fletcher, Phineas, and Giles Fletcher. *The Purple Island, or The Isle of Man: together with Piscatorie Eclogs and other Poeticall Miscellanies.* Cambridge, 1633.

———. *The Purple Island, or the Isle of Man. An Allegorical Poem. By Phineas Fletcher, Esteemed the Spenser of His Age. To Which is Added Christ's Victory and Triumph, a Poem, in Four Parts. By Giles Fletcher. Both Written in the Last Century.* London, ca. 1783.

———. *Brittain's Ida. Written by that Renowned Poet, Edmond Spencer.* London, 1728.

———. *The Locusts, or Apollyonists.* Cambridge, 1627 (see Abram B. Langdale, *Phineas Fletcher Man of Letters, Science and Divinity.* Columbia UP, 1937).

The Flying-Post: or, Weekly Medley. English and French. By a Society of Gentlemen. London, 1728–1730.

Garretson, John. *English Exercises for School-Boys.* 14th ed. London, 1716.

Gay, John. *The Shepherd's Week. In Six Pastorals.* London, 1714; 4 eds., incl. Dublin, by 1728. See bibl. C below.

———. *Poems on Several Occasions.* 2 vols. London, 1720: see for other pastoral types. See *The Shepherd's Week*, ed. Vincent A. Dearing. 2 vols. Oxford: Clarendon, 1974.

The Gentleman's Magazine. Vols. 1–70. London, 1731–1800.

Gildon, Charles. *The Complete Art of Poetry. In Six Parts.* 2 vols. London, 1718.

Gill, Alexander. *Logonomia Anglica. Qua gentis sermo facilius addiscitur conscripta.* London, 1619.

Goldsmith, Oliver. *An Enquiry into the Present State of Polite Learning in Europe.* London, 1759.

———. (ed.) *The Beauties of English Poesy.* London, 1767.

———. *An History of the Earth, and Animated Nature.* London, 1774.

Gordon, Patrick. *The First booke of the famous Historye of Penardo and Laissa other ways callid the warres, of Love and Ambitione.* London, 1615.

Gratulatio Academiae Cantabrigiensis Auspicatissimas Georgii III . . . et Serenissimae Charolottae. Cambridge, 1761.

Gray, Thomas. *Poems by Mr. Gray.* London, 1768. See *Poems of Gray, Collins, and Goldsmith,* ed. Roger Lonsdale. London: Longman, 1969. See *Correspondence,* ed. P. Toynbee and L. Whibley. 3 vols. Oxford, 1935.

Greene, Maurice (composer 1695–1753). *Spenser's Amoretti set to music by Dr Greene.* London, 1739. Cf. Greene's rendering of Spenser's sonnets 1–6 in *The Lady's Magazine* (Oct. 1794 and Jan.–May 1795), one sonnet for each issue. See 5 sonnets from Spenser's *Amoretti* "set" by Edmund Rubbra. London, 1942.

The Grub-Street Journal. 2 vols. London, 1731–1733.

The Guardian No. 40. London, 1713. Pope's celebrated mock praise of pastoralist Ambrose Philips, who earlier in the year was complimented in 5 *Guardian* essays by Thomas Tickell. Pope's own pastorals had appeared in the same volume as Philips's but were ignored by Tickell: *Poetical Miscellanies, The Sixth Part.* London, 1709. See *Guardian* nos. 30, 32, and 152 (vol. 2, 1714) for more on Spenser.

Harte, Walter. *Poems on Several Occasions By Mr. Walter Harte.* London, 1727.

Hawkins, Sir John. *The Life of Dr. Samuel Johnson* in *The Works of Samuel Johnson.* Vol. 1. London, 1787. See Bertram H. Davis' 1961 ed. of Hawkins's *Life.*

Hayward, Thomas. *The British Muse, or, a Collection of Thoughts Moral, Natural, and Sublime, Who flourished in the Sixteenth and Seventeenth Centuries.* 3 vols. London, 1738.

––––––. *The Quintessence of English Poetry: Or, a Collection of all the Beautiful Passages in our Poems and Plays: From the Celebrated Spencer to 1688.* London, 1740.

Hepwith, John. *The Calidonian Forest.* London, 1641.

Hopkins, John. *Milton's Paradise Lost imitated in rhyme. In the fourth, sixth, and ninth books; containing the primitive loves. The battel of the angels. The fall of man. By Mr. John Hopkins.* London, 1699.

Huggins, William. *The Observer Observ'd. Or, Remarks on a Certain Curious Tract intitled Observations on the Faiere Queene of Spencer by Thomas Warton.* London, 1756.

Hughes, John (ed.). *The Works of Mr. Edmund Spenser. In Six*

Volumes. With a Glossary Explaining the Old and Obscure Words Publish'd by Mr. Hughes. London, 1715. Reissued 1750. For a Life of Hughes, see vol. 1 *Poems on Several Occasions With Some Select Essays in Prose in Two Volumes.* London, 1735.

Hume, David. *Of the Standard of Taste.* London, 1757 (see *David Hume Of the Standard of Taste And Other Essays,* ed. John W. Lentz. Indianapolis: Bobbs-Merrill, 1965).

———. *The History of England, from the Invasion of Julius Caesar to the Revolution of 1688. In Thirteen Volumes . . . A New Edition.* London, 1793. See vol. 8 particularly.

Hunt, Leigh. *Juvenalia; or, A Collection of Poems: written between the ages of 12 and 16.* London, 1801.

Hurd, Bp. Richard. *Letters on Chivalry and Romance.* London, 1762; rev. and enlarged 1765; at least 12 eds. in 18th century.

———. (ed.), *Q. Horatii Flacci Epitolae ad Pisones, et Augustum: With an English Commentary and Notes.* London, 1753, "the Second Edition, Corrected and Enlarged" in 2 vols.

Jacob, Giles. *The Poetical Register.* Vol. 2. London, 1720.

Jacob, Hildebrand. *The Works of Hildebrand Jacob.* London, 1735.

Johnson, Samuel. *The Rambler* (1750–1752). 4th ed. London, 1756 (ed. Walter J. Bate and Albrecht B. Strauss. 3 vols. New Haven: Yale UP, 1969).

———. *The Idler* (1758–1760). 3rd ed. 2 vols. London, 1767. For a modern edition of the 3rd ed., see *The Idler* and *The Adventurer.* Vol. 2 of the Yale Johnson, ed. W. J. Bate, John M. Bullitt, and L. F. Powell, 1963.

———. *A Dictionary of the English Language.* London, 1755.

———. (ed.), *The Works of the English Poets.* 68 vols. London, 1779–81 (in 75 vols. in 1790).

———. *Lives of the Poets.* 10 vols. London, 1779–81, ed. G. B. Hill. 3 vols. Oxford: Clarendon, 1905. For the Johnson-Warton correspondence, see *The Letters of Samuel Johnson,* ed. Bruce Redford. 5 vols. Princeton: Princeton UP, 1992–94.

Jonson, Ben. *Works,* ed. C. H. Herford, and Percy and Evelyn Simpson. 11 vols. Oxford: Oxford UP, 1925–52.

Jortin, John (ed.). *Miscellaneous Observations upon Authors, ancient and Modern.* London, 1731.

———. *Remarks on Spenser's Poems.* London, 1734.

King, William. *The Toast, an Epic Poem in Four Books.* Dublin, 1732.

Knevett, Ralph. *Funerall Elegies, to the Memory of Lady K. Paston.* London, 1637. See C. Bowie Millican, "Ralph Knevett, Author of the *Supplement* to *Spenser's Faerie Queene,*" *RES* 14 (1938): 44–52.

Lamb, Charles. *Poems by Charles Lamb, and Charles Lloyd.* London, 1797. Added to Samuel Taylor Coleridge's 2nd ed. *Poems.*

[Lauder, William]. *An essay on Milton's use and imitation of the moderns, in his Paradise Lost....* London, 1750. Preface and postscript by Samuel Johnson.

Lloyd, Robert. *Poems by Robert Lloyd.* London, 1762.

Locke, John. *Some Thoughts Concerning Education.* 5th ed. London, 1705. See *Educational Writings: A Critical Edition,* ed. J. L. Axtell. Cambridge, 1968, a reprint of the 1705 5th ed.

The London Magazine: or, Gentleman's Monthly Intelligencer. Vols. 1–52. London, 1732–1783.

Love and Resentment: A Pastoral. London, 1717.

Mallet, David. *Amyntor and Theodora; or, The Hermit, a poem in Three Cantos.* London, 1747.

Malone, Edmond. "Rough Notes on Shakespeare," Folger Shakespeare Library ms. S.b.5. Much on Spenser therein, including identification of characters in *The Shepheardes Calender.*

[Mason, John]. *An essay on the Power of Numbers, and the Principles of Harmony in Poetical Composition.* London, 1749. Analogies to music, of course. Scansion the method.

The Maydes Metamorphosis. London, 1600.

Mendez, Moses. *The Shepherds Lottery. A Musical Entertainment....* London, 1751. Music by Dr. Boyce. Moses Mendez (ed.), *A Collection of the Most Esteemed Pieces of Poetry ... And other Contributions to Dodsley's Collection. To which this is intended as a Supplement.* London, 1767; 2nd ed. 1770.

Milton, John. *A Maske Presented At Ludlow Castle.* London, 1637.

———. *Lycidas, in Justa Edovardo King naufrago ... Obsequies to the memorie of Mr Edward King.* London, 1638.

———. *Of Education. To Master Samuel Hartlib.* London, 1644.

———. *Poems.* London, 1645.

Miscellaneous Poems and Translations. By Several Hands. London, 1712.

Monk, Mary. *Marinda. Poems and Translations upon Several Occasions.* London, 1716.

Montague, Lady Mary Wortley. *Town Eclogues with Some Other Poems.* London, 1716; pub. as *Six Town Eclogues* in 1747.

The Monthly Chronicle, for the Year MDCCXXVIII. London, 1728. 12 nos. in 1 vol. Useful books-published listing.

The Monthly Mirror. Vols. 1–8. London, 1795–1800.

The Monthly Review. Vols. 1–114. London, 1749–1800.

More, Henry. *Psychodia Platonica or a Platonicall song of the Soul.* London, 1642.

Morell, Thomas. "To Mr. Thomson on his Unfinished Plan of a Poem Called The Castle of Indolence in Spenser's Style" (ca. 1747) in Chalmers, 12, 467 (see bibl. C below).

Musae Seatonionae. A Complete Collection of the Cambridge Prize Poems. London, 1772.

The Museum: Or, the Literary and Historical Register. Vols. 1–3, London, 1746–1747.

The Musical Miscellany; Being a Collection of Choice Songs, Set to the Violin and Flute, By the most Eminent Masters. 6 vols. London, 1729.

Newberry, John. *The Art of Poetry on a New Plan: Illustrated with a great Variety of Examples from the best English Poets; and of Translations from the Ancients: Together with such Reflections and critical Remarks as may tend to form in our Youth an elegant Taste.* 2 vols. London, 1741; 2nd ed. 1762.

The New Foundling Hospital for Wit. Being a Collection of Fugitive Pieces, in Prose and Verse, . . . A New Edition, Corrected and Considerably Enlarged, in Six Volumes. 2nd ed. London, 1786 (1st ed. 1784).

New Memoirs of Literature, Containing an Account of New Books Printed both at Home and Abroad. . . . 6 vols. London, 1725–1727.

A New Miscellany of Original Poems, on Several Occasions. London, 1701.

A New Occasional Oratorio . . . the Words taken from Milton, Spenser, Etc. and Set to Musik by Mr. Handel. London, 1746.

Niccols, Richard. *The Beggars Ape*. London, 1627. Cf. Spenser's *Mother Hubberds Tale*.

Nichols, John (ed.). *A Select Collection of Poems*. 8 vols. London, 1780. See *Literary Anecdotes*, ed. Colin Clair. Carbondale: Southern Illinois UP, 1967.

The Norfolk Poetical Miscellany. 2 vols. London, 1744.

Oldham's Spencer's ghost. . . . London, 1709.

Palmer, Samuel. *Defence of the Dissenters Education in their Private Academies*. London, 1703.

Parnell, Thomas. *An Essay on the Different Stiles of Poetry*. London, 1713.

———. *Poems on Several Occasions. Written by Dr. Thomas Parnell, late Arch-Deacon of Glogher: and Published by Mr. Pope*. London, 1722.

Pasquils Palinoda, and His progresse to the Taverne. London, 1619.

Paterson, James. *A Complete Commentary . . . on Paradise Lost*. London, 1744. Contains 500 pages of notes.

Peacham, Henry. *Prince Henrie revived. Or A Poem Vpon the Birth, and in Honor of the Hopefull yong Prince Henrie Frederick*. . . . London, 1615.

———. *The Period of Mourning. Disposed into six Visions*. London, 1613. Both heavily Spenserian.

Pearch, George (ed.). *A Collection of Poems*. 2 vols. London, 1768; 1770, 1775, 1783 in 4 vols.

Pemberton, Henry. *Observations on Poetry. Especially the Epic: Occasioned by the Late Poem upon Leonidas*. London, 1738.

Percy, Thomas. *The Percy Letters: The Correspondence of Thomas Percy and Thomas Warton*, ed. M. G. Robinson and Leah Dennis. Baton Rouge: Louisiana State UP, 1951.

Philips, Ambrose. *Pastorals* in *A Variorum Text of Four Pastorals by Ambrose Philips*, ed. R. H. Griffith. *Texas University Studies in English* 12 (1932): 118–57.

Philips, John. *Poems on Several Occasions. By Mr. John Philips*. . . . 4th ed. London, 1728.

Phillips, Edward (ed.). *Theatrum Poetarum, or A Compleat Collection of the Poets . . . of all Ages*. 2 vols. London, 1675.

Pilkington, Matthew. *Poems on Several Occasions*. London, 1731.

The Plain Dealer: Being Select Essays on Several Curious Subjects. London, 1724; 1730 in 2 vols.

Poems by the Celebrated Translator of Virgil's Aneid. Together with the Jordan, a Poem; in Imitation of Spenser. London, 1756.

Poems on Several Occasions by a Lady. 2nd ed. London, 1726.

Poetical Recreations . . . In Two Parts. London, 1688.

Pope, Alexander. "Discourse on Pastoral Poetry" and *Pastorals* in *The Works of Mr. Alexander Pope.* London, 1717 (1st collected ed.). See *Pastoral Poetry and An Essay on Criticism*, ed. E. Audra and Aubrey Williams. London: Methuen, 1961. See *The Poems of Alexander Pope*, ed. John Butt. New Haven: Yale UP, 1963 (the one-volume Twickenham Text).

Prior, Matthew. *The Hind and the Panther Transvers'd to the Story of the Country-Mouse and City-Mouse.* London, 1687.

———. *A letter to Monsieur Boileau Depreaux; Occasion'd by the Victory at Blenheim.* London, 1704.

———. *Poems on Several Occasions.* London, 1709; 2nd ed. 1718.

———. *Poems on Several Occasions . . . with some additions which are not in the folio edition.* London, 1720.

———. *Poems . . . In Two Volumes. By the Late Matthew Prior . . . The Fifth Edition.* 2 vols. London, 1733.

———. *Miscellaneous Works of His Late Excellency Matthew Prior, Esq; In Two Volumes.* Dublin, 1739–40. The miscellany, perhaps a piracy, is noteworthy for its close explication of Prior's "Ode to the Queen."

———. *Works*, ed. H. Bunker Wright and Monroe K. Spears. 2 vols. Oxford: Clarendon, 1971.

Purcell, Henry. *Orpheus Britannicus. A collection of The Choicest Songs, for One, Two, and Three Voices. Compos'd by Mr. Henry Purcell. . . .* 2 vols. London, volume 1 in 1698, volume 2 in 1702.

Proposals for Printing by Subscription A New Edition of Spenser's Fairy Queen. London, 1751.

Proposals for the Reformation of Schools & Universities In Order to the Better Education of Youth. Edinburgh, 1704.

Purney, Thomas. *Pastorals.* London, 1717.

Ralph, James. *A Critical Review of the Publick Buildings, Statues, and Ornaments in and about London and Westminster.* 2 vols. London, 1734.

Ramsay, Allan. *Poems by Allan Ramsay.* Edinburgh, 1721–1728. 1st collected ed.

"A Register of Books, &c. publish'd July, 1730," *The Monthly Chronicle* No. XXXI (1730), 146.

Richardson, Jonathan (the Elder). *Two Discourses: I. An Essay on the whole Art of Criticism as it relates to Painting . . . II. An Argument in behalf of the Science of a Connoisseur.* London, 1719.

Ritson, Joseph. *Observations on the First Three Volumes of The History of English Poetry.* London, 1782. See W. C. Hazlitt's ed. of Warton's *History* 4 vols. London, 1871.

Robinson, Thomas. *The Life and Death of Mary Magdalene, Or, Her Life in Sin, and Death to Sin.* British Museum ms. Harleian 6211, ca. 1620. Heavily Spenserian.

Rowe, Elizabeth Singer. *Miscellaneous Works in Prose and Verse.* 2 vols. London, 1739.

Rowlands, Samuel. *The Famous Historie of Guy of Warwick.* London, 1609. Twelve cantos of stanzas *ababcc;* canto 4-line mottos like *The Faerie Queene.*

The St. James Magazine. Vols. 1–3. London, 1762–1764.

St. James's Miscellany: or, the Lover's Tale. Being the Amours of Venus and Adonis: or, the Disasters of Unlawful Love. London, 1732.

Settle, Elkanah. *The Fairy Queen: an Opera. . . .* London, 1692.

Sewell, George. "Life of Mr. John Philips" in Philips's *Poems on Several Occasions.* 4th ed. London, 1728.

Shenstone, William. *Essays on Men and Letters.* London, 1787.

———. *The Letters of William Shenstone,* ed. Marjorie Williams. Oxford: Blackwell, 1939.

Sheridan, Thomas. *British Education: Or, the Source of the Disorders of Great Britain.* London, 1756.

———. *Plan of Education for the Young Nobility and Gentry of Great Britain.* London, 1769.

Sidney, Sir Philip. *Sir Philip Sidney's Arcadia, moderniz'd by Mrs. Stanley.* London, 1725.

Smith, Edmund. *Miscellaneous Poems and Translations. By Several Hands.* London, 1712. (Wordsworth's copy, Lilly Library, Indiana

University.] Contains "A Poem to the Memory of Mr. John Philips. To a Friend," Pope's two-canto version of *The Rape of the Lock*, and "On a Miscellany of Poems. To Bernard Lintott," alluded to in my text.

Southerne, Thomas. *The Works of Mr. Thomas Southerne. Volume the First*. 2 vols. London, 1721.

Spence, Joseph. "An Account of the Author" (Stephen Duck) in Stephen Duck's *Poems on Several Occasions*. London, 1736. Therein, see Duck's poem on the Rev. Dr. Freind of Westminster School, 173–76.

———. *Polymetis: Or, an Enquiry Concerning the Agreement Between the Works of the Roman Poets and the Remains of the Antient Artists*. London, 1747.

———. *Observations, Anecdotes, and Characters of Books and Men*, ed. James M. Osborn. 2 vols. Oxford: Clarendon, 1966.

Spenser, Edmund. *Works* in three 17th century folio eds.: 1611, 1617, and 1679, the latter "whereunto is added an account of his life" as well as Phineas Fletcher's *Brittain's Ida*. The relevant 18th century eds. of the *Works* are the Hughes 1715 (and 1750 reissue) and the 8-vol. *Poetical Works* "From [the 1758 *Faerie Queene* edition of] Mr. Upton." Edinburgh, 1778. The major 17th century eds. of *The Faerie Queene*, other than in the *Works*, are the 1st folio ed. of 1609, the 1611–13, and the 1617 which includes *The Sheaphardes Calender*. Two early 1750s *Proposals for printing by subscription* herald the Birch, Church, and Upton eds. of 1751, 1757, and 1758 respectively. *The Sheapheardes Calender* was published in 1653 with Theodore Bathurst's Latin translation of it, *Calendarium Pastorale*. Its English-Latin pairing is continued in the 18th century with *The Shepherd's Calendar, Containing Twelve Aeglogues . . . By Edmund Spenser, Prince of English Poets. . . .* London, 1732; reissued 1735, 1758. Spenser's *Mother Hubberds Tale*, while read early in the century, does not have its separate ed. until *Mother Hubberd's Tale of the Fox and Ape; selected from the works of Edmund Spenser, with the obsolete words explained*. London, 1784.

Steele, Sir Richard (ed.). *Poetical Miscellanies, Consisting of Original Poems and Translations. By the best Hands. Publish'd by Mr. Steele*. London, 1714.

———. *The Tatler. The Lucubrations of Isaac Bickerstaff Esq; Revised and Corrected by the Author*. 4 vols. London 1710–1711. For education, see nos. 63, 173, 197, 234, 252–53. Cf. *Spectator* nos. 307, 313, 337, 353, and Steele's nos. 157, 168, 230, 294, 330, 430. London, 1712–1713. Cf. *Guardian* nos. 62, 72, 94, 105, 155. London, 1713. See *Tatler* below.

The Student; or, the Oxford and Cambridge Monthly Miscellany. 2 vols. Oxford, 1750–1751 (edited by B. Thornton and George Colman the dramatist).

Swift, Jonathan. *The Works of Jonathan Swift, D.D., D.S.P.D. In Four Volumes.* . . . Dublin, 1735.

Tasso, Torquato. *Tasso's Jerusalem, An Epic Poem. Translated from the Italian by Henry Brooke, Esq.* London, 1738. First 3 books only.

[*The Tatler*]. *The lucubrations of Isaac Bickerstaff Esq; Revised and Corrected by the Author.* 4 vols. London, 1710–1711. Addison and Steele's work.

Thompson, Isaac. *A Collection of Poems Occasionally Writ on Several Subjects.* Newcastle upon Tyne, 1731.

Tonson, Jacob (ed.). *Poetical Miscellanies: The Sixth Part. Containing a Collection of Original Poems, with Several New Translations. By the most Eminent Hands.* London, 1709. Philips's pastorals first in the volume, and Pope's (without his important preface) last.

The Town and Country Magazine. Vols. 1–22. London, 1769–1790.

The Ugly Club, a dramatic caricative [sic]. London, 1798. The Boston Public Library's copy has missing titlepage. The 35-page satire is purportedly by "Edmund Spenser the Younger," pseud.

The Universal Magazine of Knowledge and Pleasure. Vols. 1–105. London, 1747–1799.

Upton, John. *Critical Observations on Shakespeare.* London, 1746; 2nd ed. 1748.

———. (ed.), *Flavius Arrianus Epictetus.* London, 1739–41.

———. *A Letter Concerning A New Edition of Spenser's Faerie Queene.* London, 1751. A 39-page letter.

———. (ed.), *Spenser's Faerie Queene. A New Edition with a Glossary, And Notes explanatory and critical by John Upton, Prebendary of Rochester and Rector of Great Rissington in Glocestershire.* 2 vols. London, 1758. See *An impartial estimate of . . . Mr Upton's Notes on the Fairy Queen.* London, 1759. Ms. notes.

Waldron, Francis Godolphin (ed.). *Literary Museum; or Ancient and Modern Repository.* London, 1792.

Waller, Edmund. *The Second Part of Mr. Waller's Poems.* 5th ed. London, 1690.

Warton, Joseph. *Odes on Various Subjects.* London, 1746, ed. Richard Wendorf. ARS Pub. No. 197. Los Angeles: William Andrews Clark Memorial Library, 1979.

———. *An Essay on the Genius and Writings of Pope.* 2 vols. London, 1756; 3rd ed. 1782.

Warton, Thomas, the Elder. *Poems on Several Occasions.* London, 1748. Pub. by sons Joseph and Thomas.

Warton, Thomas, the Younger (ed). *The Union: or, Select Scots and English Poems.* Oxford, 1753; 2nd ed. 1759, Dublin 1761; 3rd 1766.

———. *Observations on the Faerie Queene of Spenser.* 2 vols. London, 1754; 2nd ed. 1762, 1807.

———. (ed.), *The Oxford Sausage: or, Select Poetical Pieces, Written by the most Celebrated Wits of the University of Oxford.* London, 1764; a "new edition" London, 1814.

———. *The History of English Poetry.* 4 vols. London, 1774–81 (see Warton's addendum to the History, unpub. until Rodney M. Baines's *A History of English Poetry: An Unpublished Continuation.* ARS Pub. No. 39. Los Angeles: William Andrews Clark Memorial Library, 1953, for fascinating cf. by Warton of Shakespeare's and Spenser's sonnets).

———. *Life of Sir Thomas Pope.* London, 1772.

———. *Poems. A New Edition.* London, 1777.

[Waterland, Daniel]. *Advice to a Young Student, with a Method of Study for the First Four Years.* London, 1730; 2nd ed. Oxford, 1755; 3rd ed. 1761.

Watts, Isaac. *The Works Of the late Reverand and learned Isaac Watts, D.D. . . . collected into Six Volumes.* London, 1753.

Webb, Daniel. *Remarks on the Beauties of Poetry.* London, 1762.

Welsted, Leonard. *The Works of Dionysius Longinus, On the Sublime . . . Translated from the Greek. With Some Remarks on the English Poets. By Mr. Welsted.* London, 1712.

Wesley, Samuel. *Poems on Several Occasions.* London, 1736; 2nd ed. Cambridge, 1743. See therein, "Advice to One who was about to Write, To avoid the Immoralities of the Ancient and Modern Poets."

Whaley, John. *A Collection of Original Poems and Translations. By John Whaley, M.A. Fellow of King's-College, Cambridge.* London, 1745. Among other poems of interest, Sneyd Davies' "A Voyage to Tinterne Abbey in Monmouthshire . . ." (187–91) points to Wordsworth.

Whyte, Samuel (ed.). *The Shamrock: or, Hibernian Cresses. A Collection of Poems, Songs, Epigrams &c.* . . . Dublin, 1772.

Winstanley, William. *England's Worthies. Select Lives of the most Eminent Persons of the English Nation from Constantine the Great Down to these Times.* 2nd ed. London, 1684. Has a Life of Spenser, 224–27.

Woodford, Samuel. *A Paraphrase Upon the Canticles, And Some Select Hymns Of The New and Old Testament, With other occasional Compositions in English Verse.* London, 1679. See A. C. Judson, "Samuel Woodford and Edmund Spenser," *N&Q* 189 (1945): 191–92. Woodford's *Paraphrase* contains his Spenser imitation *The Legend of Love.*

Wordsworth, William. *Lyrical Ballads, with A Few Other Poems.* Bristol, 1798.

Wray, Daniel. *The Catalogue of the Library of Daniel Wray.* London, 1790.

Young, Edward. "On Lyric Poetry" in *Ocean. An Ode . . . To which is prefix'd, An Ode to the King: And a Discourse on Ode. By the Author of the Universal Passion.* London, 1728.

———. *Conjectures on Original Composition. In a Letter to the Author* [Samuel Richardson] *of Sir Charles Grandison.* 2nd ed. London, 1759.

Zouch, Rev. Thomas. *Scheme of Study at Trinity College Cambridge.* London, ca. 1750.

Nineteenth and Twentieth Century Works Cited or Consulted

Ackermann, R. *The History of the Colleges of Winchester, Eton, and Westminster, with the Charter-house, the Schools of St. Paul's, Merchant Taylor's, Harrow, and Rugby, & the Free-School of Christ's Hospital.* London, 1816.

Aldrich, Earl A. "James Beattie's *Minstrel*: Its Sources and Its Influence on English Romantic Poets." Ph.D. diss., Harvard, 1928.

Allison, Alexander Ward. *Toward an Augustan Poetic: Edmund Waller's "Reform" of English Poetry.* Lexington: Univ. of Kentucky Press, 1962.

Altick, R. D. "Richard Owen Cambridge—Belated Augustan." Ph.D. diss., Pennsylvania, 1941.

Arnold, Thomas. "Spenser as a Textbook," *Dublin Review* 4 (1880): 321–32.

Audra, E., and Aubrey Williams (eds.). *Alexander Pope: Pastoral Poetry and An Essay on Criticism.* London: Methuen, 1961.

Bahadur, U. "Spenserian Revival in the Eighteenth Century and Spenser as an Influence throughout the Nineteenth Century." Ph.D. diss., Edinburgh, 1935.

Baker, Carlos. "The Influence of Spenser on Shelley's Major Poetry." Ph.D. diss., Princeton, 1939.

Bator, Paul G. "Rhetoric and the Novel in the Eighteenth-Century

British University Curriculum," *Eighteenth-Century Studies* 30.2 (1996–97): 173–95.

Beattie, James. *The Works of James Beattie, LL.D.* 10 vols. Philadelphia: Hopkins and Earle, 1809.

Beatty, Elsie. "The Criticism of Spenser During the Eighteenth Century." M. A. thesis, Illinois, 1925 (Dir. H. S. V. Jones).

Beers, Henry A. *A History of English Romanticism in the Eighteenth Century.* New York: Henry Holt, 1899.

Bell, Edna F. "Imitations of Spenser from 1706 to 1774" M. A. thesis. Oklahoma, 1928 (Dir. Jewel Wurtzbaugh).

Benedict, Barbara M. "Miscellanies and Canon-Formation: The Case of Browne's *Pipe of Tobacco,*" *The East-Central Intelligencer,* n.s. 10.2 (May, 1996): 9–16.

———. *Making the Modern Reader: Cultural Mediation in Early Modern Literary Anthologies.* Princeton: Princeton UP, 1996.

Blake, William. *Characters in Spenser's "Faerie Queene"* in *Blake Newsletter* 31 (1974–75), entire issue. Reproduction of Blake's tempera, with essay and comments.

Bouchier, Jonathan. "The Spenserian Stanza," *N&Q* ser. 8, vol. 3 (1887): 409, 525.

Bradley, Laurel. "Eigheenth-Century Paintings and Illustrations of Spenser's *Faerie Queene*: A Study of Taste," *Marsyas* 20 (1979–80): 31–51.

Bradner, Leicester. "Forerunners of the Spenserian Stanza," *RES* 4 (1928): 207–08.

Brauer, George C. Jr. *The Education of a Gentleman . . . 1660–1775.* New York: Bookman, 1959.

———. "Recommendations of the *Spectator* for Students During the Eighteenth Century," *N&Q* cc (May, 1955): 207–08.

Bright, James W. "Brief Mention on Some Characteristics of Spenser and on Winstanley's Editions of *The Faerie Queene,* I and II," *MLN* 31 (1916): 189–91.

Britten, Benjamin (composer). *Spring Symphony.* London, 1949. *Amoretti* sonnet incl. with pieces by 8 Renaissance writers.

Butt, John. *The Augustan Age.* New York: Norton, 1966.

Cambridge under Queen Anne, illustrated by Memoirs of Ambrose Bonwicke 1729 and Diaries of Francis Burman 1710 and

Z. C. von Uffenback 1712, ed. M. R. James. Cambridge: Cambridge UP, 1911.

Campbell, Gordon. "Imitation in *Epitaphium Damonis*" in *Urbane Milton: The Latin Poetry*, ed. James A. Freeman and Anthony Low. *Milton Studies* 19 (1984): 165–77.

Chalmers, Alexander (ed.). *The Works of the English Poets from Chaucer to Cowper*. 21 vols. London, 1810.

Charterhouse Prize Exercises, From 1814–1832. London, 1833.

Chernaik, Warren L. *The Poetry of Limitation: A Study of Edmund Waller*. New Haven: Yale UP, 1968.

Clark, Donald Lemen. *John Milton at St. Paul's School A Study of Ancient Rhetoric in English Renaissance Education*. New York: Columbia UP, 1948; repr. Archon Books, 1964.

Cohen, Gustav. *Thomson's "Castle of Indolence," eine nachahmung von Spenser's "Faerie queene."* Bonn, 1899.

Contemporary Thought on Edmund Spenser, With a Bibliography of Criticism of The Faerie Queene, 1900–1970, ed. Richard C. Frushell and Bernard J. Vondersmith. Carbondale: Southern Illinois UP, 1975.

Corder, Jim. "Spenser and the Eighteenth-Century Informal Garden," *N&Q* n.s. 6 (1959): 19–21.

Cory, Herbert E. "The Golden Age of the Spenserian Pastoral," *PMLA* 25 (1910): 241–67.

———. "The Critics of Edmund Spenser," *MP* 2 (1911): 81–182.

———. "Spenser, Thomson, and Romanticism," *PMLA* 26 (1911): 51–91.

———. *The Critics of Edmund Spenser*. Univ. California Publications in Modern Philology. Berkeley: Univ. California Press, 1917.

———. "The Influence of Spenser on English Poetry." Ph.D. diss., Harvard, 1910 (Dir. W. A. Neilson).

Courtney, W. P. (7 articles under the title of) "Dodsley's Famous Collection of Poetry," *N&Q* No. 150 ser. VI (Nov. 10, 1906): 361–63; con't. 10 ser. VI (Nov. 24, 1907): 402–03; con't. 10 ser. VII (Jan. 5, 1907): 3–5; 10 ser. VII (Feb. 2, 1907): 82–84; 10 ser. VII (Apr. 13, 1907): 284–87; 10 ser. VII (May 25, 1907): 404–05; 10 ser. VII (June 8, 1907): 442–44.

Crane, Ronald S. "Imitation of Spenser and Milton in the Early Eighteenth Century: A New Document," *SP* 15.2 (1908): 195–206.

―――. "A Neglected Mid-eighteenth-Century Plea for Originality and its Author," *PQ* 13.4 (1934): 21–29.

Curley, Thomas M. *Samuel Johnson and the Age of Travel.* Athens: Univ. Georgia Press, 1976.

Damrosch, Leopold Jr. *The Uses of Johnson's Criticism.* Charlottesville: Univ. Press of Virginia, 1976.

Davies, Phillips G. "A Check List of Poems, 1595 to 1833, Entirely or Partly Written in the Spenserian Stanza," *Bulletin of the New York Public Library* 77 (1974): 314–28.

deMaar, Harko Gerrit. *Elizabethan Romance in the Eighteenth Century.* Academisch proefschrift. Amsterdam: Zalt-Bommel, N.V. Van de Garde & Co., 1924.

―――. *A History of Modern English Romanticism.* London: Oxford UP, 1924.

Dillard, Nancy Frey. "The English Fabular Tradition: Chaucer, Spenser, Dryden." Ph.D. diss., Tennessee, 1973.

Dowden, Edward. "Spenser, the Poet and Teacher" in *The Complete Works in Verse and Prose of Edmund Spenser,* ed. Alexander B. Grosart. Vol. 1 (of 10 vols.). London, 1882–84, 304–39.

Draper, F. W. M. *Four Centuries of Merchant Taylors' School 1561–1961.* Oxford: Oxford UP, 1962.

Draper, John W. "Aristotelian *Mimesis* in Eighteenth-Century England," *PMLA* 36 (1921): 372–400.

Dryfus, Norman J., S.J. "Eighteenth-Century Criticism of Spenser." Ph.D. diss., Johns Hopkins, 1938.

Durling, Robert M. "The Bower of Bliss and Armida's Palace," *Comparative Literature* 6 (1954): 335–47.

Dyson, George (composer). *Sweet Thames run softly. Cantata for baritone solo, chorus and orchestra. Verses from the Prothalamion of Edmund Spenser.* London, 1954.

Einbond, Bernard L. *Samuel Johnson's Allegory.* The Hague: Mouton, 1971.

The English Writing-Masters and Their Copy-Books 1570–1800: A Biographical Dictionary and a Bibliography. Cambridge: Cambridge UP, 1931.

Eves, Charles Kenneth. *Matthew Prior Poet and Diplomatist.* New York: Columbia UP, 1939.

Evett, David H. "Nineteenth-Century Criticism of Spenser." Ph.D. diss., Harvard, 1965.

Fairer, David. "The Origins of Warton's *History of English Poetry*," *RES* 32 (1981): 37–63. See *Spenser Encyclopedia*.

Firth, C. H. *The School of English Language and Literature at Oxford*. Oxford: Blackwell, 1909.

Forster, John. *The Life and Times of Oliver Goldsmith*. 2 vols. 5th ed. London: Chapman and Hall, 1871.

Frushell, Richard C. "Imitations and Adaptations, 1660–1800," *The Spenser Encyclopedia*, A. C. Hamilton *et al.* (eds.). Toronto: Univ. Toronto Press, 1990, 396–403; 2nd ed. forthcoming.

———. "Spenser and the Eighteenth-Century Schools," *Spenser Studies* 7 (1987): 175–98.

———. "Native School Models and the Beginning of the Profession of English Literature," *Pennsylvania English* 17.2 (1993): 17–28.

———. and Bernard J. Vondersmith (eds.). *Contemporary Thought on Edmund Spenser*. Carbondale: Southern Illinois UP, 1975.

Fulton, E. "Spenser and Romanticism," *Nation* 92 (4 May 1911): 445.

Gleckner, Robert F. *Blake and Spenser*. Baltimore: Johns Hopkins UP, 1985.

Godley, A. D. *Oxford in the Eighteenth Century*. London: Methuen, 1908.

Godshalk, William L. "Prior's Copy of Spenser's *Works* (1679)," *PBSA* 61 (1967): 52–55.

Goldsmith, Oliver. *The Collected Works*, ed. Arthur Friedman. 5 vols. Oxford: Oxford UP, 1966.

Greene, Donald. *Samuel Johnson's Library An Annotated Guide*. Univ. Victoria Press, 1975. ELS Monograph Series, No. 1.

Greene, Herbert E. "The Allegory as Employed by Spenser, Bunyon, and Swift." Ph.D. diss., Harvard, 1888 (pub. with same title in *PMLA* 4 [1889]) (Dir. Francis J. Child, Kitteridge's teacher).

Greenlaw, Edwin A. *et al.* (eds.). *The Works of Edmund Spenser: A Variorum Edition*. Baltimore: Johns Hopkins UP, 1932–57.

———. "Proceedings of Dr. Greenlaw's Seminary C, 1926–1931," Johns Hopkins Univ. Library, Baltimore.

———. "The Shepheards Calender," *PMLA* 26 (1911): 419–51.

Griffin, Dustin. *Regaining Paradise: Milton and the Eighteenth Century*. Cambridge: Cambridge UP, 1986.

Groom, Bernard. *The Diction of Poetry from Spenser to Bridges*. Toronto: Univ. Toronto Press, 1955.

———. *The Formation and Use of Compound Epithets in English Poetry from 1579* (Society for Pure English, Tract No. 49, 295–322). Oxford: Clarendon, 1937.

Gross, Kenneth. "'Each Heav'nly Close': Mythologies and Metrics in Spenser and the Early Poetry of Milton," *PMLA* 98.1 (1983): 21–36.

Grundy, Joan. *The Spenserian Poets: A Study in Elizabethan and Jacobean Poetry*. London: Edwin Arnold, 1969.

Hagstrum, Jean H. *The Sister Arts: The Tradition of Literary Pictorialism and English Poetry from Dryden to Gray*. Chicago: Univ. Chicago Press, 1958.

Hamilton, A. C. "Spenser and the Common Reader," *ELH* 35 (Dec. 1968): 618–33. See *Contemporary Thought* above and *Spenser Encyclopedia* below.

Hard, Frederick. "Two Spenserian Imitations, by 'T. W.,'" *ELH* 5 (1938): 113–26.

Harris, Robert B. "The Beast in English Satire from Spenser to John Gay." Ph.D. diss., Harvard, 1932.

Havens, Raymond D. "Romantic Aspects of the Age of Pope," *PMLA* 27 (1912).

———. *The Influence of Milton on English Poetry*. Cambridge: Harvard UP, 1922.

———. "Thomas Warton and the Eighteenth-Century Dilemma," *SP* 25.1 (1928): 36–50.

———. "Changing Taste in the Eighteenth Century; A Study of Dryden's and Dodsley's Miscellanies," *PMLA* 44.2 (1929): 501–36.

———. "More Eighteenth-Century Sonnets," *MLN* 45 (1930): 77–84.

Helgerson, Richard. "Tasso on Spenser: The Politics of Chivalric Romance" in *The Yearbook of English Studies* 21 (special no. on "Politics, Patronage and Literature in England 1558–1658"), ed. Andrew Gurr. Leeds, England: MHRA (1991): 153–67.

Hendricks, Ira K. "The Use of the Spenserian Stanza before 1798." M. A. thesis, Stanford, 1926.

Higginson, James Jackson. *Spenser's Shepherd's Calendar in Relation to Contemporary Affairs*. New York: Columbia UP, 1912.

Hill, William R. "The Source for Dryden's *King Arthur*," *Bach* 12 (1981): 23–29.

Hoffman, Arthur W. "Spenser and *The Rape of the Lock*," *PQ* 49 (1970): 530–46.

Hook, Julius Nicholas. "Eighteenth-Century Imitations of Spenser." Ph.D. diss., Illinois, 1941.

———. "Three Imitations of Spenser," *MLN* 55 (1940): 431–32.

Hooker, Edward Niles. "The Discussion of Taste from 1750 to 1770, and the New Trends in Literary Criticism," *PMLA* 49.2 (1934): 577–92.

Houston, Percy Hazen. *Doctor Johnson A Study in Eighteenth-Century Humanism*. Cambridge: Harvard UP, 1923.

Hunt, Leigh. "English Poetry versus Cardinal Wiseman," 94-page autograph ms. ca. 1859 in Folger Shakespeare Library, N.a.74 case 84. Addressed to the editor of *Fraser's Magazine*, which publishes the defense of Chaucer and Spenser in No. 60 (1859), 747 ff.

Hunter, William B. Jr. *The English Spenserians: The Poetry of Giles Fletcher, George Wither, Michael Drayton, Phineas Fletcher and Henry More*. Salt Lake City: Univ. Utah Press, 1977.

Hurd, Richard. *Works*. 8 vols. London, 1811.

Irving, William Henry. "An Imitation of the *Faerie Queene*," *MLN* 43.2 (1928): 80.

Jackson, Wallace. *The Probable and the Marvelous: Blake, Wordsworth, and the Eighteenth-Century Critical Tradition*. Athens: Univ. Georgia Press, 1978.

Jesse, John H. *Memoirs of the Court of England: Celebrated Etonians*. 2 vols. Boston: Chester F. Rice, n.d.

Johnsonian Miscellanies, ed. George Birkbeck Hill. 2 vols. Oxford: Clarendon, 1897; repr. Barnes & Noble, 1966.

Johnson's England An Account of the Life and Manners of his Age, ed. A. S. Turberville. 2 vols. Oxford: Clarendon, 1933.

Jones, Richard F. "Eclogue Types in English Poetry of the Eighteenth Century," *JEGP* 24 (1925): 33–60.

Judson, Alexander C. "The Eighteenth-Century Lives of Edmund Spenser," *HLQ* 16 (1953): 161–81.

Kaufman, J. Paul. "The Doctrine of Neoclassical Imitation and the Theory of Original Genius in English Criticism of the Eighteenth Century." Ph.D. diss., Harvard, 1918.

Keats, John. *The Complete Poetical Works of Keats*, ed. Horace E. Scudder. Cambridge: Houghton Mifflin, 1899.

———. *Letters of John Keats*, ed. Maurice Buxton Forman. London: Oxford UP, 1947.

Kernan, Alvin. *Printing Technology, Letters and Samuel Johnson.* Princeton: Princeton UP, 1987.

Kindon, J. "Byron versus Spenser," *International Journal of Ethics* 14 (1904): 362–77.

Klein, Joan Larson. "Some Spenserian Influences on Milton's *Comus*," *Annuale Mediaevale* 5 (1964): 24–47.

Knowlton, E. C. "The Pastoral in the Eighteenth Century," *MLN* 32 (1917): 471.

Kramnick, Jonathan Brody. "The Cultural Logic of Late Feudalism: Placing Spenser in the Eighteenth Century," *ELH* 63 (1996): 871–92.

Kucich, Greg. *Keats, Shelley, and Romantic Spenserianism.* University Park: Penn State UP, 1991.

Laughlin, T. A. "Four Great Headmasters," *Studies in Education* 2 (1948): 22–31.

Lechay, Daniel T. "The Escape from the Lonely Dell: Studies in Spenser, Shakespeare, Wordsworth and Blake." Ph.D. diss., Iowa, 1975.

Leisering, Walter. "Das Motiv des Einsiedlers in der englischen Literatur des 18.Jahrhunderts und der Hochromantik." inaug. diss., Halle, 1935; pr. Wurzburg: Richard Mayr, 1935.

Linkin, Harriet Kramer. "Romanticism and Mary Tighe's *Psyche*: Peering at the Hem of Her Blue Stockings," *SiR* 35 (1996): 55–72.

Littlefield, George Emry. *Early Schools and School-books of New England.* New York: n.p., 1904.

Lowell, James Russell. "Spenser," *North American Review* 120 (1875) 334–94; pub. in *Among My Books.* 2 vols. Boston: Houghton Mifflin, 1889: vol. 2, 125–200.

Mack, Maynard. *The Garden and the City: Retirement and Politics in the Later Poetry of Pope 1731–1743.* Toronto: Univ. of Toronto Press, 1969.

McKillop, Alan Dugald. "Some Details of the Sonnet Revival," *MLN* 39 (1924): 438–40.

———. "A Critic of 1741 on Early Poetry," *SP* 30.3 (1933): 504–21.

———. *James Thomson: The Castle of Indolence and Other Poems.* Lawrence: Univ. Kansas Press, 1961.

McLachlan, Herbert. *English Education Under the Test Acts. Being the History of the Nonconformist Academies 1662–1820.* Manchester: Manchester UP, 1931.

McNeir, Waldo F., and Foster Provost. *Edmund Spenser. An Annotated Bibliography 1937–1972.* Philology Series, No. 17. Pittsburgh: Duquesne UP, 1975.

Magill, Andrew James. "Spenser and Ireland: a Synthesis and Revaluation of Twentieth-Century Scholarship." Ph.D. diss., Texas, 1967.

Mann, Elizabeth L. "The Problem of Originality in English Literary Criticism, 1750–1800," *PQ* 17 (1939): 97–118.

Marchand, Leslie A. *Byron: A Biography.* 3 vols. New York: Knopf, 1957. Leslie Marchand (ed), *Byron's Letters and Journals.* Cambridge: Harvard UP, 1973. Especially vols. 2–4.

Marples, Morris. *Romantics at School.* New York: Barnes & Noble, 1967.

Marsh, George Linnaeus. "Imitation and Influence of Spenser in English Poetry from 1765–1800." M. A. thesis Chicago, 1899.

Martz, Edwine Montague. "Bishop Hurd as Critic." Ph.D. diss., Yale, 1939.

Mehta, Ved. "Personal History A Lasting Impression," *The New Yorker.* Nov. 11, 1991, 83–110.

Melchiori, Giorgio. "Pope in Arcady: The Theme of *Et in Arcadia Ego* in his Pastorals," *English Miscellany* 14 (1963): 83–93.

Meriwether, Colyer. *Our Colonial Curriculum 1607–1776.* Washington, D.C.: Capital Pub., 1907.

Monro, John. "Spenser Allusions 1637–1709," *N&Q* 118 (1908): 121.

Moore, Thomas. *Memoirs of the Life of The Right Honourable Richard Brinsley Sheridan.* 2 vols. Philadelphia: A. Sherman, 1826.

Morton, E. P. "The English Sonnet, 1658–1750," *MLN* 20 (1905): 97–98.

———. "The Spenserian Stanza before 1700," *MP* 4 (1907): 639–54.

———. "The Spenserian Stanza in the Eighteenth Century," *MP* 10 (1913): 1–27.

Mounts, Charles E. "The Influence of Spenser on Wordsworth and Coleridge." Ph.D. diss., Duke, 1941.

Mueller, William R. *Spenser's Critics Changing Currents in Literary Taste.* Syracuse: Syracuse UP, 1959.

Murals Based upon Edmund Spenser's Faerie Queene. Baltimore: Enoch Pratt Free Library (Central), 1945. The (Spenserian) Charles Osgood wrote the section of the catalogue which describes the 18 *Faerie Queene* murals. He defines Spenser's *faerie* as "other world," namely, of the imagination which treats two basic "instincts of human nature," to fight and love (5). Osgood reports that mural artist Zeigler loved pictorial Spenser; thus his panels show chivalric moments vividly rendered. Zeigler gives two or three panels to each book of the epic, with the central mural (no. 18) over the Maryland Department (Reading) Room clock being the head of Spenser, attended by Nature, Chivalry, and Epic Poetry. The other 17 panels depict crucial points in Spenser's poem: for example, panel 1 has Redcross and Una meeting the wizard Archimago (book 1); panel 2, the House of Pride, the Seven Deadly Sins, etc.; 3, Redcross slaying the Dragon; 4, Sir Guyon (2.7) exhausted after his temptation; 5, Sir Guyon destroying the Bower of Bliss (2.12), and so on.

Musae Seatonionae. Cambridge, 1808.

The Muses Pocket Companion. Dublin, 1800.

Nitchie, Elizabeth. "Longinus and the Theory of Poetic Imitation in Seventeenth and Eighteenth-Century England," *SP* 32 (1935): 580–97.

Olson, Robert C. *Motto, Context, Essay: The Classical Background of Samuel Johnson's Rambler and Adventurer Essays.* New York: University Press of America, 1984.

Packard, Faith E. "Spenser's Influence on the Pictorial Landscape of Certain Eighteenth-Century Poets." M. A. thesis, Wellesley College, 1931.

Park, Thomas. *The Works of the British Poets.* 42 vols. London, 1808–09.

Parker, Patricia. "The Progress of Phaedria's Bower: Spenser to Coleridge," *ELH* 40 (1973): 372–97.

Peck, H. W. "Spenser's *Faerie Queene* and the Student of To-Day," *Sewanee Review* 24 (1916): 340–52.

Percy, Thomas. *The Percy Letters. The Correspondence of Thomas Percy and Edmond Malone*, ed. Arthur Tillotson. Baton Rouge: Louisiana State UP, 1944.

Phelps, William L. *The Beginnings of the English Romantic Movement*. Boston: Ginn, 1893. See ch. 5, 47–86.

Pitts, George Richard. "Romantic Spenserianism: *The Faerie Queene* and the English Romantics." Ph.D. diss., Pennsylvania, 1977.

The Poetical Register and Repository of Fugitive Poetry for 1810–1811. 11 vols. London, 1814.

Pope, Emma Field. "The Critical Background of the Spenserian Stanza," *MP* 24 (1926): 31–53.

Preston, John. "The Informing Soul: Creative Irony in *The Rape of the Lock*," *Durham University Journal* 27 (1966): 125–30.

Prettyman, Virginia. "Shenstone's Reading of Spenser" in *The Age of Johnson: Essays Presented to Chauncey Brewster Tinker*, ed. Frederick W. Hilles. New Haven: Yale UP, 1949, 227–37.

Proceedings of English Seminary C, 1926–1931 (see Edwin Greenlaw above). 5 vols. unpub. The Milton Eisenhower Memorial Library of Johns Hopkins University. See also the gathering of mss in the University Collection (137 Series 3 Box 5, of 5) that includes John C. French's 19-page account of the beginnings of the Tudor-Stuart Club, a group important for the Spenserian emphasis at Johns Hopkins for several decades after its founding (including *ELH*'s Spenser predisposition).

Provost, Foster. "Pastorals: An Exercise in Poetical Technique" in *Contributions to the Humanities* (Louisiana State Univ. Humanities Series), 5 (1954): 25–37. *Sheapheardes Calender* and Pope's pastorals. Foster Provost, see *Contemporary Thought* and Waldo McNeir above.

Radcliffe, David Hill. *Edmund Spenser A Reception History*. Columbia, SC: Camden House, 1996.

Reaney, James. "The Influence of Spenser on Yeats." Ph.D. diss., Toronto, 1958.

Reeve, Frederic Eugene Jr. "The Stanza of *The Faerie Queene*." Ph.D. diss. Princeton, 1942.

Reschke, Hedwig. *Die Spenserstanze im neunzehnten Jahrhundert* in *Anglistische Forschungen*. Heidelberg, 1918.

Reuning, Karl. "Das Altertümliche im Wortschatz der Spenser-Nachahmungen des 18.Jahrhunderts." Ph.D. diss., Univ. Giessen,

1911; pub. in Strassburg by Karl J. Trübner, 1912, No. 116 of the "Quellen und Forschungen zur Sprachund Culturgeschichte der germanischen Völker" series, ed. Alois Brandl *et al.*

———. "'The Shepherd's Tale of the Powder Plot', Eine Spenser-Nachahmung," *Beiträge zur Erforschung der Sprache und Kultur Englands und Noradamerikas* 4.2 (1928): 8–154.

Riddell, James A., and Stanley Stewart. *Jonson's Spenser: Evidence and Historical Criticism.* Pittsburgh: Duquesne UP, 1995.

Rinaker, Clarissa. "Thomas Warton's Poetry and its Relation to the Romantic Movement," *Sewanee Review* 23 (1915): 140–63.

Ringler, Richard N. "Two Sources for Dryden's *The Indian Emperour,*" *PQ* 42 (1963): 423–29.

———. "Dryden at the House of Busirane," *ES* 49 (1968): 224–29.

Roberts, W. (ed.). *Memoirs of Hannah More.* Vol. 2. London, 1834.

Ruskin, John. "Theology of Spenser" in *The Stones of Venice.* 3 vols. London, 1851–53.

Russel, Rev. M. *View of the Systems of Education at present pursued in the schools and Universities of Scotland.* Edinburgh, 1813.

Schulman, Samuel E. "The Spenserian Enchantments of Wordsworth's 'Resolution and Independence,'" *MP* 79.1 (1981): 24–44.

———. "Wordsworth's Salisbury Plain Poems and Their Spenserian Motives," *JEGP* 84 (1985): 221–42.

Scribner, Dora A. "The History of Spenser's Literary Reputation with Especial Study of 1579–1700." M. A. thesis, Chicago, 1906.

Sells, Lytton. *Oliver Goldsmith His Life and Works.* New York: Harper & Row, 1974.

Sen, Dilipkumar. "A Critical Study of Spenserian Imitations from 1700 to 1771." M. A. thesis, London, 1952.

Sherburn, George. "The Early Popularity of Milton's Minor Poems," *MP* 17 (1919–20): 259–78, 515–40.

Shih, Chung Wen. "The Criticism of *The Faerie Queene.*" Ph.D. diss., Duke, 1955.

Sipple, William L. *Edmund Spenser 1900–1936: A Reference Guide.* Boston: G. K. Hall, 1984.

Smith, J. W. Ashley. *The Birth of Modern Education: the Contribution of the Dissenting Academies 1660–1800.* London: Independent Press, 1954.

Snyder, Edward D. *The Celtic Revival in English Literature 1760–1800*. Cambridge: Harvard UP, 1923. Outgrowth of 1913 Harvard diss.

Southey, Robert. *Specimens of the Later English Poets*. 3 vols. London, 1807.

Spenser Allusions in the Sixteenth and Seventeenth Centuries, ed. William Wells *et al*. Chapel Hill: Univ. of North Carolina Press, 1972. Part 2: 1626–1700, special no. *SP* 69.5 (1972): 175–351.

Spenser, Edmund. *Catalogue of an Exhibition of the Original Editions of the Works of Edmund Spenser* [held at] . . . *The Grolier Club* . . . *May 5th to* . . . *May 20th, 1899*. New York, 1899. In commemoration of the 300th anniversary of Spenser's death.

————. *The Works of Edmund Spenser: A Variorum Edition*, ed. Edwin Greenlaw *et al*. 12 vols. Baltimore: Johns Hopkins UP, 1932–55. See Greelaw above.

The Spenser Encyclopedia, ed. A. C. Hamilton *et al*. Toronto: Univ. Toronto Press, 1990; 2nd ed. (paperback) forthcoming. See especially articles by Joann Peck Krieg on "America to 1900," Richard C. Frushell on "Imitations and Adaptations 1660–1800," Reginald Berry on John Dryden, Howard Erskine-Hill on Alexander Pope, Claudia L. Johnson on Samuel Johnson, David Fairer on Thomas Warton the Younger, and Donald G. Marshall on Richard Hurd.

"Spenser in the Eighteenth Century," *The Saturday Review* 41 (1876): 640–41.

Spenser Parodies (mostly 19th century) File. Lilly Library, Indiana University: PN6110.P3, Box 23 No. 23. (1) Colin Cloute, (2) Calling Over the Goals, (3) Pope's The Alley, (4) Britannia Liberatrix, (5) The Holidayer, (6) Imitation of Spenser by John Keats, (7) The Irish Schoolmaster by Thomas Hood, (8) North Beach by Brete Harte, (9) The Old Bachelor, (10) Old Mother Hubbard, (11) The Shewe of Faire Seeming by Leigh Hunt, (12) Spenser Describeth a Grass-Cutting Machine, (13) A Spenserian Fragment, (14) Stanzas on Charles Armitage Brown by John Keats, (15) To a Lady with the Sonnets of Petrarch in the Manner of Spenser by Peter Pindar, (16) Una and the British Lion, (17) Unified and the Lion, (18) Velvet and Iron, (19) The Virtuoso by Mark Akenside, (20) Ye Cruelle Coxwayne.

Spenser: The Critical Heritage, ed. R. M. Cummings. New York: Barnes and Noble, 1971.

Squire, James R. "History of the Profession" in *Handbook of Research on Teaching the English Language Arts*, ed. James Flood *et al*. New York: Macmillan, 1991, 1–17.

Steadman, John. "Timotheus in Dryden, E. K., and Gafori," *TLS* (Dec. 16, 1960): 819.

Stock, A. G. "Yeats on Spenser" in *In Excited Reverie: A Centenary Tribute to William Butler Yeats, 1865–1939*, ed. A. Norman Jeffares and K. G. W. Cross. New York: Macmillan, 1965, 93–101.

Straus, Ralph. *Robert Dodsley Poet, Publisher and Playwright*. London, 1910.

Stroup, Thomas B. "*The Cestus*: Manuscript of an Anonymous Eighteenth-Century Imitation of *Comus*," *SEL* 2 (1962): 47–55.

Sutherland, James R. "Shakespeare's Imitators in the Eighteenth Century," *MLR* 28 (1933): 21–36.

———. *A Preface to Eighteenth-Century Poetry*. Oxford: Oxford UP, 1963 (repr. of 1948 ed.).

Taboureux, Etienne. "The Spenserian Stanza," *Revue de L'Enseignement des Langues Vivantes*, 15 (1899): 499 ff.; 16 (1899): 14 ff., 112 ff., 163 ff.

Tanner, Lawrence E. *Westminster School A History*. London: Country Life, Ltd., 1934.

Tennyson, Alfred Lord. *Poetical Works*. London: Oxford UP, 1953.

Todd, Rev. Henry John (ed). *Works of Edmund Spenser*. 5 vols. London, 1805.

Tompson, Richard S. "English and English Education in the Eighteenth Century" in *Popular Education in the Age of Improvement*. A 14-page printed handout given at the ASECS meeting at McMaster University, Canada, 1973.

Tucker, Herbert F. Jr. "Spenser's Eighteenth-Century Readers and the Question of Unity in *The Faerie Queene*," *UTQ* 46.4 (1977): 322–41.

Turnage, Maxine. "Samuel Johnson's Criticism of the Works of Edmund Spenser," *SEL* 10 (1970): 557–67.

Vaughan, Robert. "Popular Education in England," *British Quarterly Review* 4 (1846): 444–508.

Wasserman, Earl R. "The Scholarly Origin of the Elizabethan Revival," *ELH* 4 (1937): 213–43.

————. *Elizabethan Poetry in the Eighteenth Century*. Urbana: Univ. Illinois Press, 1947.

Watkins, W. B. C. *Johnson and English Poetry before 1600*. Princeton: Princeton UP, 1936. Reprinted by Gordian Press, 1965.

Watson, Foster. *The Beginnings of the Teaching of Modern Subjects in England*. London: Pittman, 1909.

————. "The Curriculum and Textbooks of English Schools in the First Half of the Seventeenth Century," *Transactions of the Bibliographical Society* 6.2 (1903): 159–267.

Weinbrot, Howard D. "'An Ambition to Excell': The Aesthetics of Emulation in the Seventeenth and Eighteenth Centuries," *HLQ* 48.2 (1985): 121–39.

————. *Britannia's Issue*. Cambridge: Cambridge UP, 1993.

West, S. George. "A Study of the Life and Works of William Julius Mickle, Translator of the Lusiad." M. A. thesis, London, 1932.

————. "The Works of William Julius Mickle, the First Anglo-Portugese Scholar," *RES* 10.4 (1934): 385–400.

Williams, Raf Vaughan (composer). *Epithalamion* (a cantata based upon the masque *The Bridal Day* "words by Edmund Spenser"). London: Oxford UP, ca. 1957.

Wilson, John. "Spenser and His Critics" in *Critical Essays of Early Nineteenth Century*, ed. R. M. Alden. New York: Scribners, 1921.

————. "Spenser," Nos. 1–7 *Blackwood's Edinburgh Magazine*: 34 (Nov. 1833), 224–56; 36 (Sept. 1834), 408–30; 36 (Nov. 1834), 681–714; 36 (Dec. 1834), 716–37; 37 (Jan. 1835), 49–71; 37 (March 1835), 540–56; 37 (Apr. 1835), 659–76.

Wiseman, Cardinal Nicholas P. S. *On the Perception of Natural Beauty by the Ancients and the Moderns: Two Lectures*. London, 1856. See Hunt above.

Wordsworth, Christopher. *Scholae Academicae: Some Account of the Studies of English Universities in the Eighteenth Century*. Cambridge: Cambridge UP, 1877.

Wordsworth, William. *Faerie Queene* 1.1–9 ms. prose redaction in the Wordsworth Collection, Lilly Library, Indiana University. Ms. dated 16–30 Sept. 1835.

————. *The Poetical Works of William Wordsworth*. 6 vols. London, 1832.

———. *Literary Criticism of William Wordsworth*, ed. Paul M. Zall. Lincoln: Univ. Nebraska Press, 1966.

———. *The Letters of William and Dorothy Wordsworth: The Early Years, 1787–1805.* 2nd edition ed. E. de Selincourt, rev. Chester L. Shaver. 4 vols. Oxford: Clarendon, 1967.

Wurtsbaugh, Jewel. "The 1758 Editions of *The Faerie Queene,*" *MLN* 48 (1933): 228–29.

———. *Two Centuries of Spenserian Scholarship (1609–1805).* Baltimore: Johns Hopkins UP, 1936. Reprinted by Kennikat Press, 1970 (Her book was first a Johns Hopkins Ph.D. diss., 1932, same title.).

Wyld, Henry Cecil. "Spenser's Diction and Style in Relation to Those of Later English Poetry" in *A Grammatical Miscellany Offered to Otto Jespersen on His Seventieth Birthday*, ed. N. Bogholm *et al.* Copenhagen: Levin & Munksgaard, 1930, 147–65. Good on Spenser in Pope.

Yeats, William Butler (ed.). *The Poems of Spenser Selected and with an Introduction by W. B. Yeats.* London, 1906.

Yost, C. D. "The Poetry of the *Gentleman's Magazine.*" Ph.D. diss., Pennsylvania, 1936.

Zimmerman, Dorothy W. "Romantic Criticism of Edmund Spenser." Ph.D. diss., Illinois, 1957.

Bibliography C

Eighteenth Century Imitations and Adaptations

The following list of 318 imitations and adaptations for the entire chronological eighteenth century augments my original bibliography published in *The Spenser Encyclopedia* by some 30 percent and is, so far as I know, complete. I have read most items herein. Included, but in addition to the 318 total above, are 20 representative seventeenth century imitations intended to give something of the inheritance of Spenser imitations for the eighteenth century; no claim is made for direct influence upon any one imitator or sort of imitation. As this listing makes clear, the latter part of the century was not the only active time for Spenser imitations, which heretofore was the usual understanding. The bibliography is organized by name or title rather than by date since references to the imitations in my text are usually made thusly. Even though all the major romantic poets imitated Spenser, they mostly did so after the turn of the century. I list only their Spenser imitations before 1800, fully aware that a more satisfying bibliography of imitations would reach to the end of the first quarter of the nineteenth century, beyond the limit of my study.

The information within entries is at times incomplete since many imitations were often reprinted; no attempt is made at a publication stemma. A typical entry includes author's name (if known); date when written or first published; author, date, and title of a work in which it appeared (most often the one I have examined or know the work to be in) if not published separately; place of publication; statement on its form and other annotations. Page numbers are most often omitted.

For other relevant information, see the Spenser bibliographies of William Sipple 1984 (for studies 1900–1936), Waldo McNeir and Foster Provost 1975 (for 1937–1972), and the *Spenser Newsletter* since 1970. See also Phillips G. Davies 1973 "Check List of Poems . . . in the Spenserian Stanza" and Julius Nicholas Hook's 1941 dissertation (University of Illinois). Other unpublished theses and dissertations that I have read which touch or center on the topic include those of George Linnaeus Marsh (1899, University of Chicago), Herbert Cory (1910, Harvard University), Karl Reuning (1911, University of Giessen), Edna Bell (1928, University of Oklahoma), C. D. Yost (1936, University of Pennsylvania), Norman Dreyfus (1938, Johns Hopkins University), Dilipkumar Sen (1952, University of London), and Charles E. Mounts (1941, Duke University): see bibliography B above for each. My indebtedness to individual scholars who provided information on imitations is given in the introduction.

Spenser imitations are included in collections published under formulaic titles such as *Poems on Several Occasions*, collected works of individual imitators, and periodicals such as *The Gentleman's Magazine* (abbreviated here as *Gent M*) and *The European Magazine* (*Eur M*). The other major repository is anthologies. The Dodsley collections (continued by Pearch) are of course primary examples. Over half of the century's Spenser imitations were first published in the collections of (alphabetically) Robert Anderson, John Bell, Alexander Chalmers, Robert Dodsley, Moses Mendez, George Pearch,

James Ralph, and Samuel Whyte (see bibliography B for full publication information). The following anthologies are cited more than once in the accompanying list: John Bell, 1789–90 *Classical Arrangement of Fugitive Poetry*, vols. 10–11 (vol. 10 titled *Poems in the Stanza of Spencer*, vol. 11 titled *Poems in the Stanza of Spenser; and, In the Manner of Milton*), 14 vols. (London); Alexander Chalmers, 1810 *The Works of the English Poets from Chaucer to Cowper*, 21 vols. (London); Robert Dodsley, 1751–63 *A Collection of Poems in Six Volumes, by Several Hands* (5th ed. London); George Pearch, 1783 *A Collection of Poems in Four Volumes, by Several Hands*, 4 vols. (London); James Ralph, 1729 *Miscellaneous Poems, by Several Hands* (London); Samuel Whyte, 1772 *The Shamrock: or, Hibernian Cresses* (Dublin); *The British Magazine and Review*, 1782–83, 3 vols. (London).

Ager, Thomas. 1794. "The Schoolmaster, a Poem in Imitation of Spenser's Style" in *Musae Berkhamstediensis* (London). Spenserian stanzas.

Akenside, Mark. 1745. *Odes on Several Subjects* (London). Several odes are reminiscent of Spenserian and Prior stanzas. "Ode VIII: On Leaving Holland" is in 4 stanzas, *ababcdcdC*, an adaptation of the Spenserian stanza. "Ode to Sleep" (rpt. in Pearch 1783 vol. 3) is in 6 Prior stanzas.

———. 1737. "The Virtuoso" *GentM* 7:244. In 10 Spenserian stanzas.

———. 1758. *An Ode to the Country Gentlemen of England* (London). *ababccdeeD*.

Andrews, James. 1789. "A Description of the Fairy Morgana" (trans. from Boiardo) in *Anecdotes, &c. Antient and Modern, with Observations* (London). *ababcddc*.

[Armstrong, John]. 1748. "An Imitation of Spencer Written at Mr. Thomson's Desire, to be Inserted into the Castle of Indolence" in *Miscellanies, by John Armstrong, M.D. in Two Volumes I* (titled *Imitations of Shakespeare and Spencer*) (London 1770). Four Spenserian stanzas, the final ones for Thomson's *Castle of Indolence* canto 1 (see Thomson 1748, below).

[Arnold, Cornelius]. 1755. *The Mirror: A Poetical Essay, in the Manner of Spenser* (London). In 44 Spenserian stanzas. A burlesque.

Atwood, William. See Matthew Prior.

Aylett, Robert. 1621. *The Song of Songs, Which was Salomons, Metaphrased in English Heroicks . . . With Certayne of the Brides Ornaments* [repr. 1654 as *Divine, and Moral Speculations*]. Imitation of "Prothalamion" in Spenserian stanzas; *The Brides Ornaments* in Spenserian stanzas and owes to *Faerie Queene* 1.10. 1625 *The Brides Ornaments*, books 3 and 4 in Spenserian stanzas. 1622 *Thrifts Equipage* [repr. 1654 as *Divine, and Moral Speculations*] in Spenserian stanzas (the 5th meditation, "Of Death," an adaptation of *Faerie Queene* 1.9).

Bagot, Lewis. 1755. "Imitation of the Epithalamion" *Gratulatio Academiae Cantabrigiensis* (Cambridge). *Epith.* stanza.

Barbauld, Anna. ca. 1780. "Love and Time, to Mrs. Mulso" in her *Works* (London 1802). *ababcc.*

———. "Stanzas in the Manner of Spenser." Five Spenserian stanzas.

[Baynes, John]. 1782. *An Archaelogical Epistle to the Reverend and Worshipful Jeremiah Milles D.D. Dean of Exeter* (London). *ababcc.*

Beattie, James. 1771. *The Minstrel, or The Progress of Genius: A Poem, Book the First* (Edinburgh). In 60 Spenserian stanzas.

———. 1774. *The Minstrel, or The Progress of Genius, the Second Book* (London). In 63 Spenserian stanzas. Four eds. of book 1 by 1774, when book 2 was pub. Rpt. of books 1–2 in Bell 1789–90, vol. 10.

Beaumont, Joseph. 1702. *Psyche, or Love's Mystery, in XXIV. Cantos: Displaying the Intercourse betwixt Christ, and the Soul* (Cambridge) 2nd ed. (first ed. 1648, in 20 cantos). Spenser imitation in stanzas *ababcc.*

Bedingfield, Robert. 1747. "The Education of Achilles" in Bell 1789–90 vol. 11. In 14 Spenserian stanzas. First pub. in *The Museum* 3 (1747). Cf. West's *Education.*

[Bicknell, Alexander?]. 1779. *Prince Arthur: An Allegorical Romance; The Story from Spenser, in Two Volumes* (London). Prose. Donald Cheney has determined that aside from title page differences this is the same work as *Una and Arthur* 2 vols. in 1 (Cambridge 1779).

Bidlake, John. 1797. *The Country Parson* (London). In 48 Spenserian stanzas.

Blacklock, Thomas. 1746. "Hymn to Divine Love" in his *Poems on Several Occasions* (Glasgow). *ababbcc*.

———. 1752. "Philantheus" in his *Poems* (Edinburgh 1754). *ababbcc*.

Blake, William. 1783. "An Imitation of Spenser" in his *Poetical Sketches* (London). In 6 near-Spenserian stanzas.

Bowdler, Jane. 1786. "Envy: A Fragment" in her *Poems and Essays by a Lady* (Bath). In 14 Spenserian stanzas.

Bowles, William Lisle. 1796. "Hope, an Allegorical Sketch, on Recovering Slowly from Sickness" in his *Poetical Works* (London 1885) vol. 1. In 30 Prior stanzas.

Boyd, Henry. 1780a. *Orlando* (London). In 92 Spenserian stanzas (part of this poem is appended to his 1785 tr. of Dante's *Inferno* [London]).

———. [1780]b. *The Woodman's Tale, after the Manner of Spenser* (London 1805). In 325 Spenserian stanzas.

———. 1793. "Specimen of the Captives, a Romance" in his *Poems* (Dublin). In 123 Spenserian stanzas.

[Boyse, Samuel]. [1736]a. *The Olive: An Ode, Occasion'd by the Auspicious Success of His Majesty's Counsels, and His Majesty's Most Happy Return, in the Stanza of Spenser* (London 1737). Prior stanzas.

———. [1736]b. "Part of Psalm XLII, in Imitation of the Style of Spenser" in his *Translations and Poems, Written On Several Occasions* (London 1738). *ababcc*.

———. 1740a. "The Character and Speech of Cosroes the Mede: An Improvement in the Squire's Tale of Chaucer, in the Manner of Spenser, Inscrib'd to George Ogle, Esq" *GentM* 10:404–05. In 18 Prior stanzas.

———. 1740b. "An Ode Sacred to the Birth of the Marquis of Tavistock" *GentM* 10:83–84. In 12 Prior stanzas.

———. [ca. 1740]. "The Vision of Patience, Sacred to the Memory of Mr Alexander Cuming, A Young Gentleman Unfortunately Lost in the Northern Ocean on his Return from China, 1740" in Bell 1789–90, vol. 11. In 26 Prior stanzas.

———. 1743. "Stanza's from Albion's triumph: An Ode, Occasioned by the Happy Success of His Majesty's Arms on the Maine" *GentM* 13:378. In 5 Prior stanzas, nos. 13–15 and 19–20 *Albion's Triumph . . . in the Stanza of Spencer* (London 1743); this poem is mostly in Prior stanzas also.

———. 1748. "Irene: An Heroic Ode, in the Stanza of Spencer" *GentM* 18:517. Three Prior stanzas, part of a longer *Irene: An Heroic Ode, in the Stanza of Spencer* (London 1748).

———. [ca. 1738]. "Stanzas Occasioned by Mr. Pope's Translation of Horace, Book IV, Ode 1, Addressed to the Honourable Mr. M–" in his *Translations* (1783; see Boyse [1736]b above). Prior stanzas. See "To a Lover" below.

Boyse, Samuel and George Ogle. See Joseph Sterling.

The British Hero, or The Vision: A Poem, Sacred to the Immortal Memory of John, Late Duke of Marlborough 1733. (London). *aabbccb*. [by Francis Manning?]

Browne, Moses. 1729. *Piscatory Eclogues* (London). Couplets and varying stanzas. Cf. his Spenserian 1755 "Percy-lodge . . . a Poem" (London).

Burges, Sir James. 1800. *Richard the First: A Poem* (London). In 1,849 Spenserian stanzas.

———. 1796. *The Birth and Triumph of Love* (London). In 112 Spenserian stanzas (with P. Tomkins's plates).

Burns, Robert. 1784. "Stanzas on the Same Occasion [i. e., the prospect of death]" in *Poems, Chiefly in the Scottish Dialect, by Robert Burns* (Edinburgh 1787). In 3 Spenserian stanzas.

———. 1786. "The Cotter's Saturday Night, Inscribed to R.A.****, Esq" in *Poems Chiefly in the Scottish Dialect, by Robert Burns* (Kilmarnock). In 21 Spenserian stanzas.

Calendarium Pastorale . . . Nunc autem eleganti Latino carmine donatae a Theodoro Bathurst, ed. John Ball. [1730]. (London; another ed. in 1732 and a reissue in 1735). Latin-English ed. of Spenser's *Shepheardes Calender* has a biographical sketch (in Latin only): "De Vita Spenseri, & Scriptis." *SC* is in Latin-English facing, with a glossary of "uncommon words" in *SC*, but one "which may be also of Use for the better understanding the Fairy Queen, and other Writings of *Spenser*" (247). The black-white pictures, one for each eclogue, by P. Fourdrinier, should be compared to Hughes (1715) and Birch-Kent (1751): some show rustics in early 18th century dress; others are in Elizabethan dress (e. g. April eclogue). All are dressed; none looks like a shepherd; a few have a simple, childlike allegorical overlay (e. g. March eclogue).

Cambridge, Richard. 1736. "The Marriage of Frederick" in Chalmers 1810 vol. 18. Prior stanzas.

————. [ca. 1740]. "Archimage" in Chalmers 1810 vol 18. In 29 Spenserian stanzas.

Cary, Henry F. 1789. sonnets in his *Memoirs* (London 1847) vol. 1. Two Spenserian sonnets.

Case, W. Jr. 1800. "Descriptive Sketch" in *Poetical Register . . . for 1801* (London). In 17 Spenserian stanzas.

The Cetus: A Mask ca. 1783? British Library Egerton MS 3507. A three-act imitation of *Faerie Queene* 2, 4 and Milton's *Comus*.

Chatterton, Thomas. ca. 1770. In 1777 *Poems*: some Rowley poems are imitations. See "Elinour and Juga" below.

Chettle, Henry. 1600. *Englands Helicon*, wherein "A Pastorall Song betweene Phillis and Amarillis," an imitation of *SC* August.

Coleridge, Samuel Taylor. 1795. "Epistle IV, to the Author of Poems Published Anonymously at Bristol, in September, 1795" in his *Poems* (1796; see Coleridge [1796?] below). Five Spenserian stanzas. Called "Lines Addressed to Joseph Cottle" in the 2nd ed. (1797). Cottle, Coleridge's friend, was a poet who wrote "Monody on John Henderson" in Spenserian stanzas.

————. [1796?]. "Effusion XXIV, in the Manner of Spenser" in his *Poems on Various Subjects* (London 1796) [very rare]. Five Spenserian stanzas, addressed to the Rev. W. L. Bowles, himself a Spenserian.

Colin Clout's Madrigal, on the Auspicious First of March,1727–8, Being the Anniversary of Her Majesty's Birthday. 1728. (London).

Collins, William. 1739. *Eclogues* (London 1742). Rpt. in 1757 as *Oriental Eclogues* and in Pearch 1768 *Collection of Poems*.

————. 1747. *Odes on Several Descriptive and Allegoric Subjects* (London). Lonsdale 1969 demonstrates how imitative of Spenser are Collins 1739 and Collins 1747.

Combe, William. 1775. *Clifton: A Poem, in Imitation of Spenser* (Bristol). In 30 Spenserian stanzas. Cf. Henry Jones 1773. *Clifton: A Poem, in Two Cantos* 2nd ed. (Bristol), which does not appear to be a Spenser imitation.

"The Consolation." 1729. *The Flying-Post, or Weekly Medley* (12 July). Four Prior stanzas.

"The Contest, A Pastoral." 1777. In *Town and Country Magazine* (London) 9:439. Couplets.

Cottle, Joseph. See Samuel Taylor Coleridge.

"The Country Curate." 1737. *GentM* 7:52–53. In 12 stanzas *ababbcC*.

"The Country Meeting." 1787. In *EurM* 12:233. In 12 stanzas *ababbcdcdd*. Signed "T. J." A burlesque.

"The Country Parson." 1737. *GentM* 7:52–53. Twelve stanzas *ababbcC*.

"The Court of Excess." 1800. *EurM* 38:128–30. In 21 stanzas *ababcdcD*.

"The Court of Truth, In the Manner of Spenser." ca. midcentury. In *Poetical Amusements at a Villa Near Bath* (London 1776 3rd ed.) vol. 2. Eight Spenserian stanzas.

Courtier, P. L. 1800. *The Pleasures of Solitude*. Supposedly in Spenserian stanzas, but not found in Courtier's 2-vol. *Lyre of Love* (London 1806).

"The Courtier." 1729. In Ralph 1729. Seven pp. of blank verse.

[Cowper, William]. 1781. *Anti-Thelyphthora: A Tale in Verse* in his *Poetical Works* (London 1867) vol. 2. Couplets.

[Croxall, William]. 1713. *An Original Canto of Spencer, Design'd as Part of His Fairy Queen, but Never Printed, Now Made Public, by Nestor Ironside, Esq* (London 1714). On dating, see D. F. Foxon 1975 *English Verse 1701–1750: A Catalogue* (Cambridge) p. 154. In 46 Spenserian stanzas. See *The Examiner Examin'd, in a Letter to the Englishman: Occasion'd by the Examiner of Friday Dec. 18, 1713, upon the Canto of Spencer* [by Samuel Croxall] 1713 (London).

————. 1714a. *Another Original Canto of Spencer, Design'd as Part of His Fairy Queen, but Never Printed, Now Made Publick, by Nestor Ironside, Esq* (London). In 54 Spenserian stanzas.

————. 1714b. *An Ode Humbly Inscrib'd to the King, Occasion'd by His Majesty's Most Auspicious Succession and Arrival, Written in the Stanza and Measure of Spenser, by Mr. Croxall, Author of the Two Original Canto's, Etc* (London). Dedicated to the Rt. Hon. Thomas, Earl of Wharton, Lord Privy Seal. In 42 Spenserian stanzas.

————. [ca. 1720]. "On Florinda Seen While She Was Bathing" in *The Fair Circassian: A Dramatic Performance . . . to Which Are Added Several Occasional Poems* (London 1720).

Davison, Francis. 1602. *A Poetical Rapsody Containing Diuerse Sonnets, Odes . . . and other Poesies*, wherein Eclogue 1 imitates Jan. and Nov. eclogues of *SC*; 2nd ed. of 1608, wherein "A Complaint Of which all the staves end with the words of the first, like a

Sestine," an imitation of stanza 1 of Spenser's sestina of *SC* Aug. Eclogue.

Denton, Thomas. 1754. "Immortality, or The Consolation of Human Life: A Monody" in Dodsley ed. 1758–63 vol. 5. In 31 Prior stanzas.

―――. 1762. "The House of Superstition: A Vision" in Bell 1789–90 vol. 11. Thirteen Prior stanzas (the Catholic Church cf. to Spenser's Errour).

Dermody, Thomas. 1792. *Poems Consisting of Essays, Lyric, Elegiac, Etc* (Dublin 3 includes 3 imitations). (1) "Sonnet." One Spenserian stanza against hunting. Poetic diction perhaps reaches its nadir with "fatal tube" for gun. In his "Postcript" to "Memory: A Poem" in this volume, Dermody's sentimentality is clear. After confessing to copying the "language of sweetness" of Spenser's age, he allows that "One tear [shed over his poem on "Memory"] from the eye of feeling, is, in my opinion, more precious than the superfluous plaudits of a million." (2) "Sonnet, to the Rev. Mr. Sterling." Two Spenserian stanzas. (3) "To the Right Honourable the Countess of Moira [*nee* Lady Elizabeth Hastings, his patron]." One Spenserian stanza serving as dedication to the volume. Dermody published his poems in several editions from 1792 to 1802. Many of his many imitations are in the 2-vol. ed. of his works, titled *The Harp of Erin* (London 1807): "The Cave of Ignorance, in Two Cantos" in 24 Spenserian stanzas; "Farewell to Joy," "The Winter's Night," "The Progress of Pedantry," "The Vanity of Hope," "The Cave of Patronage," and "Prince Scrapin or the Enchanted Hind," all in *ababbcdcdd*; "The Vision of Fancy" in 10 Spenserian stanzas; "The Coffee House" in near-Prior stanzas.

―――. [ca. 1792]a. "The Enthusiast" in his 1802 *Poems on Various Subjects* (London). In 16 Spenserian stanzas. This series of "delightful dreams" and "faery scenes" has been read as a satire on liberalism.

―――. [ca. 1792]b. "The Pleasures of Poesy, in Spenser's Stanza" in his *Poems on Various Subjects* (1802; see Dermody [ca. 1792]a above). In 16 Spenserian stanzas.

"De Sacrobosco" [John Holywood?]. 1794. "The Trumpet-Call—1794" in *GentM* 67 (1797):324. Six Prior stanzas.

[Dodsley, Robert]. 1744a. *Melpomene, or The Regions of Terror and Pity: An Ode* (London 1757). *ababccdD*.

―――. 1744b. "On the Death of Mr. Pope" *GentM* 14:447. *ababcC*. Two stanzas of 1 section are imitative of *SC*.

————. 1745. "Pain and Patience: An Ode" in his *Trifles* (London). Seventeen stanzas of *ababcC*. On Spenser imitations in Dodsley's *Collections*, Lord Byron in an 1814 letter to publisher John Murray judges that "Dodsley was I believe the last decent thing of the kind, & his [anthologies] had great success in its day and lasted several years; but then he had the double advantage of editing and publishing—the 'Spleen' and several of Gray's odes, much of Shenstone and many others of good repute, made their first appearance in his collection": quoted by W. P. Courtney in "Dodsley's Famous Collection," 361: see bibliography B.

Downman, Hugh. 1768. *The Land of the Muses: A Poem in the Manner of Spenser, with Poems on Several Occasions* (Edinburgh). In 85 Spenserian stanzas, changed to couplets in his *Poems* 1791. Downman 1790 *Poems* (Exeter), writes this to another Spenserian, "To Dr. Blacklock," on imitating Spenser: ". . . and dress'd my thoughts in *Spenser's* antique style, / 'Twas but a frolic task, a youthful play. . . ."

Doyne, Philip. 1763. *The Triumph of Parnassus: A Poem on the Birth of His Royal Highness the Prince of Wales* (London). Noteworthy only because in both Prior and (18) Spenserian stanzas. See "Irene" below.

Drayton, Michael. 1748. *Works* (1st collected ed., London). Printed by Spenser editor John Hughes.

Edwards, Thomas. 1765 and 1780. sonnets in *The Sonnets of Thomas Edwards* (1765, 1780) ed. Dennis G. Donovan, Augustan Reprint Society 64 (Los Angeles 1974). Four of Edwards's 52 sonnets are in the Spenserian *ababbcbccdcdee*; most are Petrarchan. Among the "irregular" sonnets is "Sonnet VIII: On the Cantos of Spenser's Fairy Queen, Lost in the Passage from Ireland" in Robert Dodsley 1748 *A Collection of Poems in Three Volumes, by Several Hands* 2nd ed. (London) vol. 2. See Hester Chapone's reaction to reading Edwards' sonnets: *Miscellanies* (London 1775) 127–28 and his response to her on p. 129.

"Elinour and Juga; Modernized from Chatterton." 1790. In *EurM* 18:224. *ababbcc*.

[Emily, Charles]. 1755. "The Praises of Isis: A Poem, Written MDCCLV, by the Same" (i. e., by same author as the previous poem *Death*; see Emily 1762, below) in Pearch 1783 vol. 1. Blank verse. Emily 1762 *Death* in Pearch 1783 vol. 1. In 18 sonnets considered by Hook to be imitative of Spenser; their rhyme scheme, however, is *ababcdcdefefgg*, the Shakespearean or English form, of course.

Enort, Thomas. 1797. "Sonnet to the Sky-Lark by Thomas Enort" *EurM* 32:40. One Spenserian sonnet.

Epicedia Oxoniensa. 1751. (Oxford) has several imitations in several Spenser and Prior forms.

"Epithalamium." 1729. In Ralph 1729. Couplets. Marginally an imitation.

"Epithalamium, by the Same ["Mr. D–"]." [ca. 1758]. In Dodsley ed. 1758–63 vol 5. Irregular stanzas.

Erskine, Andrew. 1757. "Ode to Fear" *GentM* 27:228. In 10 ten-line stanzas, some of which are Prior stanzas.

Fanshawe, Sir Richard. 1648. *Il Pastor Fido,* 2nd ed. wherein "The Progress of Learning" in Spenserian stanzas, as is the adaptation of Spenserian stanza in "The Fourth Booke of Virgills Aeneis On the Loves of Dido and Aeneas."

———. 1648. *The Faerie Leveller . . . A lively representation of our times* (London).

[Fenton, Elijah]. 1707. "An Ode to the Sun, for the New Year, 1707" *Poems on Several Occasions* (London 1717). Several of the 24 stanzas, numbered from 1 to 3 cyclically throughout, are Prior stanzas.

Fergusson, Robert. 1773. "The Farmer's Ingle" in his *Poems* (Edinburgh). *ababcdcdD.*

Fletcher, Giles, and Phineas Fletcher. 1783. *The Purple Island, or The Isle of Man: An Allegorical Poem* [1623], *by Phineas Fletcher, Esteemed the Spenser of His Age; To Which Is Added Christ's Victory and Triumph* [1610]: *A Poem, in Four Parts, by Giles Fletcher, Both Written in the Last Century* (London). Rpt. of 17th century Spenser imitations. *The Purple Island* is in eight-line modified Spenserian stanzas.

Fosbroke, Thomas Dudley. 1796. *The Economy of Monastic Life* (London 1802). In 85 Spenserian stanzas.

"Fragment, in the Style of Spenser, Being an Introduction to an Intended Continuation of the Canto of Mutability." 1789. In *A Collection of Poems, Mostly Original* (Dublin). Poem signed "W. B."

"Fragment of Horace's Ode, in Praise of Pindar." 1771. *GentM* 41:327. *ababcC.*

Gay, John. 1714. *The Shepherd's Week, in Six Pastorals, by Mr. J. Gay* (London). Couplets. Cf. Lady Mary Wortley Montague 1747

Six Town Eclogue with Some Other Poems (London) (in the manner of Gay's Monday–Saturday approach, but quite distant from Spenser), pub. as *Town Eclogues* in 1716.

Gibbons, Thomas. 1750. "An Elegiac Ode on the Death of the Reverend Mr. Mordecai Andrews" in his *Juvenelia* (London?). *ababcC*.

Godwin, William. 1784. "Inkle and Yariko" in *Four Early Pamphlets 1783–84*, ed. Burton R. Pollin (Gainesville FL 1966). Eight Spenserian stanzas.

Gray, Thomas. 1742–68. *Poems by Mr. Gray* (London 1768). Lonsdale 1969 shows how imitative of Spenser Gray was in his hymns, *Elegy* and odes (both "regular" and Pindaric). Especially impressive is Gray's detailed knowledge of Spenser's works other than *FQ*. See Dodsley above.

Green, Maurice. 1739. *Spenser's Amoretti, A Collection of Twenty-Five Sonnets* (London). With music.

[Hamilton, William]. 1748. "On Seeing a Lady Sit to Her Picture, in Imitation of Spencer's Stile" *Poems on Several Occasions* (Glasgow). *abab*.

Hayes, Samuel. See James Scott.

Henry and Minerva: A Poem. 1729. (London). Couplets ["B.J.," Esq."]

Holywood, John. See "De Sacrobosco."

Hoole, Samuel. 1787. "Edward, or, the Curate" (London). *ababcdcd*.

"The House of Care, in Imitation of Spenser's Faery Queen." 1786. *GentM* 60 (Aug.): 696–97. Eight Spenserian stanzas.

Hunt, Leigh. 1786. "The Palace of Pleasure" in *Juvenalia, or a Collection of Poems, Written between the Ages of Twelve and Sixteen* (London 1801). In 130 Spenserian stanzas.

Hunt, "Miss." 1786. "On Visiting the Ruins of an Ancient Abbey in Devonshire, September, MDCCLXXXVI, by a Young Lady" *GentM* 60 (Oct.): 885. Six Spenserian stanzas.

An Hymn to Harmony, in Imitation of Spencer. 1729. (London).

"An Imitation of Spencer's Fairy Queen: A Fragment, by a Gentleman of Twenty." 1729. In Ralph 1729. Decasyllabic couplets rendering *FQ* 7.7. Davies identifies as by T. Gardner.

"An Imitation of Spenser." 1750. *The Student, or The Oxford and Cambridge Monthly Miscellany* 5 (31 May): 198–99. Six Spenserian stanzas.

"Industry and Genius, or The Origin of Birmingham: A Fable, Attempted in the Manner of Spencer, to Mr. Baskerville." 1751. *The London Magazine* 20:37. Seven Spenserian stanzas.

"Irene, A Canto, on the Peace, Inscribed to the Provost and Fellows of Trinity College." ca. 1772. In *The Shamrock* (Dublin). In 49 Spenserian stanzas. Davies gives the author as Samuel Whyte, Hook as Philip Doyne.

Jones, Henry. See William Combe.

Jones, Sir William. 1767. "The Seven Fountains" and 1769 "The Palace of Fortune" in *Poems* (Oxford 1772). Both in couplets.

Jortin, John. 1729. *A Hymn to Harmony* (London). *ababbcc.* Foxon mentions the ode as advertised "in imitation of Spencer."

Knevett, Ralph. 1637. *Funeral Elegies*, number 3 of which is in 20 Spenserian stanzas.

Lamb, Charles. 1797. "A Vision of Repentance" in *Poems, by S. T. Coleridge, Second Edition; To Which Are Now Added Poems by Charles Lamb, and Charles Lloyd* (London). In 6 *ababcc* stanzas and 23 octosyllabic couplets. See Lamb's comparison of Cowper to Spenser: "To the Poet Cowper on His Recovery from an Indisposition" *Monthly Magazine* (Dec. 1796).

Leapor, Mary. [ca. 1743]. "The Temple of Love" in her *Poems upon Several Occasions* (London 1748). Couplets.

"Liberty, In the Manner of Spenser." 1783. In *British Magazine and Review* (London) vol. 2. Six Prior stanzas signed "A. Z."

Lloyd, Charles. 1794. "A Poetical Effusion, Written after a Journey into North Wales, February, 1794" in his *Poems* 3rd ed. (London 1819). Dated Feb. 1794. Six Spenserian stanzas. This is the first poem in this volume which is quite reminiscent of Wordsworth. A four-stanza version of it ("Stanzas, Written after a Journey into North Wales") is in *Poems, by S. T. Coleridge* 2nd ed. (see Lamb 1797 above).

———. 1799. "Lines to a Brother and Sister, Written Soon after a Recovery from Sickness" in his 1819 *Poems*. Signed "6th April, 1799." Ten Spenserian stanzas.

———. 1795. *Oswald: A Poem* (Carlisle) in his 1797 *Poems* (Bristol). In 46 Spenserian stanzas.

———. 1819. "Stanzas. Let the Reader Determine Their Title" in *Poems*. In 28 Spenserian stanzas.

Lloyd, Robert. 1751. *The Progress of Envy: A Poem, in Imitation of Spenser, Occasioned by Lauder's Attack on the Character of Milton, Inscribed to the Right Honourable the Earl of Bath* (London). The dedication identifies the Earl of Bath as "Patron of Milton, and his Vindicators." Poem in 30 altered Spenserian stanzas: *ababcdcdD*. Cf. Lloyd, *The Connoisseur* 67 (1755) on Spenser imitations.

Llwyd, Richard. ca. 1790. One Spenserian stanza in his *Poetical Works* (London 1837).

Lowth, Robert (the Rev. Dr. Lowth was Bishop of London). 1747. "The Choice of Hercules" in Bell 1789–90 vol. 11 (first pub. in Joseph Spence 1747 *Polymetis* [London]). In 27 Prior stanzas. Cf. Shenstone "Judgment of Hercules"; the anon. "Choice of Hercules" above. Cf. the indebted ca. 1772 anon. "The Choice of Hercules, An Ode, for Music" in *The Shamrock* (Dublin 1772); Walpole discloses that "part of this poem has been set to music by Handel." Irregular stanzas. Cf. 1761 anon. Spenser burlesque "A Familiar Epistle, from a Law-student in the Country, to His Friend, at the Temple" in *The Shamrock* (see above): 285–303. Spenserian William Mason (memoir in Spenserian William Whitehead's *Poems*, vol. 3.18) calls Lowth's poem a school exercise. See Mason and Whitehead below.

MacDonald, Andrew. 1782. "Velina" and "Minvela" in *Miscellaneous Works* (London 1791). In 99 and 19 Spenserian stanzas respectively.

———. 1791. "New Probationary Odes for the Laureateship" in *Miscellaneous Works* (London). Six Spenserian stanzas.

Mackenzie, Henry. ca. 1765. "The Old Batchelor, After the Manner of Spenser" and ca. 1765 "The Old Maid, After the Same Manner" in his *Works* (London 1808), vol. 8. In 14 and 8 Prior stanzas respectively. Both are burlesques of Spenser.

[Mason, William]. [ca. 1744]. *Musaeus: A Monody to the Memory of Mr. Pope, in Imitation of Milton's Lycidas* (London 1747). 3 eds. by 1748. The first 2 stanzas of Colin Clout's speech "as they relate to Pastoral, are written in the measure which Spenser uses in the first eclogue of the *Shepherd's Calendar*; the rest, where he speaks of Fable, are in the stanza of the *Faery Queen*." Thomas Gray considers the imitation as "a promise at least of something good to come." See Mason as imitator in William Rider 1762 *An Historical and Critical Account of the Living Authors of Great-Britain* ed. O. M. Brack Jr., Augustan Reprint Society 163 (Los Angeles 1974). "In the year of his death [1771] William Mason presented to the College [Pembroke] some chairs for the Master's lodge and a painting of Edmund Spenser, a copy made by Benjamin Wilson from an original now lost": *Pembroke College Cambridge: A Short History*, ed. S. C. Roberts (Cambridge: Cambridge UP, 1936), 102.

Melmoth, William. [ca. 1743]. "The Transformation of Lycon and Euphormius" in Bell 1789–90 vol. 10. Previously pub. in *Fitzosborne's* [Melmoth's pseudonym] *Letters 2* (London 1749). In 19 Spenserian stanzas.

Mendez, Moses. [ca. 1748]. Spenserian stanza on Thomson in *EurM* 22 (1792):517. One stanza.

———. 1751. *The Seasons* (London, rpt. [anonymous] Dublin 1752). In 35 Spenserian stanzas (8 for each season and 3 more as an introduction which testily strikes at critics of the four seasons to follow).

———. [ca. 1751]. "The Squire of Dames: A Poem, in Spenser's Stile" in Robert Dodsley 1755 *A Collection of Poems in Four Volumes, by Several Hands* 4 (London) rpt. in Dodsley ed. 1758–63. In 82 Spenserian stanzas in imitation of *FQ* 3.7 (5 stanzas of prologue, canto 1 of 35 stanzas, canto 2 of 42 stanzas).

———. 1752–58. "The Blatant Beast: A Poem, in Spenser's Style" *EurM* 22 (1792) 331–36, 417–22. Canto 1 in 48 Spenserian stanzas, canto 2 in 46.

Merivale, John H. [ca. 1798]. "The Minstrel" in his *Poems Original and Translated* (London 1806). In 69 Spenserian stanzas owing to Beattie's *Minstrel*. In this volume are two other of his imitations (both in variant Spenserian stanzas): "St. George and the Dragon" and "St. Denis and the Mulberry Tree." *abbaccdde*.

[Mickle, William Julius]. 1767. *The Concubine: A Poem, in Two Cantos, in the Manner of Spenser* (pub. separately at Oxford and Cambridge). At least four editions by 1772; rev. as *Sir Martyn: A Poem, in the Manner of Spenser, by William Julius Mickle* (London 1777). In two cantos of 73 and 64 Spenserian stanzas.

———. ca. 1770. "An Inscription on an Obelisk at Langford" in Chalmers 1810 vol. 17:523. One Spenserian stanza.

———. 1776. "On the Neglect of Poetry" in Chalmers 1810 vol. 17:553. Eight Spenserian stanzas.

Miller, J. 1754. "The Sloe-Ey'd Maid: A Pastoral" in his *Poems on Several Occasions* (London). Couplets.

More, Henry. 1647. *A Platonick Song of the Soul*. Spenserian stanzas.

Morell, Thomas. [ca. 1747]. "To Mr. Thomson, on His Unfinished Plan of a Poem Called the Castle of Indolence, in Spencer's Style" in Chalmers 1810 vol. 12:467. Spenserian stanzas.

————. 1742. "Verses on a Silk Work." Four stanzas.

"Morning: An Ode, Written by a Student Confined to College." 1770. *GentM* 40:232. *ababcC.*

Mother Hubbards Tale of the Ape and Fox, Abbreviated from Spenser. 1715 (London). These eight pages are supposedly a "Jacobite parody of Spenser's poem" according to British Museum Catalogue. Octavo ed. "with the obsolete words explained" pub. London 1784. Cf. 1733 "Part of Mother Hubbard's Tale, from Spencer" *London Magazine* 2 (Sept. 1733).

A New Occasional Oratorio, As It Is Perform'd at the Theatre-Royal in Covent-Garden, the Words Taken from Milton, Spenser, Etc. and Set to Musik by Mr. Handel. 1746. (London). On the "suppression of the Rebellion" according to British Museum Catalogue.

Niccols, Richard. ca. 1603. *The Beggars Ape* (London 1627). Imitation of *Mother Hubberds Tale.*

"Ode on British Freedom." 1772. In *The Shamrock* (Dublin) 207–16. Near-Spenserian stanzas.

"Ode on the King's Nuptials." 1772. In *The Shamrock* (Dublin) 352–56. *ababcC.*

"Ode to Genius." 1792. In *Poems, Chiefly by Gentlemen of Devonshire and Cornwall* (Bath). Near-Spenserian stanzas.

Ogilivie, John. 1769. "Solitude, or the Elysium of the Poets" in *Poems on Several Subjects* (London). *abab.*

"On Happiness and Palinodia." 1731. In James Husband *Miscellany of Poems by Several Hands* (London). *ababcC.*

"On Hope." ca. 1730. In *The Polite Correspondence* n.d. One 8-line stanza *ababcdcd.*

"On the Tree." 1799. In *Monthly Mirror* 7 (1799) 107. *ababbacc.* Signed "C. L."

"P." 1755. "Sonnet, by Dr. P–, Occasioned by Leaving B-X-N, July 1755, the Author Telling the Ladies 'He Looked upon Himself in a Worse Situation than Adam Banish'd Paradise,' Was Enjoined by Them to Give His Reasons in Verse" in Pearch 1783 vol. 3. *ababbcbccdcdee.*

Park, Thomas. 1797. "Stanzas on the Death of Dame Morris" in *Sonnets and Other Small Poems* (London). *ababbcbcc.*

Pasquils Palinodia, and His progresse to the Taverne. 1619. (Parody of the opening of *Faerie Queene*).

"A Pastoral: Digon Davy and Colin Clout." [1743?]. In Timothy Silence, ed. 1764 *The Foundling Hospital for Wit, Intended for the Reception and Preservation of Such Brats of Wit and Humour, Whose Parents Chuse to Drop Them, Number V* (London).

"A Pastoral, in Imitation of Spenser." 1741. *The Publick Register, or The Weekly Magazine* (7 March): no page. In 22 stanzas *ababcc.*

Peacham, Henry. 1613. *The Period of Mourning. Disposed into six Visions,* the 3rd of which is an imitation of *Faerie Queene* book 1's Wood of Error and Cave of Despair.

———. 1615. *Prince Henrie revived* (Heir Apparent to Frederick Count Palatine and Princess Elizabeth). Four Spenserian stanzas and an imperfect 5th (8 lines): one stanza of which is an encomium on the late Queen Elizabeth.

"The Peasant's Sabbath" (after Robert Burns's *The Cotter's Saturday Night*). ca. 1799. In *Poetical Magazine* 4 (1811) 167. In 21 Spenserian stanzas signed "M."

Penrose, Thomas. 1781. "The Hermit's Vision" in his *Poems* (London). *ababcc* usually.

Percy, Thomas. [ca. 1755]. Two Spenserian sonnets in Pearch 1783 vol. 3.

Philips, Ambrose. 1709. *Poetical Miscellanies: The Sixth Part, Containing a Collection of Original Poems, with Several New Translations, by the Most Eminent Hands* (London). (Also includes Pope's *Pastorals*.) Six pastorals of decasyllabic couplets in imitation of *SC*. In his Life of Philips, Dr. Johnson avers that "Philips had taken Spenser and Pope took Virgil for his [pastoral] pattern."

["Philisides"]. 1758. *The Shepherd's Calender, Being Twelve Pastorals Attempted in Blank Verse, the Subjects Partly Taken from the Select Pastorals of Spenser and Sir Philip Sidney* (Dublin). Blank verse.

Philpot, Charles. See James Scott.

"A Pindarick Ode in Imitation of Spencer's Divine Love, Inscrib'd to Mrs. Katherine Bridgemann, Unfinish'd." 1726. In *Poems on Several Occasions, by a Lady* [Elizabeth Thomas?] (London). *ababb.*

[Pitt, Christopher]. 1747. "The Jordan" in *Poems by the Celebrated Translator of Virgil's Aneid; Together with The Jordan: A Poem, in Imitation of Spenser, by—, Esq* (London 1756). Six Spenserian stanzas. Cf. 1768 anon. Spenser burlesque "The Hermite's Addresse to Youthe" in *London Magazine* 37 (Aug.) 438.

Polwhele, Richard. 1795–96. "The Ancient and Modern Patriot Contrasted, 1795" in his *Poetic Trifles* (London 1796). Six Spenserian stanzas. Contains other imitations in Spenserian stanzas ("The Banished Poet" in 2 stanzas, "A Swiss Scene" in 4 stanzas) including, in 2nd ed., Polwhele 1798 "The Influence of Local Attachment, with Respect to Home: A Poem, in Seven Books." In 166 Spenserian stanzas. Originally part of the preceding poem is "Ellen and Danvert, A Tale" in 29 Spenserian stanzas (1798 rev. edn. vol. 2).

———. 1799. "Grecian Prospects" (London). Spenserian stanzas.

Pope, Alexander. [ca. 1706]. "The Alley" in Motte 1727 *Miscellanies in Prose and Verse* 4 (London). Six Spenserian stanzas.

Porteus, Beilby. See James Scott.

Potter, Robert. 1749. *A Farewell Hymne to the Country, Attempted in the Manner of Spenser's Epithalamion, by Mr. Potter* (London). In 19 irregular stanzas, most long.

———. 1758. *Kymber: A Monody to Sir Armine Wodehouse* (London). Long stanzas.

———. ante 1774. "An Imitation of Spenser" in his *Poems* (London 1774). Long stanzas.

Prior, Matthew. 1706. *An Ode, Humbly Inscrib'd to the Queen, on the Glorious Success of Her Majesty's Arms, 1706, Written in Imitation of Spencer's Stile* (London). For a long explication of this ode, see his *Miscellaneous Works* vol. 1 of 2 (Dublin 1739?). Prior's ode, a panegyric of both Queen Anne and Marlborough, is in 35 Prior stanzas: 10 lines *ababcdcdeE*, the last alexandrine. For a contemporary attack on Prior's influential *Ode*, see William Atwood 1706 *A Modern Inscription to the Duke of Marlborough's Fame, Occasion'd by an Antique, in Imitation of Spencer* (London).

———. [ca. 1718]. *Colin's Mistakes, Written in Imitation of Spenser's Style* (London 1721). In 11 Prior stanzas.

The Progress of Time; or An Emblematical Representation of the Four Seasons and Twelve Months . . . in Imitation of Spencer's Fairy Queen. 1743. (London).

A Protestant Memorial: or, The Shepherd's Tale of the Pouder-Plott: A Poem in Spenser's Style. 1713. (London). Couplets; imitation of *SC*. Doubtfully by Dr. William Bedell, the title-page attribution (on Hook's authority).

Pye, Henry J. 1787. "The Parsonage Improved" in his *Poems on Various Subjects* (London). In 32 Spenserian stanzas.

Ralph, James. 1729. "Zeuma" in *Miscellaneous Poems, by Several Hands* (London). One section of canto 3 imitates *FQ* 2.12.60–61. Blank verse.

Reid, W. H. 1790. "Stanzas for the Festival of Christmas" in *EurM* 17:58. Three stanzas *ababbcdcdd*.

Rider, William. 1755. "Westminster Abbey" *GentM* 25:373. Ten stanzas *ababbccC*.

Ridley, Glocester. 1747. "Psyche, or The Great Metamorphosis" in *The Museum* (London); rpt. in Bell 1789–90 vol. 10. These 51 Spenserian stanzas are a Spenserian imitation in form and method especially, but heavily indebted to *Paradise Lost* as well, particularly book 9's temptation scene and book 10's postlapsarian nature transformation.

———. [ca. 1772]. *Melampus, or The Religious Groves: A Poem in Four Books, with Notes* (London 1781). In 260 Spenserian stanzas.

Robinson, Mary. 1806. *Poetical Works* (London). Includes "The Cavern of Woe" 1:49. In 15 near-Spenserian stanzas. Also includes "The Foster-Child" 2:52 (ca. 1790). In 53 Spenserian stanzas.

Robinson, Thomas. ca. 1620. *The Life and Death of Mary Magdalene* BL Ms. Harleian 6211: an imitation of *Faerie Queene's* House of Pride, Cave of Despair, Bower of Bliss, and Castle Joyous.

Rowlands, Samuel. 1609. *The Famous Historie of Guy Earle of Warwick*, an imitation of *Faerie Queene's* four-line mottos before each canto; there are 12 cantos in the *Historie*, with six-line stanzas *ababcc*.

"The Ruins of Time." 1729. In Ralph 1729 *abab*.

St. James's Miscellany, or The Lover's Tale, Being the Amours of Venus and Adonis, or The Disasters of Unlawful Love. 1732. (London). Four parts in couplets: pt. 2 House of Sleep; pt. 4 Dungeon of Despair. Although the preface says that Virgil and Homer are "the noblest Patterns for our Imitation," the Morpheus and Despair sections may be considered imitations of Spenser.

Scott, James. 1761. "Ode on Sleep" in his *Odes on Several Subjects* (London). *ababcC*.

———. [ca. 1761?]. "A Spousal Hymn, Addressed to His Majesty [George III] on His Marriage" in Pearch 1783 vol. 3. In 19 Prior stanzas. See Scott's award-winning (Cambridge University) imitations, "Heaven: A Vision" (1760) [in 3 Prior stanzas indebted to *FQ* 2.12] and "An Hymn to Repentance" (1762), both in Prior stanzas, in *Musae Seatonionae* 1808 vol. 1; this collection also contains Beilby Porteus's 1759 "Death," a blank-verse imitation. Prize imitations in Prior stanzas in vol. 2 are Samuel Hayes 1783 "Hope" and Charles Philpot 1790 "Faith: A Vision."

Scott, John. ca. 1765. "The Shepherd's Elegy" in his *Poetical Works* (London 1782). *ababbcc.*

Seward, Anna. [ca. 1765]. "Knowledge, A Poem in the Manner of Spenser" in her *Poetical Works* (Edinburgh 1810) vol. 1. Five Spenserian stanzas.

———. 1772. "To Time Past, Written Dec. 1772" in *Works* (see above). *ababccbdd.*

Sewell, George. [ca. 1710]. "The Force of Musick: A Fragment after the Manner of Spenser" in his *A New Collection of Original Poems, Never Printed in Any Miscellany, by the Author of Sir Walter Raleigh* (London 1720). Couplets.

Shenstone, William. 1737. "The School-Mistress: A Poem, in Imitation of Spenser" in Robert Dodsley 1748 *A Collection of Poems in Three Volumes, by Several Hands* 2nd ed., vol. 1 (London). In 35 Spenserian stanzas (which Thomas Gray called "Excellent in its kind and masterly"). Cf. Thomas Hood's early 19th century bittersweet 29 Spenserian stanzas on "The Irish Schoolmaster." And cf. 1755 anon. "The School-master, a Characteristical Poem. By a Gentleman of Cambridge" (London). See Dodsley above.

"Sir Salvadore, An Allegoric Poem, Canto the First." 1780. In *Ingratitude, an Ode; and Sir Salvadore* (Lincoln). Spenserian stanzas.

"Slander or the Witch of Wokey." [ca. 1768]. In Pearch 1768 vol. 1. *aabccb.*

Smart, Christopher. 1752. *Poems on Several Occasions, by Christopher Smart, A. M. Fellow of Pembroke-Hall, Cambridge* (London). Includes "Epithalamium."

———. 1755. "Secular Ode" and 1756 "Hymn to the Supreme Being on Recovery from a Dangerous Fit of Illness" in Robert Anderson 1795 *The Works of the British Poets* (London) 11:136. *ababcc.* See "Untitled Spenserian stanza" below.

Smith, Charlotte. 1787. "Sonnet XLII. Composed during a Walk on the Downs, in November 1787" in *Elegiac Sonnets* (London).

Smith, Elizabeth. ca. 1792. "The Sun Just Rising" in her *Fragments* (London 1811). Six Spenserian stanzas.

"Sonnet, by Spenser, Never before Printed." Before 1727. In Curll 1727 *Miscellanea, in Two Volumes, Never before Published* vol. 1 (London). Eleven couplets.

"Sonnet, to a Lady of Indiscreet Virtue, in Imitation of Spenser." [1755?]. In Pearch 1783 vol. 3. *ababbcbccdcdee.*

"Sonnet to Sleep." 1800. *EurM* 38:368. Spenserian sonnet signed "W. F."

Sotheby, William. 1798. *Oberon* (London 1810). *abbaccddc.*

[Southey, Robert]. 1800. "St. Juan Gualberto" in *The Annual Anthology* vol. 2 (Bristol). *ababcc.*

Spencer's Fairy-Queen, Attempted in Blank Verse, Canto 1. 1774. (London). Eighteen pages of blank verse.

Spencer Redivivus; Containing the First Book of the Fairy Queen; His Essential Design Preserv'd, but His Obsolete Language and Manner of Verse Totally Laid Aside, Deliver'd in Heroick Numbers, by a Person of Quality. 1687. (London). Paraphrase in some 4,600 couplets of *FQ* 1.

Spenser's Fairy Queen Attempted in Blank Verse, with Notes, Critical and Explanatory. 1783. (London). Blank-verse version of *FQ* 1.1–4.

Sterling, Joseph. [1782?]. "La Gierusalemme; Soggettita" in *The Poetical Register for 1805* (London 1807). In 56 Spenserian stanzas. See Sterling's five sonnet imitations in his *Poems* (Dublin 1782).

———. 1785. *Cambuscan; or, The Squire's Tale of Chaucer, Modernized by Mr. Boyse, Continued from Spenser's Fairy Queen, by Mr. Ogle, and Concluded by Mr. Sterling* (Dublin). In Prior stanzas, as was its prototype: Samuel Boyse and George Ogle 1741 "Cambuscan" in Ogle's *Canterbury Tales of Chaucer Modernis'd* (London).

———. 1768. *Bombarino, A Romance: with Poems on the Four Sister Arts* (Dublin). Couplets, wherein Spenser is the native writer imitated (the Italians otherwise).

Stone, Jerome. 1755. "Albin and the Daughter of Mey: An Old Tale, Translated from the Irish, by the Late Mr. Jerome Stone" in Moses Mendez 1767 *A Collection of the Most Esteemed Pieces* (London). Prior stanzas.

[Tait, John]. 1775. *The Land of Liberty: An Allegorical Poem, in the Manner of Spenser. In Two Cantos, Dedicated to the People of Great Britain* (London). In 120 (poor) Spenserian stanzas.

"The Temple of Glory, Inscribed to the Meritorious." ca. 1772. In *The Shamrock* (Dublin 1772). In 28 Spenserian stanzas. Davies attributes this poem to Samuel Whyte, I suppose because of Whyte's editorship of *The Shamrock* and his other Spenser imitations: good grounds for the attribution I believe.

"Thales: Sacred to the Memory of Pococke, D. D." 1751. In Bell 1789–90 vol. 11. In 16 stanzas *ababbccc*. First pub. as *Thales: A monody, Sacred to the Memory of Dr. Pococke, in Imitation of Spenser, from an Authentic Manuscript of Mr. Edmund Smith* (London 1751).

"Thames: A Canto, on the Royal Nuptials in May 1737, in Imitation of Spenser." 1737. *The Publick Register, or The Weekly Magazine* (May): 296–99. In 25 Spenserian stanzas.

Thelwall, John. 1787. "The Metamorphosis" (*ababcc*), "Pastoral" (dictional imitation), "The Tears of the Genii" (Spenserian stanza) and Epilogue (*ababbcC*) in *Poems* (London) 2 vols.

Thompson, Alexander. 1796. *The Paradise of Taste* (London). In 33 Spenserian stanzas.

Thompson, Isaac. 1731. "An Epithalamium," "Colin's Despair," and *A Pastoral Ode* in his *A Collection of Poems Occasionally Writ on Several Subjects* (Newcastle-upon-Tyne). The seven pastorals of the *Ode* are "Spring," "Parting," "The Pensive Swain," "The Complaint," "Friendship," "The Letter," and "Absence."

Thompson, William. 1736a. "An Epithalamium on the Royal Nuptials" in his *Poems on Several Occasions* (London 1758). In 25 Spenserian stanzas.

———. 1736b. "The Nativity" in *Poems on Several Occasions* (London 1758). Twenty Spenserian stanzas.

———. 1740. *An Hymn to May, by William Thompson, M.A. of Queen's College Oxon.* (London, n.d.): One of the century's finest imitations of Spenser, *An Hymn* also includes an important preface. In 72 stanzas *ababccC* (adaptation of *Fowre Hymnes*), expanded to 75 stanzas in Bell 1789–90 vol. 11. See also Thompson's two Spenserian sonnets (ca. 1763) in his *Poetical Works* (1807).

Thomson, James. 1748. *The Castle of Indolence: An Allegorical Poem, Written in Imitation of Spenser* (London and Dublin). In 158 Spenserian stanzas. See Bertram Dobell, *The Dreamer of The Castle of Indolence and Other Poems* (1915).

Tighe, Mary. 1795. *Psyche* (London 1805). In 372 Spenserian stanzas.

"To a Lover," "The Hermite's Addresse to Youthe," and "The Hospital Oake." ca. 1770. In Pearch 1775 vol. 4. All three *ababcc* [by Samuel Boyse?].

"To Dr. Beattie." 1783. In *GentM* 5 (Oct.) 870. Six Spenserian stanzas signed "N. T.," followed by "Sonnet to Dr. Beattie." One Spenserian stanza.

"To Mr Urban, on the Conclusion of His Vol. XIII for the Year 1743." 1743. *GentM* 13: no page. Ten Prior stanzas.

"To Samuel Rogers, Esq. Author of the Pleasures of Memory, on His Ordering a Short Great Coat Called a Spenser." 1795. *EurM* 27:418. Three Spenserian stanzas. Signed "P," who says that Samuel Rogers is better as a Spenserian than either Mason or Shenstone.

"To the Authoress of the Victim of Fancy." In *GentM* 57 (1787) 260. *abbacc*. Signed "Y. E."

Turnbull, Gavin. 1788. *Poetical Essays* (Glasgow). Includes "Pastoral 1," "The Bard," and "The Cottage." Couplets, 22 Spenserian stanzas, and 4 Spenserian stanzas, respectively.

The Ugly Club: A Dramatic Caracature in One Act Performed on the 6th of June, 1798, . . . Drury Lane. Founded on the Seventeenth Number of the Spectator. By Edmund Spenser the Younger. (London).

Untitled Spenserian stanza. [1756]. On flyleaf of *Universal Visiter and Memoralist* 1756. Not seen by me nor Davies. Hook speculates the stanza may be by Christopher Smart.

[Upton, John]. 1747. *A New Canto of Spencer's Fairy Queen, Now First Published* (London). In 42 Prior stanzas. The following year Upton, the century's finest Spenser editor, shows himself to be a busy critic of Renaissance literature when he publishes his *Three Plays of Benjamin Jonson* (London, 1749).

Vernon, William. 1758. "The Parish Clerk" in Pearch 1783 vol. 2. In 28 stanzas *ababcc*.

"Verses on Hope, in the Manner of Spencer." [1741]. In *The Polite Correspondence, or Rational Amusement* (London, n.d.). One stanza *ababcdcd*. Perhaps by John Campbell.

"The Village Sunday, A Poem Moral and Descriptive, In the Manner of Spenser": cited by Hook but not seen by Davies or me. Spenserian stanzas.

Warton, Joseph. 1746. *Odes on Several Subjects* (London). Thoroughly Spenserian.

Warton, Thomas, the elder. 1706. "Philander: An Imitation of Spencer, Occasioned by the Death of Mr. Wm. Levinz, of M. C., Oxon,
Nov. 1706" in his *Poems on Several Occasions* (London 1748).
ababcc.

Warton, Thomas, the younger. [ca. 1745]. "Morning" *The Student
or The Oxford and Cambridge Miscellany* 1 (1750). *ababcC*.

———. 1753. "A Pastoral in the Manner of Spenser" in *The Union,
or Select Scots and English Poems* (Edinburgh). Six stanzas *ababcc*.

———. 1777. "Sonnet in Imitation of Spenser" *GentM* 47:500.

———. 1751. "Elegy on the Death of the Late Prince of Wales" in
Poems (London 1791). *ababcC*. See his ode "Sent to Mr. Upton,
on His Edition of the Fairy Queene" therein.

———. 1761. "The Complaint of Cherwell" in 1777 *Poems* vol. 3.
ababcC.

[Wesley, Samuel]. 1723. *The Battle of the Sexes: A Poem* (London).
Originally 46 Prior stanzas. Revision in 50 Prior stanzas in Wesley
1736 (see below). *Guardian* 52 (1713) supposedly presents the
argument for Wesley's stanzas.

———. 1736. *Poems on Several Occasions, by Samuel Wesley,
A. M. Master of Blundell's School at Tiverton, Devon, Sometime
Student of Christ-Church, Oxford; and Near Twenty Years Usher
in Westminster-School* 2nd ed. (London). Includes "The Iliad in a
Nutshell, or Homer's Battle of the Frogs and Mice, Illustrated with
Notes" (in 75 Prior stanzas) and "Pastoral" (in couplets but doubt-
ful imitation of February eclogue), both written before 1736.

[West, Gilbert]. 1739. *The Abuse of Travelling: A New Canto of
Spenser's Fairy Queen* (London). Also pub. as *A Canto of the Fairy
Queen, Written by Spenser, Never before published* (London 1739).
In 58 Spenserian stanzas. Writing to Richard West in 1740, Thomas Gray remarks on the imitation: "Mr. Walpole and I have frequently wondered you should never mention a certain imitation
of Spenser published last year by a namesake of yours with which
we are all enraptured and enmarvailed": quoted by W. P. Courtney
in "Dodsley's Famous Collection," 83: see bibliography B.

———. 1751. *Education: A Poem, in Two Cantos, Written in Imi-
tation of the Style and Manner of Spenser's Fairy Queen, by
Gilbert West, Esq.* (London). Half-title adds, "Inscrib'd to Lady
Langham, Widow of Sir John Langham, Bt. [and West's mother]."
In 96 Spenserian stanzas.

Whalley, John. 1745. "Prothalamium " in his *A Collection of Original Poems and Translations* (London). In his 1805 ed. of Spenser, the Rev. Todd has "Thenot and Cuddy" as perhaps by Whalley.

White, Henry Kirke. 1798. "To the Muse" in his *Remains* (London 1807). Near-Spenserian stanza.

Whitehead, William. ca. 1730. "The Vision of Solomon" in William Mason's *Plays and Poems* (London 1774). Eight Prior stanzas.

———. ca. 1735. "Ode to the Hon. Charles Townsend" and "To the Same" both *ababcC*.

———. "Hymn to Venus" in 5 Prior stanzas. In vol. 3 of Whitehead's *Poems* (London 1888). William Mason's memoir has this important remark on Spenser in the schools (p. 18): "I take it ["The Vision of Solomon"] from a small MS. collection of his school poems, which, at the time, he thought the best worthy of preservation. . . . The critical reader will find a striking similarity between this poem and Dr. Lowth's version of the Apologue of Prodicus, published by Mr. Spence in his Polymetis. I have heard that the judgement of Hercules was originally a school exercise, though it undoubtedly afterwards received much revision, an advantage the other never obtained from its author." The other Spenser poems by Whitehead (above) also may well be school exercises. I appreciate the correspondence on this from David Hill Radcliffe. See Lowth above.

[Whyte, Samuel]. ca. 1772. "To Mr. Thomas Hickey, with Spenser's Fairy Queen" in *The Shamrock* (Dublin 1772). Spenserian sonnet. Cf. "Irene" and "The Temple of Glory" above.

Wilkie, William. 1759. "A Dream in the Manner of Spenser" in his *Epigoniad* 2nd ed. (Edinburgh). In 18 Spenserian stanzas.

Wilson, Alexander. [1790]. "The Suicide" *The Scots Magazine* 53 (1791): 138. Ten Spenserian stanzas.

[Wolcott, John]. 1786. "To a Lady, with the Sonnets of Petrarch. In the Manner of Spencer. By Peter Pindar" in *An Asylum for Fugitive Pieces* (London). Burlesque Spenserian sonnet.

———. 1789. "In Imitation of Spenser, Written at Santa Cruz, . . . and sent to . . . a Spanish Young Lady" in *An Asylum* (see above).

Woodford, Samuel. 1679. *Epodē: The Legend of Love* in his *A Paraphrase upon the Canticles, and Some Select Hymns of the New and Old Testament, with Other Occasional Compositions in English Verse* (London) pp. 54–118. There are 189 Spenserian stanzas in 3 cantos.

Wordsworth, William. [1791–94]. "The Female Vagrant" in *Lyrical Ballads, with a Few Other Poems* (Bristol 1798). In 26 Spenserian stanzas. This poem was pub. in revised form as *Salisbury Plain* in 54 stanzas, and then as *Guilt and Sorrow* in 74 stanzas (1793–98).

"Written in Mr Stanyan's Grecian History, by a Gentleman Lately Deceased, to the Rev. Thomas Burton, A. M. Student of Christ Church, Oxford." 1755. *GentM* 25:420–21. Seven Prior stanzas.

Wynne, John Huddlestone. 1782. "The Four Ages" in *British Magazine and Review* (London) vol. 1. *ababcC*.

———. 1783. "The Temple of Freedom, A Vision, in Spenser's Stile" in *British Magazine and Review* vol. 2:295. *ababcC*.

INDEX

Note: This index covers items found in chapters 1–4 only. For additional references to particular authors or texts, please consult bibliographies A, B and C.

ABOUT THE AUTHOR

Richard C. Frushell is associate professor of English and comparative literature at The Pennsylvania State University. Formerly, he was Andrew H. Sherratt Professor of English at Rockford College. Dr. Frushell is a member of the advisory board for the journal *Classical and Modern Literature,* and he coedited *Contemporary Thought on Edmund Spenser,* an edition of Spenser criticism.